# Quality Management: Applications for Therapeutic Recreation

# Quality Management: Applications for Therapeutic Recreation

edited by Bob Riley

Venture Publishing, Inc.
State College, PA

Cover Design: Sikorski Design
Production: Bonnie Godbey
Printing and Binding: BookCrafters, Inc., Chelsea, MI

Library of Congress Catalog Number 91-66102
ISBN 0-910251-47-9

This work is dedicated, in loving memory, to

## Jessie Riley

Inspiration drawn from her short but coura-
geous life served as the impetus for the
completion of this project. The meaning and
importance of quality assurance were well
learned by observing her struggle for a quality
life. This has been an invaluable lesson, one
which shall stay with her dad forever.

# Notes From The ATRA Publication Committee

The Publication Committee of the American Therapeutic Recreation Association is pleased to present the publication *Quality Management: Applications in Therapeutic Recreation*. The state-of-the-art information to be found within this publication is of both theoretical and practical application, and reflects the commitment of the American Therapeutic Recreation Association to the professional development of its membership.

At a time when professional accountability is of paramount importance to quality health care, therapeutic recreation professionals must strive to appropriately evaluate and document their unique contribution to client/patient care. By doing so, therapeutic recreation practitioners may effectively establish the need for their services, establish standards for quality and appropriateness of care, demonstrate effectiveness and outcomes of services, and illuminate resources necessary for the provision of services. *Quality Management: Applications for Therapeutic Recreation* presents the standards and procedures by which such accountability may be achieved.

Keith S. Savell, Ph.D.
Chair, Publication Committee
San Jose State University

# TABLE OF CONTENTS

## SECTION ONE
## QUALITY ASSURANCE PERSPECTIVES

# SECTION TWO
## QUALITY ASSURANCE OUTCOME MEASURES

# SECTION THREE
## QUALITY ASSURANCE MANAGEMENT APPLICATION

# FORWARD

In June of 1986 I had the distinct pleasure to be involved in the workshop "Evaluation of Therapeutic Recreation Through Quality Assurance" held at Green Mountain College. As President of the American Therapeutic Recreation Association (ATRA), I was invited to open the workshop with a presentation entitled "The Role of Quality Assurance in the Professionalization of Therapeutic Recreation" and also provide remarks at the conclusion of the workshop. In 1987 the proceedings of this workshop were published and *Evaluation of Therapeutic Recreation Through Quality Assurance* became part of our professional literature. It was exciting to be part of what I considered to be a significant contribution to our professional body of knowledge and to ultimately improve quality service for our clients.

It is equally exciting to be invited to contribute these remarks to *Quality Management: Applications for Therapeutic Recreation*. As I write these comments I am struck with the historical significance of what has occurred since the "Evaluation of Therapeutic Recreation Through Quality Assurance" workshop at Green Mountain College in 1986. Two national workshops on quality assurance, one at Montclair State College in New Jersey and one at Stanford University in Palo Alto, California, as well as about thirty presentations/seminars have been conducted around the country since 1986. The Quality Assurance Committee of the Therapeutic Recreation Association, chaired by Bob Riley, has been involved in all of these activities. It is clear that quality assurance is a significant focus of this profession and gratifying that the attention given to this important concern has increased during the past four years.

In the comments I made in 1986, I identified that people's understanding and expectations for therapeutic recreation have changed and the demands for accountability as a treatment service have increased. In our early history as a health care service we were expected to provide recreation services as an aspect of a therapeutic milieu. Today, in many systems, we are expected to deliver treatment services (recreation therapy), as an aspect of an individualized treatment plan (based upon an individualized assessment), designed to improved the physical, mental, emotion, and/or social functioning. In short, we are expected to deliver treatment services as an aspect of reasonable, necessary medical care and, in some setting, to also provide opportunities for recreation. Health care financing concerns and societal trends have added additional pressures from accountability. This has resulted in the following developments:

1. Discussion and debate about philosophy and definition;
2. Expansion of our literature and body of knowledge;
3. Development and compliance with standards;
4. Certification of practitioners; and
5. Increasing emphasis on issues relevant in clinical settings such as reimbursement, etc.

Market forces affecting health care and human services will continue to influence the evolution of the therapeutic recreation profession. I challenge professionals to continue to make quality assurance a primary and major focus of the therapeutic recreation profession, to demonstrate the efficacy of our service and to measure the outcome of our service to provide accountability to our clients and our service systems. I further challenge the profession to remember that as professionals we have a collective responsibility to regulate ourselves to ensure the quality of the services provided to our clients.

We have seen many changes since 1986 in both the health care industry and in the therapeutic recreation profession. Health care is increasingly market driven, consumer-oriented and very concerned about financing. Health care is an increasingly complex business. Concerns about customer service, bottom lines, profit margin, outcome in comparison to resources invested, and quality care continue to be influential forces and will be for years to come.

Therapeutic recreation has also evolved. The American Therapeutic Recreation Association has grown into a strong national professional association making major contributions to effort including: development of a definition of service; activities to advance our body of knowledge; improved efforts with the Joint Commission of Accreditation of Health Care Organizations (JCAHO) and the Commission of Accreditation of Rehabilitation Facilities (CARF); legislative advocacy, development of standards for marketing/public awareness efforts, development/promotion of a code of ethics, support for reimbursement and development of a vision statement are some of the many activities supported by ATRA to advance the profession as a quality health care service. These activities have occurred because of a collective commitment on the part of therapeutic recreation professionals to provide services to our clients. As a profession we are being driven by the forces shaping health care, but we are also being influenced by a professional commitment to provide the highest quality service possible to our clients.

This publication is an excellent example of a continuing dedication of therapeutic recreation professionals to improving the quality of client services. Many related topics are covered by professionals who have specific expertise in the subject area.

Notice the breadth of topics ranging from general perspectives about quality assurance to management applications of quality assurance. Also note the depth of coverage given to outcome measurement. This text is an excellent compliment to *Evaluation of Therapeutic Recreation Through Quality Assurance* and a significant contribution to our professional literature. It is also ATRA's client centered focus. Congratulations to Bob Riley and all contributors for a job well done! I will end my remarks with the same statements in 1986, since they are still so evident today. *The challenge is still before us. We must continue...to actively pursue the issue of quality assurance. If we lose sight of the necessity to deliver quality services to our clients we are lost. It has to be a primary focus of all we do.*

I am very proud to be associated with professionals who are dedicated to quality client services and who will continue to be in the future.

Ray West
North Carolina Memorial Hospital
Chapel Hill, NC

# PREFACE

Several years ago, while attending a conference on future health care trends, the significance of the term "quality assurance" (QA) was introduced to me for the first time. The year was 1982 and the conference reflected a mood of impending change. In addition to QA, the other topics that dominated the discussion were cost containment and accountability. It was projected that during the era of the 80s, health care services would be transformed into a cost efficient and effective commodity. Now nearly a full decade has passed since my baptism into the realm of QA. Reflecting back upon that time period, I am struck by how much therapeutic recreation has adapted to the call for the delivery of more appropriate and quality based services. I am also sobered by the realization of how much has yet to be done.

During the past five years, primarily through the efforts of its QA committee, ATRA has spearheaded the movement toward improving the quality of therapeutic recreation services. This is evident, in part, by the support and encouragement that the ATRA Board of Directors has provided to the QA committee in its pursuit of vital QA projects. The primary purpose of the QA committee is to keep abreast of new and changing quality related strategies within the general health care environment. A secondary purpose, equal in importance to the first, is to disseminate such information to the membership. Toward completion of the goal, the committee has sponsored several national conferences and dozens of regional workshops, conducted related research, and has generated two publications. Information contained in volume is a direct outgrowth of many of the projects sponsored by the QA committee during recent years.

This publication is designed to provide the reader with a better understanding of the concept of Quality Management and its application to the field of therapeutic recreation. Quality Management is viewed as part of the quality improvement era that was born in the 70s, developed during the 80s, and is projected to continue well into the 90s. As such, Quality Management and its related component (Quality Assurance and Quality Assessment), serve as essential tools for professional; accountability and advancement. As therapeutic recreation moves forward in its quest for professional recognition and acceptance, Quality Management will undoubtedly continue to play a vital role. As such, this edited volume extends beyond the basic tenants of quality assessment and the process of monitoring and evaluation. It takes the reader beyond current practices of QA and presents a platform for quality service for the next decade. The purpose of this volume is to stimulate broader thinking regarding Quality Management and its relevance to providing quality therapeutic recreation service.

The chapters contained within set forth an agenda for professional development that is deemed essential for therapeutic recreation practitioners. The establishment of valid protocols of service, measurement of outcomes of care and implementation of clinical privileging transcend the scope of many existing therapeutic recreation departments. These issues are only now beginning to be addressed by professional organizations concerned with the advancement of therapeutic recreation. Accelerated and widespread usage of these strategies, among others discussed within this book, are considered essential by experts within the general health care industry.

The information presented within this volume was written by individuals who share a positive vision of therapeutic recreation for the future. The authors, who are representative of the many aspects of the profession, envision therapeutic recreation emerging as a vital professionally delivered service, characterized by high quality in terms of both effectiveness and efficiency. As such, these authors believe in the need for establishing and implementing valid quality improvement strategies and programs throughout therapeutic recreation delivery systems.

The divergent topics and areas of concern regarding Quality Management and Quality Assurance that have been addressed by the authors are organized into three major sections, each containing interrelated themes. The first section presents four papers that present the perspectives of the QA movement in therapeutic recreation. Exploration of the concept of outcome measurement and its application to service delivery follows in the second section. Finally, the five chapters of section three address effective strategies for use within the realm of Quality Management in therapeutic recreation. The fifteen chapters cumulatively provide a stimulating and informative discussion of the critical issues of quality improvement that need to be incorporated into the infrastructure of all therapeutic recreation service organizations.

This book challenges each therapeutic recreation professional to engage in the "risk of commitment" to ensure quality therapeutic recreation services. Success in quality performance is often marked by a ground swell of commitment by all involved. As such, the quest for quality within therapeutic recreation must become contagious and reach epidemic proportions. Professionals are encouraged to take the time to share their quality improvement efforts with one another, as well as with the authors of this volume. It is only through a process of open exchange and unilateral commitment that therapeutic recreation will emerge as a bench mark of quality service by the close of this century. It is toward this end that we must all unify our effort.

In conclusion, I would like to thank several individuals for their assistance and guidance for making this book a reality: the ATRA Board of Directors (1987 through 1990) for their continuous support of the QA committee and its various project; Steve Wright and Ann Huston for the critical role they have played in my understanding of the QA process; Karen Callahan for her many hours of work in preparing the written manuscript; certainly, the authors and contributors of his volume for their unselfish giving of time and energy to help make this project a success; and to Devin and Maria Riley for their continued support and good cheer.


Bob Riley
Middletown Springs, Vermont
Winter, 1990

# SECTION ONE
# QUALITY ASSURANCE PERSPECTIVES

# CHAPTER ONE

# Advancing Therapeutic Recreation Through Quality Assurance: A Perspective on the Changing Nature of Quality in Therapeutic Recreation

NANCY NAVAR, Re.D., C.T.R.S.

## Introduction

A friend commented, as he emerged from an hour long drive in New York's rush hour traffic, "It's difficult knowing how to get where you are going if you don't know where you are." This unusual twist with a goal-oriented statement speaks to the importance of perspective and the importance of taking a few moments to reflect on the past and present status of quality assurance in therapeutic recreation before speculating on the future status of quality assurance in therapeutic recreation. This chapter attempts to place the issues of both quality service and quality assurance in a historical perspective with the evolution of the profession of therapeutic recreation over the last several years. Rather than providing a strict accounting of historical events, most of the examples provided are drawn directly from the experiences and opinions of the author.

The chapter is divided into the following topical areas related to therapeutic recreation: quality assurance, body of knowledge in therapeutic recreation, philosophy of therapeutic recreation, pressures influencing the practice of therapeutic recreation, directions and strategies for advancing quality assurance in therapeutic recreation. For each section, an attempt is made to discuss the meaning of *quality* for that topic and to discuss the methods of *quality assurance* that were commonly used throughout the given era of therapeutic recreation. No assumption is made that the author's experiences or opinions are reflective of the entire profession of therapeutic recreation. Rather, a personal historical perspective is used as the main method of discussion. Therefore, much of the remaining text is written in the first person.

## Quality Assurance in Therapeutic Recreation

For many of us, the initial motivation for providing quality therapeutic recreation services was to help others. We wanted to provide the best possible services because our clients deserved the best. Two decades ago, the measures that we had for quality services included subjective statements such as "She really cares about her clients," "He works so well with people," or "She's so energetic, creative, motivating . . . " One objective measure seemed to be whether or not one was educated in therapeutic recreation. If formal education in therapeutic recreation was absent, then one's actual knowledge of a variety of activities or motivation techniques was used. The main method of quality assurance was verbal approval from other disciplines.

The next measure of quality seemed to focus on one's knowledge of professional issues and one's professional behaviors surrounding these issues. I was a high-quality professional in some people's opinion because I was registered at the national level as a Therapeutic Recreation Specialist and later as a Master Therapeutic Recreation Specialist. In the early and mid-1970s many professionals were actively organizing therapeutic recreation sections within the state recreation and park organizations. A high measure of quality occurred if an adequate number of practitioners attended those section meetings. At this same time, we felt quite successful when new positions in therapeutic recreation were created. I applied for an Occupational Therapist position and successfully convinced the program director of the alcoholism unit that she really needed to hire a Therapeutic Recreation Specialist instead. The subsequent addition of two more therapeutic recreation positions was a sure measure of high quality programming. It was proof that others were convinced that we were an important addition to the treatment team. That external sanction was a very important and common measure of the quality of therapeutic recreation services.

In the mid-1970s, another measure of quality that was both desired and received was the verbalized respect and approval I (synonymous with therapeutic recreation in the agency) received from team members: the therapists liked my in-service training on the role of therapeutic recreation; the head nurse made sure that patients were sent to my programs; the program director invited me to attend team meetings; therapeutic recreation acquired a permanent time slot in the required education program for patients. These were exciting times for patients and staff. The quality assurance mechanisms included verbal feedback of my performance at staffings or staff meetings, verbal feedback or written surveys of patient satisfaction, and verbal and written evaluations from selected therapists, nurses or interns. Having therapeutic recreation chosen as the allied health discipline that would train first-year medical students in interpersonal relations with patients was certainly a measure of quality.

A fourth measure of quality in the 1970s was the comprehensiveness of the therapeutic recreation program. It was professionally quite important to offer more than bowling, crafts or special events. It was also a sign of quality when we really began to feel like we were improving the client's condition. It was the ultimate acknowledgment of quality when the newly created outpatient (by referral only) leisure counseling group had a waiting list of patients.

In 1980, when I was introduced to the term *quality assurance* during a visit to the Joint Commission on Accreditation of Healthcare Organizations (JCAHO or Joint Commission), my colleague[1] and I were fairly certain that we understood the term. We understood the term "quality assurance" to mean an overall measure (probably nebulous) of good programs for patients. We initially equated the term "quality assurance" with program evaluation. When we realized that the Joint Commission was using the term "quality assurance" to imply a very specific process, I began calling professional colleagues for clarification of the meaning of quality assurance. No clarification was gained from seeking the advice of physical therapists, nurses, occupational therapists, psychotherapists, or medical records personnel. My personal physician finally enlightened me by saying "Oh, don't worry about quality assurance; that's just something for physicians." At least we knew that we weren't the only profession that was unclear about quality assurance standards.

Although the Joint Commission had introduced quality assurance standards with the audit approach in 1979, it wasn't until 1984 that they introduced the problem focused approach to quality assurance. Given that short history of formalized quality assurance, therapeutic recreation was on time and on target with its first quality assurance book published in 1980.[2] However, there was a large variance of compliance with standards in therapeutic recreation practice. While some therapeutic recreation practitioners immediately began addressing the standards of regulatory agencies (i.e., JCAHO and CARF) or *Therapeutic Recreation Professional Standards of Practice* (National Therapeutic Recreation Society), other practitioners did not seriously document compliance with established standards .

About this same time, the Joint Commission distinguished "quality" and "appropriateness." While quality was the degree of adherence to standards of good practice, appropriateness referred to providing the right patient with the right service and the right time in the right setting at the right intensity and for the right duration. To some practitioners, it looked as if the Joint Commission changed their quality assurance expectations almost annually. While there is some truth to this outlook, the truth also lies in the fact that the Joint Commission was also learning about quality assurance at the same time. There was a somewhat constant interplay between providing quality assurance standards that would stretch the field to improve services and attempting to be responsive to the field wanting or needing further clarification of standards. To some, the term "quality assurance" became the same as "quality assessment" or the same as meeting the Joint Commission standards. To others, quality assurance took on a global meaning and "monitoring and evaluation" became the newer buzz words to describe the Joint Commission's process.

In 1986, the Joint Commission published quality assurance standards that used an ongoing monitoring and evaluation approach. With this approach, therapeutic recreation was introduced to the concept of "important aspects of care." Those practitioners that stayed current went beyond the "problem focused" approach to quality assurance and began monitoring important aspects of care that were "high risk," "high volume" and/or "problem prone." Also during this era, Bob Riley (1987) helped us see the difference between the comprehensive concept of quality assurance and the more specific process of "quality assessment," such as the ten step process prescribed by the Joint Commission. In 1987, we started looking at "structure, process, and outcomes" as different measures of quality. The structures (i.e., TR is included in the treatment plan) and processes (i.e., TR conducts a valid and timely assessment on each client) looked at the question "*Can* we provide quality TR services?" The outcomes (which are still in the novice stage of quality improvement) look at the question "*Do* we provide quality?"

According to the Joint Commission, the quality assurance process should measure four different areas: good professional performance, efficient use of resources, reduction of risk, and patient/family satisfaction. The more sophisticated therapeutic recreation departments measure these areas both on a department or service level and at the aggregate or agency level.

A few years ago, quality assurance seemed so simple. Today there are so many different levels of quality assurance and several different methods for demonstrating improvement in service provision. In fact, the more acceptable term is "quality improvement," since it is very difficult to "assure" quality. A practitioner in an agency accredited by the Joint Commission must understand the monitoring and evaluation system of quality improvement. Regardless of setting, therapeutic recreation professionals should understand the concept of structure, process and outcomes as they concern quality improvement. On a broader scale, it is helpful to understand global quality assurance. In some ways, the evolution of quality assurance is like an infection. Once we got started, QA kept spreading; it was contagious and we really couldn't contain it at either the conceptual level or the implementation level. In another sense, some people perceived QA as undesirable. This view sometimes occurred when practitioners saw QA as a paper work exercise where the original intent of quality was sacrificed. Bob Riley once stated that, "Quality Assurance is the conscience of our profession." I agree. When so many pressures exist in our agencies and in health care, quality assurance remains a strong bureaucratically sanctioned and mandated method that we can use to "do good things for clients" and at the same time be accountable for our professional behaviors.

## Body of Knowledge and Quality

The body of knowledge in therapeutic recreation has greatly influenced our understanding of quality in therapeutic recreation services. This section discusses the evolving content of the body of knowledge during the past several years and relates these changes to the changing perception of quality in therapeutic recreation.

Historically, practitioners believed that recreation activity involvement is beneficial to people and that persons with illnesses and/or disabilities need recreation too. Our body of knowledge originally included the selection and adaptation of recreation activities to meet the needs and skill levels of persons with differing abilities. In this era, a measure of quality included the ability of the practitioner to select and/or adapt activities for a variety of individuals.

We then learned the basic facts about disabilities, although at first in a very cursory way. Looking back, it is amazing that we attempted to cover all the facts about all disabilities in one chapter of a textbook or one unit of an undergraduate college course. Although in the 1990s most therapeutic recreation curricula spend a great deal more time learning about disabilities (i.e., specifically designed courses), much of the working knowledge a practitioner uses is still learned during the internship or during on the job training. One measure of quality, then, is the level of a practitioner's knowledge about disability etiology, characteristics, prognosis and related precautions.

Activity analysis formally became part of therapeutic recreation's body of knowledge in the early 1970s.[3] Many times, the ability to functionally and practically analyze an activity was the cause of one's initial professional success. When I could describe activities as "intragroup" or "aggregate" (according to Avedon's social interaction patterns), my colleagues somehow were impressed and invited me into professional decision-making arenas. The body of knowledge in therapeutic recreation paralleled what practitioners were doing and what was expected of us in the job. For example, as Therapeutic Recreation Specialists learned about treatment plans, we were included on the treatment teams. As we were included in the treatment teams, we learned more about interdisciplinary functioning. The body of knowledge was expanding unevenly in different areas of the country. A measure of quality in one state was possibly unheard of in another state.

Fortunately, in my early professional training I learned the systems approach to program planning. This was probably the earliest formal method of quality assurance that was actually taught in therapeutic recreation curricula. The first time that this topic gained widespread use in therapeutic recreation was in 1979 with the publication of Peterson's systems approach to program planning.[4] Even today, when practitioners want to know where and how to start to be accountable, this systems approach provides an understand able, useable model of accountability and quality assurance. The parallels between the quality assurance literature and the systems literature are many. While QA talks about "outcomes," systems uses "terminal performance objectives" or "performance measures." When QA talks about "processes," the systems literature has incorporated "teaching/learning activities" or "content and process" as forms of documentation. It seems important to use our professional body of knowledge as a basis for interpreting the other functions we are required to learn during professional practice.

The next era of our body of knowledge concerned clinical quality. This was measured by the presence of progress notes (originally called anecdotal records) and charting. At first we documented attendance. Then we learned to document progress toward or regression from an individual's goals. Later we learned various methods for writing progress notes and treatment plans. Also included in this clinical quality was knowledge about medications and their side effects. The inclusions of families and significant others put therapeutic recreation at the forefront of milieu programming. It wasn't until years later that psychotherapy or rehabilitation would regularly join us in that effort. I'm not sure we ever took enough credit for knowing the importance of including family and friends in a recovery or rehabilitation process.

Our body of knowledge expanded to include knowledge of legislation. Certainly having therapeutic recreation included in national legislation (P.L. 94-142 and the Rehabilitation Act) was a measure of quality. We learned about this legislation, yet we failed to adequately monitor and evaluate our involvement or successes in the implementation of these important legislative milestones.

More recent body of knowledge concerns include client assessment, comprehensive program planning, treatment plans, client progress monitoring, professional standards, advocacy, fiscal reimbursement, quality assurance, liability, risk management, facilitation techniques, and leisure education. Other concerns include professional issues such as credentialling, philosophy, the development of protocols, and marketing. External regulatory standards are certainly a part of our body of knowledge.

As a practitioner, I believe it takes an extra effort to stay current, to keep up with the recent literature in therapeutic recreation. A practitioner who is aware of current issues affecting therapeutic recreation is demonstrating a measure of quality. A better measure of quality exists when the practitioner is actually doing something about these issues at their particular facility. A broader measure of quality exists when one is knowledgeable and active at either a local, state or national professional level.

The challenge of ensuring quality in the practice of therapeutic recreation becomes greater when many college curricula have only three content courses in therapeutic recreation in which to include much of this information. The actual body of knowledge in therapeutic recreation is much greater than our present academic curricula can accommodate. To ensure quality in practice, students must learn how to learn on their own after graduation. Colleges can be selective in approving internships so that only the best facilities in therapeutic recreation are eligible to receive student interns. Agencies can be selective in accepting students so that only top-notch curricula have access to high quality internship sites. Quality assurance for colleges should exist on a regular basis. Measures such as NRPA-AALR accreditation of recreation curricula, student evaluations, practitioner evaluations of curricula can all be included as quality assurance measures. It will be interesting to see how curricula that have a high percentage of graduates passing the new NCTRC certification exam use that information as a measure of a quality curriculum. In most cases, the method of quality assurance of academic curricula depends upon the faculty's commitment to measuring such.

The method to be used for quality assurance in clinical facilities is dictated by regulatory agencies. If an agency is not accredited (i.e., group homes, community therapeutic recreation programs) the therapeutic recreation professionals need to then self-regulate in the quality assurance process. The method of quality assurance for the profession is presently the use of verbal and written rhetoric by persons who are critical of the professional organizations. Another measure of quality in the profession is the high level of hard work and commitment by many local, state and national leaders in therapeutic recreation–until they burn out. I am concerned about the "lack of aging" within the therapeutic recreation profession. I believe that if we could develop ongoing methods for monitoring and evaluating our professional progress (i.e., expansion of body of knowledge, increased professionalization), the profession would more readily retain quality professionals. We need to focus on our collective professional accomplishments as well as engage in problem-solving and taking corrective action. It might be very interesting to attempt to apply the Joint Commission's ten step quality assurance process to the overall profession of therapeutic recreation.

### Philosophy and Quality

Philosophy has a great deal of influence on our concept of quality. Differing philosophical orientations often use different measures of quality. Rather than repeating or attempting to summarize the current philosophies that exist within the profession of therapeutic recreation,[5] I'll briefly share my changing philosophical orientations over the span of twenty years. For each major shift in philosophy, I'll comment on a corresponding measure of quality.

My first philosophic orientation could be summarized as "education through recreation involvement." In the early 1970s, this was logical since my undergraduate degree was in education. I focused on being able to teach physical skills (i.e., coordination or fitness), social skills (i.e., cooperation or sharing) and appreciation skills (i.e., music or nature) through the use of recreation activities. The measure of quality was how much a client learned.

A few years later, I learned about and became committed to the importance of leisure in the lives of my clients. Yet I never thought that it was really enough to have my clients simply experience leisure in a treatment setting. I thought it was very important to help clients prepare for leisure post discharge. So teaching about leisure became more intricate and more complex than only providing leisure experiences for clients. Yet, the focus of my therapeutic recreation programs really depended on the type of clients I was serving. For example, with alcoholics, the major form of therapeutic recreation treatment was leisure education–preparation for post discharge. The method included some prescribed involvement in recreation activities and much group processing and values clarification. With autistic, emotionally disturbed, or speech and hearing impaired children, play was both a means and an end. With hearing impaired adults, recreation activities were the means of practicing and expanding social skills. It's no news that different clients have different needs. Peterson and Gunn's (1984) therapeutic recreation service continuum became a cornerstone for both my philosophy and quality assurance. Quality became defined as the provision of all three types of service described in the therapeutic recreation continuum (therapy, leisure education, recreation participation). As practitioners became more sophisticated in philosophy, a higher measure of quality became the separation of therapy, leisure education and recreation and participation.

The following quote(s) from Kinney and Shank (1987) have relevance to the relationship between philosophy and quality:

> "There still exists a large void in the translation of a comprehensive service model into the terminological understanding suitable to guide professional practice . . . (Therapeutic Recreation) needs deeper exploration and understanding of the process inherent in each of the service components, thereby allowing the process to be modified and manipulated as appropriate to a specific context . . . It's not a question of what's the best role for the Therapeutic Recreation Specialist, it's a question of what role is most appropriate to the clients' needs in a particular context . . . (It is important to) recognize the plurality within the discipline . . ." (1987, p. 73)

We as a profession have not skillfully monitored nor evaluated much of what we've created. Even our useful philosophical models have not received the depth of development that would provide us with useful information related to quality therapeutic recreation service provision. It's easy to criticize a service model or professional standards of practice and it's just as easy to defend them. Without ongoing monitoring and evaluation of our professional "tools," neither criticism nor support are terribly valid. Quality assurance must start to permeate our professional philosophies and practices.

Presently, NTRS formally provides the profession with a written philosophy while ATRA formally provides the profession with a written definition of therapeutic recreation. In brief, the NTRS philosophy addresses leisure-ability through the provision of therapy, leisure education and recreation participation; the ATRA definition addresses independence through both treatment and recreation services. Which should one espouse? I personally believe that the NTRS philosophy and the ATRA definition of therapeutic recreation are compatible. I believe that leisure is important and that improved functioning is essential. Often times we don't debate smartly. We need to "wise up" enough to know which audiences need which vocabulary and which concepts emphasized. This does not mean that we change our basic professional beliefs each time there is pressure to adjust or conform. We do need to know which disabilities need which service goals and which settings need to emphasize specific services. This is not a license to do what we want regardless of professional advancement. I believe we have an obligation to be current and then accommodate diversity within our profession. The late psychiatrist, Paul Haun, addresses this issue with the following words:

> "Occasionally we confuse (this) splendid freedom of choice with
> the notion that a similar latitude exists with respect to the respon-
> sibilities and the privileges of specific occupations . . . It takes a partic-
> ularly unclear type of thinking to argue that the first baseman . . .
> while covering first, also be allowed to pitch since he is just as fine
> a (person) as the pitcher . . . It would be a mistake to assume that
> recreation workers deal with identical problems in every setting
> where ill or disabled persons are cared for . . ." (1977, p. 93)

Our philosophy of therapeutic recreation must reflect the broad scope of settings where therapeutic recreation exists. As the medical profession is expanding its views of medicine, we must not become so narrow (i.e., only treatment focused) as to philosophically become out of sync with the very profession from whom we seek increased recognition. At the same time, we must be specific and clear about which type of service we do offer. If we do this, succinct measures of quality will become possible. If we continue to attempt to be all things to all people within the same program, the measurement of quality becomes an impossible task.

In relation to philosophy and quality, our vocabulary often hinders communication. I am continuously amazed at the frequent occurrence of vocabulary problems within our profession. While riding on a bus with a nationally known therapeutic recreation philosopher, I couldn't resist asking, "So what is your philosophy of therapeutic recreation?" He responded with words that I thought showed agreement between the two of us. One half hour later, I realized that he was using the same words but they had different meaning to each of us. When I use the word "treatment," I'm referring to planned pre-determined purposeful intervention. When he was using the word "treatment," he meant that any recreation activity is inherently therapeutic. In another meeting with a national leader at a conference banquet, two of us debated over the concept of leisure-ability. When I use the term, I'm referring to preparation of the individual for post discharge leisure functioning (i.e., decision-making skills, leisure awareness, knowledge of resources, etc.). My colleague agreed with the concept, yet not the term. In this later case, there was agreement in concept but not in the use of terms while in the prior example there was use of the same terms but they referred to different concepts.

How can we as a profession begin to measure quality if we have such difficulty communicating? I think we can. Other professions have ongoing vocabulary and philosophical debates. For example, psychology accommodates the behaviorist, the gestaltist and the cognitive therapist all within one profession. Our solution lies not in having iron clad clear vocabulary (as nice as that may sound) but in being willing to accommodate differing opinions within our philosophical models. We need to think and look beyond our particular agencies and accommodate the scope of the profession. Just as different clients have different needs, different aspects of the therapeutic recreation profession have different measures of quality. As Kinney and Shank explain, " There is a gap between theory and practice, partially due to the 'contextless individual.' Our models don't adequately account for situational variables. There is great diversity in practice. Insisting on a single conceptualization and philosophy may stifle discovery and growth of our helpful but immature discipline." (1987, p. 72)

Measuring quality means then that we (in our agencies) define the purpose of our program and implement our programs using the same goals. It doesn't mean that I claim to do treatment and offer mass programming of bowling for everyone. It doesn't mean that I say I help prepare clients for a leisure lifestyle and then just offer recreation participation activities. Quality assurance means evaluating our programs according to results (outcomes) of the client. In addition, quality assurance means documenting our program methods (lesson plans, protocols, systems, etc.) so that we can replicate successful programs. It truly is a "cop out" to claim that "each individual is different" as an excuse for not documenting program methods. Of course each individual is different. A dentist knows that each person's mouth is different, yet he or she can pick the right tool through guidelines, not through unlimited choices. Therapeutic recreation needs to define the parameters of the profession and the tools available for use within the scope of our services. As technology and our body of knowledge grow, we need to keep current. When we are current and choose the appropriate methods to achieve the goals that will meet our clients' needs within the delimited parameters of our profession, then quality is possible.

## Pressures Affecting Quality

During my graduate school days, there was great pressure for therapeutic recreation to gain an identity distinct from the general field of recreation. For hours we debated "Is all recreation therapeutic?" Seldom is this debate current among therapeutic recreation professionals. However, I find myself every few years being pulled into that same old debate with a general recreation colleague or a local professional from another human service occupation. Quality in this context refers to the extent that therapeutic recreation has an established identity in its own right.

A major continuing pressure concerns the concept of accountability. This concept spans topics such as therapeutic recreation budgets, staff time, programming, treatment outcomes and so on. Documentation pressures, finding valid assessments and being included in the treatment plans or staffings are all related to accountability issues. We've all heard or read about increased competition in health care, hospitals and institutions servicing the more acutely ill or more severely disabled clients, and the trends toward more outpatient and home-based programs. As therapeutic recreation becomes more "clinically" accountable we begin to make great strides in areas that have been either neglected or floundering over the past several years. The emerging advocate in this arena is the American Therapeutic Recreation Association (ATRA). Caution, however, is warranted. We as a profession should not think or act as if all of health care were inpatient oriented. As health care expands to include home care, outpatient care, day treatment and other newer structures, therapeutic recreation must not focus solely on inpatient treatment. We must act as if and believe that the quality health care programs of the upcoming decade will be ones that include therapeutic recreation services. That means that therapeutic recreation professionals need to now be included in the planning stages of whatever new program structures are being discussed in each facility and community.

As we focus on being more clinically accountable, we quickly learn to address the area of fiscal responsibility and eventually third party reimbursement. Some therapeutic recreation programs are successfully receiving third party reimbursement. This is a measure of quality. However, the absence of third party reimbursement does not necessarily indicate the absence of quality therapeutic recreation services. I'll not enter into a detailed discussion about the scope or methods of obtaining third party reimbursement or other methods of fiscal accountability. I will however briefly relate three current thoughts on reimbursement to the issue of quality in therapeutic recreation.

Therapeutic recreation experts in third party reimbursement have introduced us to such publications as the *ICD-9 manuals,* which often serve as a basis of coding for fiscal reimbursement. These experts say "If we could just redefine our services in *functional terms*, we would then have a better chance at receiving reimbursement." I conditionally agree. While it is important for therapeutic recreation to develop, refine and incorporate functional terminology into our professional practice and documentation, we should only do that for *some* of our services. Not all services in therapeutic recreation should be functionally oriented. To me, the measure of quality becomes: "Are we using functional measures in the appropriate areas of therapeutic recreation service?"

The second concern often cited in relation to reimbursement discussions is truly more of a quality assurance topic. Experts claim that, "If we just had well-formulated outcomes in therapeutic recreation, we would be more accountable and

more reimbursable." Again, I conditionally agree. This issue becomes complicated when we admit that some of the outcomes we'll be striving for in therapeutic
recreation will not be realized until after discharge from an agency. For example,
the alcoholic's ability to use solid decision-making skills in relation to the use of
alcohol and leisure resources will often not be tested until an inpatient treatment
program is completed. A person with a spinal cord injury needs the ability to seek
out accessible resources and practice social skills with a newly acquired disability.
We may not be able to measure or receive reimbursement for such outcomes. Yet
it is important to continue to work toward such outcomes.

The third quality related message is centralized in the old statement: "If we
could just demonstrate the need for our services, we would be able to receive
reimbursement in therapeutic recreation." Again I extend only conditional agreement. The demonstration of need does not necessarily result in payment of
services. My personal experience with my HMO testifies to this. As I made a
very logical and well substantiated argument requesting a referral for services
offered outside my HMO, my physician frankly stated, "You may need those
services but we don't always get what we need in life." My request for referral
and payment for such services was denied.

Therapeutic recreation will make a grave mistake if the profession begins to
equate quality with reimbursement. Some of our needed high quality therapeutic
recreation services may never get reimbursed. Does this mean we stop delivering
those services? In some settings, that might be a reality. Yet if we really assume a
visionary stance and attempt strategic planning, maybe we need to be focusing on
service delivery structures that go beyond the inpatient reimbursement nightmares.
As inpatients are "sicker" and have a shorter stay, therapeutic recreation may need
to focus less on the inpatient services. Many of our professional outcomes are
more long range. We need to be thinking about outpatients, homecare, hospice,
group homes, residential facilities and structures that do not yet even exist yet. We
need to be involved on the ground floor of newer health care delivery structures.
The "illness of preference" might need to be an illness where therapeutic recreation can make an impact given the length of stay, and the specific environment or
setting.

Quality then is matching the appropriate therapeutic recreation service with
the designated disability, illness or condition. Quality assurance then involves the
monitoring of therapeutic recreation's participation in these newer programs. This
monitoring needs to precede any evaluation of the effectiveness of therapeutic
recreation services. Temple University's upcoming conference (1991) on efficacy
in therapeutic recreation is the first national effort to share the results of monitoring and evaluation of therapeutic recreation services' efforts in rehabilitation.
Additional efficacy studies would also enhance our knowledge about quality in
therapeutic recreation. Yet, we have many other methods of quality assurance or

quality improvement available to us as a profession. Individually and collectively, we as therapeutic recreation professionals must regularly use these quality assurance methods.

## Directions and Strategies in Quality Assurance

Which is the best or the most practical quality assurance method available to therapeutic recreation specialists? Which quality assurance methods will health care be using during the next several years? Dr. Dennis O'Leary, President of the Joint Commission on Healthcare Organizations provides us with insight to these questions: "Faced with a compelling need to develop rigorous methods for evaluating the quality and appropriateness of care, we have no science to draw upon. That science can and will be developed, but fruition is a decade or more away." (1988, p. 32)

Certainly therapeutic recreation specialists will need to utilize the quality assurance methods that are required by regulatory agencies or the employing agency. Yet beyond these specific quality assessment methods, therapeutic recreation specialists can and should address quality assurance on both organizational and attitudinal levels.

Organizationally, therapeutic recreation must be active at both a national and local level. For example, at the national level both ATRA and NTRS need to be working to eventually develop agreed upon standards of practice for the entire profession. On a local level, I can provide input to the development of these national standards of practice. I can also document the goals, content and process that I use in my therapeutic recreation programs. I can keep an updated "written plan of operation" for my therapeutic recreation department so that at least at the agency level, I become accustomed and comfortable with following professional therapeutic recreation standards.

In another example, ATRA is in the process of developing protocols for therapeutic recreation practice. Again at the local level, I can provide input into the development of these protocols. I can also begin to develop agency level protocols. It is a sign of quality to act before one is required to act. If therapeutic recreation specialists are proactive in relation to the development of protocols and standards of practice, a quality assurance mechanism will be developing simultaneously.

A third example of an organizational strategy for therapeutic recreation's quality assurance efforts involves the initiation and coordination of efficacy research. When we discover that "therapeutic recreation works" or directly contributes to the improved condition of clients, this information needs to be readily available and understandable by therapeutic recreation specialists. A national clearinghouse that monitors current relevant research would be exceptionally useful. On the local level, therapeutic recreation specialists can be laying the groundwork for efficacy information without being involved in formal research studies. The thorough documentation of our therapeutic recreation programs in relation to specific disabilities or specific client goals would provide useful information at the agency level. In addition, we need to implement the most current quality assurance information available even before we are required to do so. Bob Riley once said it will take five years for the therapeutic recreation field to catch up with the content of the last ATRA quality assurance conference. I will be pleased if the entire profession of therapeutic recreation incorporates current quality assurance information within five years.

There are many ways that our individual attitudes affect the quality of our therapeutic recreation programs. Three attitudes in particular have direct relevance to quality assurance in therapeutic recreation.

First, we need to "stop thinking so black and white." There are not right and wrong answers for our profession. Terminology is a relevant example of black and white thinking. Some therapeutic recreation specialists insist on using the phrase "functional improvement" as the ultimate purpose in therapeutic recreation. Functional improvement may be appropriate in a rehabilitation setting. In a residential center for severely and profoundly retarded individuals, the term "habilitation" may be more appropriate. In an alcoholism treatment center the term "leisure lifestyle" may have the most relevance. Some therapeutic recreation specialists say that we are in the business of "medicine." Others claim we are in the business of "wellness." Others prefer the term "health care" to encompass both the medical and the wellness aspects of therapeutic recreation services. Still others prefer the even broader term of "human services" to describe our professional affiliations. We each have a frame of reference. We can disagree. I do not need to shut down communications because our vocabulary or concepts differ.

The second attitudinal block that directly influences our quality assurance efforts is censorship. We need to "stop trying to censor." Having strong convictions is commendable. Yet we each need to be able to talk with someone who thinks differently. We need to be open to the process of being influenced by them. We need the freedom to grow, to change, to expand, and to say "oops!"

The earlier example of the field of psychology has relevance to therapeutic recreation. The cognitive oriented psychologist helps clients gain insight or think differently in order to improve their lives. The behavioral-oriented psychologist may focus on environmental or behavioral changes of the client. The affectively-oriented psychologist emphasizes the identification and expression of feelings as a means toward improvement. Not only do the methods drastically differ, the stated goals or outcomes may differ. The same is true in therapeutic recreation. While we each may be striving for an improved quality of life, the methods and outcomes will differ. The profession must be able to accommodate such diversity and not believe that only one way is the correct way of functioning professionally. This tolerance and even cherishing of diversity is basically attitudinal.

A third attitude which influences our quality assurance efforts is an "attitude of power." We as a group of professionals and individually as therapeutic recreation specialists, need to feel empowered. We can't be powerful in every area. Yet if we possess a strong sense of powerlessness, there's little chance that we'll initiate something like a new quality assurance program. If I feel powerless, is it because I'm not involved with other professionals who can educate and inspire me? Is it that I'm choosing the wrong battles or the wrong time to do battle? When I feel powerful, I'm more creative, energetic and less defensive. I'm able to examine and monitor aspects of my program and look for areas to improve. I'm also able to take credit for areas of my program when I operate from a core of confidence.

Related to this attitudinal arena, I believe there are some professional "obligations" and some professional "smart moves." For example, an obligation for therapeutic recreation specialists working in facilities accredited by the Joint Commission is to know the quality assurance standards and the ten step QA process of the Joint Commission. A smart move for these same practitioners is to attend a conference on quality assurance in therapeutic recreation. Another smart move is to systematize one's therapeutic recreation programs. A third smart move is to keep current with the development of professional standards of practice and protocols in therapeutic recreation.

An obligation related to quality assurance is one's professional reading. I believe that each therapeutic recreation specialist has an obligation to read regularly the current literature in therapeutic recreation. Without current information, we attempt to practice from a position of outdatedness or ignorance.

Another obligation is to maintain current membership in professional therapeutic recreation organizations. Regardless of my own professional training or credentialling eligibility, I can make a commitment to the future advancement of therapeutic recreation. Professional membership and certification are accepted as state of the art measures of quality in most human service professions. Therapeutic recreation needs this quality improvement effort from each person working in therapeutic recreation.

A final "smart move" is to think aloud with fellow therapeutic recreation professionals. I believe it is important to share ideas with new colleagues, even those who think a little differently than I might. Many times I believe we have the right answers. Maybe we just need to learn to ask the right questions. How do we find the myriad of right questions concerning quality improvement in therapeutic recreation? We need to start monitoring and then evaluating what we are professionally doing now at an agency, professional organization and personal level. Once we acquire the habit of such a practice, high quality service will be inherent in therapeutic recreation programs.

## Endnotes

1. Nancy Navar and Julie Dunn, on behalf of the National Therapeutic Recreation Society, made official contact with Richard Weedman, then Associate Director of the Accreditation Program for Psychiatric Facilities of the Joint Commission on Accreditation of Hospitals.
2. The first quality assurance book in therapeutic recreation is presently out of print: Navar, N. and Dunn, J. (Eds.) *Quality Assurance: Concerns for Therapeutic Recreation.* Champaign, Illinois: Department of Leisure Studies, University of Illinois, 1980.
3. Both the first (1979) and second (1984) editions of the following text include a complete chapter on activity analysis in therapeutic recreation. Peterson, Carol A. and Scout L. Gunn, *Therapeutic Recreation Program Design : Principles and Procedures.* Englewood Cliffs, NJ: Prentice Hall, 1984.
4. Peterson provides a detailed explanation of a systems approach to program planning that has great utility in therapeutic recreation services (same text listed in Endnote 3).
5. A summary of four current philosophical approaches to therapeutic recreation can be found in the following text. Reynolds, Ronald P. and Gerald S. O'Morrow, *Problems, Issues and Concepts in Therapeutic Recreation* Englewood Cliffs, NJ: Prentice Hall, 1985.

## References

Haun, P. (1977). *Recreation: A Medical Viewpoint.* (Fourth Printing) Columbia University, NY: Teachers College Press.

Kinney, W. and Shank, J. (1987). On The Neglect Of Clinical Practice, In Sylvester, C.; Hemingway, J. L.; Howe Murphy, R.; Mobily, K.; and Shank, P. (Ed.) (1987). *Philosophy Of Therapeutic Recreation: Ideas and Issues.* Alexandria, VA: National Recreation and Park Association.

Navar, N. and Dunn, J. (1980). *Quality Assurance: Concerns for Therapeutic Recreation.* Champaign, IL: Department of Leisure Studies, University of Illinois.

O'Leary, D. (1988). The Need for Clinical Standards of Care, *Quality Review Bulletin*, February, 1988.

Peterson, C. A. and Gunn, S. L. (1984). *Therapeutic Recreation Program Design: Principles and Procedures.* Englewood Cliffs, NJ: Prentice Hall.

Reynolds, R. P. and O'Morrow, G. S. (1985). *Problems, Issues and Concepts in Therapeutic Recreation*. Englewood Cliffs, NJ:  Prentice Hall.

Riley, B. (Ed.) (1987). *Evaluation of Therapeutic Recreation Through Quality Assurance*. State College, PA:  Venture Publishing, Inc.

Scalenghe, R. (1988). Unpublished Presentation at ATRA Quality Assurance Conference, Palo Alto, CA.

Sylvester, C.; Hemingway, J.L.; Howe Murphy, R.; Mobily, K.; and Shank, P. (Ed.) (1987). *Philosophy Of Therapeutic Recreation: Ideas and Issues*. Alexandria, VA:  National Recreation and Park Association.

# CHAPTER TWO

# "Vision Statements" and "Mission Statements": Macro Indicators Of Quality Performance

CARMEN V. RUSSONIELLO, C.T.R.S.

**The soul .... never thinks without a picture.**
**Aristotle**

## Introduction

During the past several years there has been much talk in the therapeutic recreation profession about the need to be accountable. Most of this effort has concentrated on establishing measurable goals and/or clinical indicators. These micro approaches are very important and essential components of quality care. Yet, they are only a part of the total synergistic process.

Current thinking, outcropping from progressive corporations and researchers in the field of leadership and organizational theory (Bass, 1985, Wolfe, 1985, Roberts, 1987 and Gardner, 1990), portend that micro indicators of quality must be superseded by macro indicators. These macro indicators, they assert, are not only the catalyst for the generation of micro indicators, but also provide a benchmark to measure individual and organizational desired outcomes.

Applicable macro indicators are the concepts reflected in "Vision" and "Mission" statements. While these statements defy strict monitoring and can only be loosely measured, they nonetheless provide a cauldron from which micro indicators originate. Vision and mission statements also affirm the existence and importance of individual and collective values. Furthermore, they speak to the nature of the business we are in. Put another way, a collective mission statement and vision statement can provide the therapist, recreational therapy department or an organization with a global "picture" from which quality care can emanate. The purpose of this paper is to explore vision and mission statements and their relationship to quality assurance in therapeutic recreation.

## Vision Statement Defined

A vision statement is a description of a desired state that an organization or therapeutic recreation department commits to. It represents the organizational assertion of where a particular therapeutic recreation service wants to be. A common belief is held "that this vision will be good for the individual, good for the unit, and good for the organization" (Block, 1987, p. 101). Vision statements are often a one or two sentence collective interpretation of what constitutes quality service. They are based on patient, employee, and organizational values.

While it may be true that organizations and/or departments can survive without a clearly defined vision statement, the corollary, is often fragmentation and ultimate dysfunction. In other words, when there is no clear picture of what one hopes to achieve, then quality cannot be assured. If one patient program follows one set of expectations and other programs follow different sets, then continuity is ambiguous or nonexistent. To counteract this outcome, Riley (1987) proposes "establishing mutually acceptable standards that constitute quality care" (p. 9). Indeed, a vision statement is a communication of mutually acceptable standards based on individual and organizational values.

Practically speaking, an adolescent unit in an acute care psychiatric facility is most assuredly going to have different program goals than a geriatric program serviced by the same therapeutic recreation department. Rather than focusing on these differences the vision statement concentrates on the commonalities of the overall service such as providing equitable services in a caring, compassionate manner. In essence, the vision statement helps define what quality really means to those who provide the service. When these similarities are not clearly identified and continually articulated, employee motivation is detrimentally affected due to therapist dissonance. In turn, patient care and organizational values are sacrificed.

Therefore, in addition to providing a macro level indicator of quality and an affirmation of values, a vision statement provides motivation. Tichy and Devanna (1986) assert that this motivation comes in two forms. "First, it provides the challenge for which the organization and its members strive, it is the reach for excellence and the source of self-esteem for the members. The second purpose is to help provide a conceptual road map or a set of blue prints for what the organization will be in the future" (p. 128). Hence, a vision statement is an affirmation of values, a macro level indicator of quality and a motivator.

## Vision Statement Development

Figure 2.1, Perspective on Macro Level Indicators (Block, 1987) represents a visual description of contrasting macro indicators. The picture demonstrates a fusion of three macro indicators (vision, mission, objectives) and how they commingle for a synergistic relationship. For example, therapeutic recreation departments should develop their vision statement from both personal and organ-

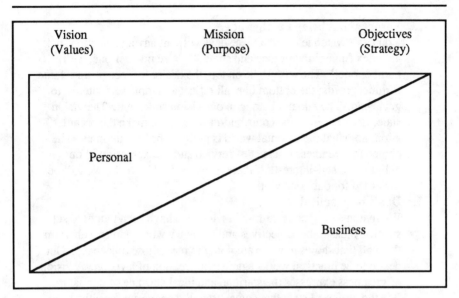

| Vision | Mission | Objectives |
|--------|---------|------------|
| (Values) | (Purpose) | (Strategy) |

Figure 2.1–Perspective on Macro Level Indicators

izational values. The dominant influence, however, should be personal values. Huston (1987) recognized the importance of this process when she stated, "(P)rofessional staff must collectively identify those aspects of care they consider most important" (p. 69).

Ask yourselves whether you care about the people you serve? If you do care, in what ways? Should all patients be treated equally? Do your patients deserve cost effective services? A vision statement is the collective identification of those aspects of care that recreational therapists feel are critical in the quest for quality.

Figure 2.1 further demonstrates that a department should compose a mission statement which reflects equally how the recreational therapist believes the department should be run and the expected outcomes of the business. As a recreational therapist, you have a purpose for practicing. This purpose needs to be woven together with the purpose of the business. The mission statement is a collective identification of these purposes. Finally, objective strategies should be created in order to carry out the responsibilities of the department. Review Navar (1987) and the Joint Commission for the Accreditation of Healthcare Organizations (1989) for excellent guidelines from which a written plan of operation can be developed.

A vision statement can usually be developed during one staff meeting. Both credentialed and noncredentialed staff should have input. Peter Block (1987), a strong proponent of the vision, offers the following pointers when creating your collective "vision of greatness":

1. **Forget about being number one.**
   You can't watch television these days without having someone stick an index finger in your face and shout, "We're number one, we're number one!" The wish to be on top, the desire for recognition, fame, fortune, profits; the bottom line, all reflect a myopic self-interest to get ahead. They do not belong in our vision statement. The vision statement expresses the contribution we want to make the organization, not what the external world is going to bestow upon us. The choice for greatness is an act of service and an expression of our enlightened self-interest. If there is justice in this world, we will be rewarded for our good work.

2. **Don't be practical.**
   We live in a pragmatic culture in which we have been taught to set specific measurable objectives and to have a work plan or a chart on the wall that shows how we are going to meet those objectives. Our desire to be practical works against the creation of a vision. A vision of greatness expresses the spiritual and idealistic side of our nature. It is the preferred state that comes from the heart, not from the head.

3. **Begin with your customers.**
   The long term survival of an organization is dependent upon how well the organization stays in touch with and serves its internal and external customers. In the short run, it can sustain itself through price increases, cost control, or a friendly banker (administrator), but ultimately the reality of the marketplace determines the organization's future. This also applies to department operating within the larger organization.

4. **You can't treat your customers any better than you treat each other.**
   An additional vital element in our vision is how we treat each other within the unit. Each of our customers wants a unique and understanding response from us. If, within the unit, we are cautious, competitive, and judgmental with each other, we won't be able to give the customers the response they want . . . . Our own unit is also our testing ground for discovering what is possible for organizations. One of our primary purposes is to create within our own unit a model of how we want the whole organization to function.

5. **If your vision statement sounds like motherhood and apple pie and is somewhat embarrassing, you are on the right track.**
   A vision is an expression of hope and idealism. It oversimplifies the world and implies that anything is possible (pp. 112-115).

If your statement is first, from your collective hearts; second, is unique to your service; and third, is compelling, then you have it (Block, p. 115). Your vision statement can now serve as a source of motivation, a macro indicator of quality and an affirmation of personal and organizational values. Couple this with a pithy mission statement that expounds on your department's business and you will have two excellent macro indicators of quality performance. Write both statements down. Congratulate yourselves. You are on the cutting edge of organizational development. Now every time you develop programs and/or clinical indicators and wonder whether you are providing quality look to your vision and mission statement. They will provide a place to begin to evaluate your efforts as well as the outcomes of your service. The following statement serves as an example of a Department Vision Statement.

## Vision Statement

The recreational therapy department at Chrisville Hospital will continually strive to provide excellent and equitable service to all patients by assimilating state-of-the-art professional techniques and applying them in a caring and compassionate manner. We are intent on treating each other with dignity, respect and empathy. Consequently, the patients we serve will be treated in a similar manner.

### Department Mission Statement

The mission statement can be developed during the same meeting as the vision statement. As indicated earlier both vision and mission statements convey important macro indicators of quality (See Figure 2.1). Yet, vision and mission statements differ significantly. Whereas "a vision is really a dream created in our waking hours of how we would like the organization to be, the mission is a statement of what business we are in and sometimes our ranking in that business" (Block, p. 107). Again, vision and mission go "hand in hand," but the vision statement represents a desired future, where as the mission statement represents the type of therapeutic recreation business you represent.

The mission statement should tell something of the recreational therapy business you are in. It should reflect how it is perceived in comparison to competitors as well as denote what the consumer can expect as a result of the service. Potential consumers of therapeutic recreation service will not pay money for a treatment from a service that can not articulate what business they represent. Consumers will not be trusting that outcomes compatible with their needs are going to be reached when such outcomes have not been predetermined. Consequently, the perception of this program, in regard to other programs or competition, will be negatively viewed. One excellent way to avoid this problem is to develop a mission statement that articulates the business you are in and sets the parameters on which the business or department operates. An example of a mission statement is presented as follows.

## Mission Statement

The Chrisville Hospital recreation therapy department's mission is to lead all other therapies in providing quality, cost effective, health care services that ultimately increase the patient's independent functioning while providing a profit for the organization and opportunities for the growth of the employees.

This particular mission reflects a health care business that provides professional, caring services while seeking a reasonable profit. It also clearly indicates that opportunities for employee growth are directly tied into the success of the business. Therefore, when goals and objectives (micro indicators/strategies) are developed, they will need to reflect these macro indicators.

Earlier, during the discussion involving vision statements, an adolescent and geriatric psychiatric unit were used to draw a comparison to demonstrate the need for a mechanism to articulate a synergistic model of recreational therapy structure. The same example can also demonstrate how micro indicators originate, are shaped, or are rejected. If you look at the Chrisville, "vision and mission," statements you will see that this therapeutic recreation department states that maximizing individual independent functioning in a cost effective manner is critical to the success of this business.

Therefore, questions such as: "Does the geriatric program maximize independent functioning for clients?" or "Is the treatment provided cost effective?" become logical probes that help staff focus on the purposes of the department. If the Chrisville Therapeutic Recreation Department is not meeting these goals, then what different programs could be developed for success? (origination of micro indicators), can the existing program be modified? (shaping of micro indicators), and finally, should this program be terminated? (rejection of micro indicators).

Obviously, the situation becomes complicated when the adolescent program objectives are included in this scheme. Now you have to balance the needs of two departments. Certain decisions will have to be made that will affect the patient, the staff and the organization. As long as you include the consumer's needs (cost effective treatment), the consideration of staff values (treat all patients equally and in a caring, compassionate manner), the organization goal (profit), this department should not have difficulty making decisions. In fact, if vision and mission statements are truly part of the overall organizational culture, which they should be, then it should be easy to tell if particular actions or programs are in line with what this department has defined as quality.

In conclusion, a vision is a collective statement of where the department or organization wants to be. It enhances motivation and provides a benchmark for value measurement. A mission statement, on the other hand, sets the tone of what business you are in and provides several overall goals of that service. Together, vision and mission statements serve as macro indicators from which micro indicators originate.

Vision and mission statements assure quality of services. These macro indicators are essential to the development of a sound management strategy and an effective quality assurance program. Without a clear mandate and sense of purpose, many therapeutic recreation programs will potentially experience major setbacks. In a competitive health care market, this is a situation that therapeutic recreation services can ill afford.

## References

Bass, B.M. (1985). *Leadership and Performance Beyond Expectations*. New York, NY: The Free Press.

Block, P. (1987). *The Empowered Manager*. San Francisco, CA: Jossey-Bass.

Gardner, J.W. (1990). *On Leadership*. New York, NY: The Free Press.

Huston, A.D. (1987). "Clinical Application of Quality Assurance in the Therapeutic Recreation Setting. " In Riley, B. (Ed). *Evaluation of Therapeutic Recreation Through Quality Assurance*. State College, PA: Venture Publishing, Inc.

Joint Commission for Accreditation of Healthcare Organizations, (1989). Proposed Principles of Organizational and Management Effectiveness for Health Care Organizations. *News About the Agenda for Change*. 3:1, p. 5-6.

Navar, N. (1987). Therapeutic Recreation's Written Plan of Operation: The Step Before Quality Assurance. In Riley, B. (Ed). *Evaluation of Therapeutic Recreation Through Quality Assurance*. State College, PA: Venture Publishing, Inc.

Riley, B. (1987). Conceptual Basis of Quality Assurance: Application to Therapeutic Recreation Service. In Riley, B. (Ed). *Evaluation of Therapeutic Recreation Through Quality Assurance*. State College, PA: Venture Publishing, Inc.

Roberts, W. (1987). *Leadership Secrets of Attila The Hun*. New York, NY: Warner.

Tichy, N.M. and Devanna, M.A. (1986). *The Transformational Leader*. New York, NY: John Wiley & Sons.

Wolfe, R.O. (1985). The Synergistic Model of Organizational Structure. *Planning & Changing*, 16, Spring, p. 51-59.

CHAPTER THREE

# The Joint Commission's "Agenda for Change" as Related to the Provision of Therapeutic Recreation Services

RICHARD SCALENGHE, RMT*

## Introduction

For reasons familiar to us all, the health care environment is rapidly changing bringing about a growing public interest in the quality of health care and a related increase in demand for public accountability for quality. Health professionals share this concern and are beginning to ask important questions: How good is the care being provided?

How is it changing over time? By geographic area? By type of provider? What response is expected when care is found to be substandard? Are these responses effective in improving care? As an integral part of the health care delivery team, today's Therapeutic Recreation professional finds him/herself confronted with these issues and is attempting to demonstrate accountability for the services that he/she provides.

Previously, there has been an implicit assumption of high quality in the health care system, based largely upon public trust in health care professionals (especially physicians) and health care institutions. Now as awareness grows that there is wide variability in utilization rates, practice patterns, and clinical results, the public (through government, business, insurers, consumers, and other interest groups) is seeking information concerning how much of this variation reflects actual quality differences.

The issue is further sharpened by the current major restructuring of the health care system. Service diversifications, managed care, risk sharing, vertical and horizontal integration, and "corporatization" of care all add new variables to an already complex equation. Broader choices for health care purchasers haveled these decision-makers to seek reliable guidance in evaluating and reconciling

---

\* Richard Scalenghe has adapted this chapter to the field of Therapeutic Recreation from various articles and papers developed by the Joint Commission's Department of Research and Development.

cost *and* quality considerations. As these forces place a spotlight on the quality of health care, sharply defined but difficult questions emerge. Who is assuming responsibility for the quality of a patient's care as the patient traverses multiple health care settings, organizations and practitioners? Are existing systems of information diffusion sufficient to assure that current knowledge is consistently utilized in day-to-day clinical decision-making? Do the information and decision-making systems in health care organizations provide adequate support for rigorous, day-to-day attention to the quality of care? To what extent do the expectations for health care services differ among practitioners, consumers, businesses, insurers and government? Indeed, what are the service priorities among these groups, and how does each of them define quality in health care? Can existing differences be reconciled and then be reflected in meaningful approaches for monitoring the quality of care? And can the objective of a better informed public be met in a substantive fashion acceptable to providers and consumers?

The initial step for therapeutic recreation in approaching this task is to start with a critical review of similar endeavors attempted by other health care professional organizations. A careful review of the experience of others should reduce the unnecessary duplication of effort, limit the foreseeable roadblocks and pitfalls and reduce the need for "reinventing the wheel."

Health care professionals should appreciate that the cornerstone of accountability is evolution. Systems should develop over time to become more sophisticated approaches for monitoring and evaluating the quality and appropriateness of care.

As a start, the therapeutic recreation profession should take a critical look at its standards of practice. Do they adequately reflect today's provision of service? Are they comprised of structure, process and outcome expectations? Are they too general or specific? Do they provide any guidance for the management and administrative components which enable the provision of quality therapeutic recreation services? Could they be used as a basis for assessing accountability?

In addition to professional standards of practice, a significant amount can be learned from understanding and appreciating the evolution of the Joint Commission standards. During the past, as is true today, the resources necessary for assessing quality have been limited. Most standards are based on either structure (e.g., a resource) or process (e.g., an event of activity) standards. An example of a structure standard is: "Activity schedules are posted in places accessible to patients and staff" (JCAHO, 1987). An example of process standards is: "An assessment of the patient's leisure, social, and recreational abilities, deficiencies, interests, barriers, life experiences, needs and potential" (JCAHO, 1988).

At present, Joint Commission accreditation attests to an institution's or clinical department's compliance with accepted standards of structure and process and answers the basic question: *"Can* this organization/department provide quality health care?" For Therapeutic Recreation, there is a consensus that the above structure and process standards (at least) should be in place for quality therapeutic recreation services to be provided.

However, public government, business insurers and other consumers today are asking more than the above "can" question. The Joint Commission is attempting to help institutions answer the questions, *"Does* this organization provide quality health care?" Therefore, within therapeutic recreation, it is no longer sufficient to demonstrate that structures and processes are in place but, in addition, to demonstrate that the patient changed as a result of such care.

Drawing upon the rapidly evolving clinical and organizational research literature and recognizing the importance of more direct evaluation of performance, the Joint Commission intends, through a project entitled, "THE AGENDA FOR CHANGE," to move beyond the current primary focus on evaluating a health care organization's *capability* of delivering quality care to the monitoring and evaluation of *clinical and organizational performance.* This initiative involves the development of a more precise and objective evaluation of clinical and managerial performance. The purpose is to substantially improve the Joint Commission's capability to aid and stimulate health care organizations to provide high quality care.

Health care quality is often analyzed by the use of measures related to the structures, processes, and outcomes of assessment/diagnosis and treatment protocol as well as by the interrelationships among these precesses. Clinical excellence, in turn, relies upon and is supported by the quality of the organizational environment within which patient care is delivered. Both clinical and organizational excellence are essential components of quality, and the Joint Commission is convinced that it is appropriate and timely to encourage a more direct assessment of both.

The Joint Commission is not developing a capability to judge, on its own part, the actual quality of care provided by an organization seeking accreditation. Rather, the Joint Commission is committed to developing more accurate methods to evaluate the effectiveness of those governance, management, clinical and quality assurance activities which are most important in assuring the provision of high quality care.

Specifically, the above outlined developmental efforts, if successful, will allow the Joint Commission to:

- Use valid and reliable clinical indicators as screening devices to identify potential problems in the organization, provision or monitoring of care;
- Apply more relevant organizational standards and related indicator measures in evaluating the effectiveness of the governance and management of health care institutions; and
- Render accreditation decisions that reflect more accurately the adequacy of an organization's attention to providing high quality care.

## AGENDA FOR CHANGE

Five components, described in more detail below, comprise the research and development activities related to the Agenda for Change:

1. Identification and selection of clinical indicators
2. Identification and selection of organizational and management indicators
3. Development of risk adjustment methods
4. Establishment of an ongoing monitoring and evaluation process
5. Modification of survey and accreditation procedures

### Clinical Indicators

The Joint Commission intends to formulate a system which provides for more effective and accurate evaluation of an organization's clinical performance through the use of carefully selected clinical indicators. These indicators are to be identified by task forces of carefully chosen clinical experts, all having extensive experience in evaluating the quality of care in their clinical settings.

Clinical performance may be monitored by analyzing data concerning structures, processes and outcomes of diagnosis/assessment or treatment (Table 3.1). Although measurement of clinical activities (processes) is one step removed from measurement of clinical results (outcomes), process measures are often the most direct measure of what health care practitioners contribute to the care of the patient. Timely and effective delivery of health care services, including preventive care, is also essential to the avoidance/reduction of complications and to the promotion of good health.

An indicator is defined as a measurable dimension of the quality or appropriateness with respect to an important aspect of patient care. Indicators describe measurable care processes, clinical events, complications, or outcomes for which data should be collected to allow comparison against an established threshold. Examples of indicators include death, hospital-acquired infection, severe adverse drug reaction, and return to the operating room from the recovery room. Valid and reliable data concerning desired/expected results and undesired/unexpected results (whether measured with reference to the occurrence of single "sentinel events," rates of occurrence of clinical events, or changes in health status, quality of life, level of function, or patient satisfaction) can play an important role in a comprehensive monitoring and evaluation system.

From the Joint Commission's perspective, clinical indicator data are important only in the context of a meaningful quality assurance system which itself serves as the index as to how effectively a health care organization is measuring the quality of its care. Clinical indicators are not direct measures of quality; any determination about actual quality of patient care can only be made as part of a case-oriented peer review process. Quality of care judgements require individual decisions about acceptability of treatment processes and results.

Table 3.1–Issues Which Could Be Addressed Through Use of
Clinical Indicators

|  | Assessment/Diagnosis | Treatment |
| --- | --- | --- |
| **Structure** | • Availability of resources (staff, equipment) for accurate assessment/ diagnosis<br>• Assessment/Diagnostic protocols | • Availability of needed therapeutic resources;<br>• Treatment plans |
| **Process** | • Accuracy, timeliness, and technical skill in applying assessments diagnostic protocols | • Skill and technical quality of therapeutic interventions |
| **Outcome** | • Correctness of clinical formulation of assessment/ diagnosis | • Improvement in the patient's functional or health status/ symptom remission |

The proper use of clinical indicators requires that they be used only as objective screens for identifying those cases needing in-depth professional scrutiny. Indicators provide for an efficient mechanism and focus for the health care organization's peer review process by "flagging" instances of apparent substandard care or outcomes. The Joint Commission's interest lies principally in the quality of the organization's response to the potential problem highlighted by aberrant indicator data.

Unfortunately, at present there is no national consensus regarding a uniform set of valid and reliable clinical indicators. Measures which have been utilized by individual organizations are often administrative rather than clinical in nature, and are focused on technical quality control rather than patient-directed quality assurance, or are oriented heavily toward clinical processes rather than results. Utilizing expert task forces and real-world pilot testing, the Joint Commission is in the process of identifying the best available clinical indicators for use in the quality assurance programs of accredited organizations. Through this process, the Joint Commission believes it can improve both its own evaluative capability and that of the organization it surveys.

Critical clinical indicators, whether they reflect aggregated rates or single sentinel events, are to be pre-established to monitor diagnostic and treatment activities as shown in Table 3.1. For high volume and/or high risk and/or potentially problematic care, indicators should be selected which have relevance for organization-wide review, for cross-department review, or for specialty-specific review. Several examples of each type are presented in Table 3.2.

Table 3.2–Examples of Clinical Indicators

| Hospitalwide Clinical Indicators | Cross-departmental Clinical Indicators | Specialty-specific Clinical Indicators |
|---|---|---|
| For general application: | For surgical departments: | For obstetrics department: |
| • Nosocomial infection rate<br>• Deaths<br>• Neurological impairment at discharge not present at admission<br>• Patient falls<br>• Hospital-acquired decubiti | • Complications of surgery<br>• Discrepancies between pre-op diagnosis and pathology findings<br><br>For medical departments:<br><br>• Drug interactions and and reactions<br>• Complications of IV and other lines | • Eclampsia<br>• Hyaline membrane disease after elective C-section<br>• Antibiotics after term vaginal delivery<br>• APGAR 3 at five minutes |

The clinical indicators initiative is aimed at redressing an imbalance in current Joint Commission accreditation activities, which currently focus on organizational structures and processes. Emphasis on the use of clinical indicators to track important clinical processes and outcomes is not intended to eliminate the Joint Commission's attention to structure and function. It still recognizes that all three aspects of care must be examined in an ongoing monitoring system in order to provide an accurate assessment of an organization's quality. The fundamental purpose of this monitoring activity is to prompt health care organizations to improve care through continuing education, structural changes, managerial improvements, and competence-based clinical privileging/job assignments.

## Organizational and Management Indicators

There are two necessary but not independently sufficient ingredients for patient care quality: excellence in clinical care and excellence in the governance and management of the environment within which clinical practice occurs. As described above, the intent in the area of patient care assessment is to add a valid clinical evaluation component to the Joint Commission accreditation process. The intent in the organizational arena is to provide more effective monitoring of critical organizational events and, equally important, to revise and improve the Joint Commission's traditional standards by focusing on the elements of structure and function which are most critical to the delivery of high quality care.

Although current accreditation manuals now describe many of the organizational structures and functions necessary to organize and administer an effective health care institution, these standards do not adequately discriminate "better" from "poorer" performing organizations–and therefore do not stimulate improvement in the latter. With assistance from an expert task force, the Joint Commission intends to identify the key dimensions of organizational function which exert the greatest influence on quality of care. These organizational characteristics will then be used to provide a template for reviewing current accreditation standards and for developing a more relevant, "streamlined" set of standards.

Some of the same organizational characteristics used to guide the revision of accreditation standards will be translated into indicators that can support the monitoring of governance/managerial effectiveness. The expert task force is utilizing two approaches in selecting organization and management quality indicators. The first approach focuses upon developing indicators that correspond to "traditional" administrative behaviors:  goal setting, planning, resource allocation, personnel management, financial management, evaluation, etc. This would essentially involve operationalizing "effective health care management," using measures that address the management activities that are believed (in light of expert opinion, experience, and/or organizational research findings) to directly influence quality of patient care.

The second approach involves the use of research literature to first identify characteristics of "successful" organizations, particularly health care organizations, second to develop indicators that operationalize these discriminating factors. The literature suggests that key characteristics may include the creation of mechanisms for conflict resolution; the setting of high internal standards; timely and accurate feedback to employees; more formal staff organization; and a participatory organizational culture, etc. Although such phenomena may not be easy to measure, nevertheless, application of such parameters may prove to be effective in simply stimulating improvement in organizations which are not optimally managed.

## Risk Adjustment Methods

There is a growing body of clinical research which clearly identifies significant variations in clinical practice. Because variation has been shown to exist for nearly any parameter which has been measured, we can safely predict that the same will occur to some of the indicators contemplated for use by the Joint Commission (e.g., mortality, nosocomial infections, anesthesia complications,

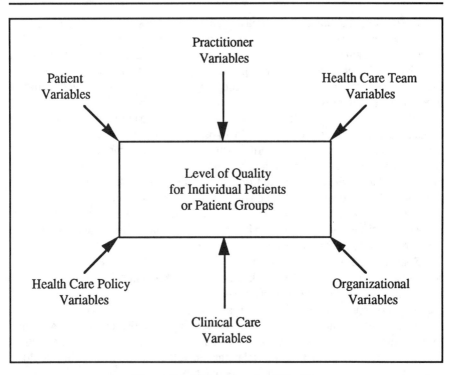

Figure 3.1–Determinants of Quality

Caesarian-section rates, etc.). This variance may reflect actual difference in quality of care–some of high quality, some of lower–or it may relate to differences in the case mix among patient populations being treated in different settings.

As presented in Figure 3.1, there are six major classes of variables that interact to influence quality of patient care. Organizational variables, both structural and procedural, have historically been the primary focus of Joint Commission standards and survey processes. Although practitioner, team, and clinical care variables have also been addressed in Joint Commission standards to a modest extent, a major challenge for the Agenda for Change is to identify a set of clinical indicators that will help shift attention from organizational capability to actual clinical performance.

But if cross-organizational comparisons of clinical indicator data are to be applied equitably, adjustment for patient variables (severity of illness, case complexity, etc.) is clearly required. Further, severity of illness adjustment becomes important in ensuring that screening data generate only *relevant* questions for additional investigation by accredited organizations. Thus, in addition to recommending clinical indicators, the expert task forces are also being asked to identify patient covariates that are associated with each clinical indicator.

The development of sound case complexity or severity of illness adjustment techniques should permit the Joint Commission to reduce the confounding effect of relevant patient characteristics upon measures of the performance of the organization. Likewise, with appropriate control for patient covariates, each organization will be better able to compare its performance to performance data from other providers.

"Severity adjustment" systems currently on the market have been designed primarily to address needs other than the purposes contemplated for both the Joint Commission's analysis of indicator data and the individual organization's internal quality assurance mechanisms. In fact, different risk adjustment methods may be required in various settings of care (ambulatory, hospice, nursing home) or for various hospital services (e.g., pediatrics, surgery, ICU).

With assistance from experts in the field, the Joint Commission intends to investigate techniques currently in use and then select, modify, or create the most feasible adjustment methodologies in order to minimize both false positives and false negatives that can emerge from review of indicator data. These risk adjustment approaches are to be tested and refined during pilot testing and field testing phases of the developmental process.

## Ongoing Monitoring and Evaluation Process

The Agenda for Change anticipates that the Joint Commission and accredited institutions will jointly participate in a continuous-flow monitoring system in which clinical *and* organizational data are periodically and regularly transmitted from the field, entered in a Joint Commission database, aggregated and analyzed, and then fed back to the organizations.

Data relative to specified indicators would be routinely and continuously collected by the institution and, at regular intervals throughout the period of accreditation, these clinical and organizational data would be submitted to the Joint Commission, either in writing or by computer. The periodicity of this transmission has yet to be established, and will be determined in view of cost, feasibility, and the need for timely analysis by the Joint Commission.

Upon receipt of clinical or organization/management data, the Joint Commission will process the information and provide timely feedback to the health care organization as additional input to its ongoing self-monitoring process. This cyclical collection and reporting of data would permit feedback of three general types, each involving an associated comparison of interest:

- The organization could promptly compare its performance to internal expectations as an "early warning system;"
- The organization could compare its performance to external expectations. Such external expectations, based on national performance criteria or "thresholds of acceptable performance," would include sufficient flexibility to permit local application; and

- The Joint Commission could summarize the indicator data and provide "norm-referenced" summaries. Each organization would then see its standing relative to the distribution of indicator data from similar (but anonymous) peer group institutions. This approach could be utilized whenever external evaluation criteria were lacking; at the least, empirical data would provide a base of actual experience from which to develop judgments of achievable, expected performance.

The design of the data retrieval, collection and transmission process, and of the data base itself, should allow each organization to build efficiently on its existing quality assurance activities. An effective monitoring and evaluation system requires valid clinical and managerial indicators. Irrespective of Joint Commission requirements, health care organizations should be collecting and analyzing important screening data for internal use. Although an ongoing interactive system may be more data intensive for both the provider and the Joint Commission, relatively little incremental time or cost should be required to advise the Joint Commission of indicator data already known to the organization.

As the implementation phase of this project approaches, the Joint Commission intends to provide health care organizations with the technical assistance they will need to smooth the interaction between existing "internal" QA programs and the Joint Commission's monitoring activities. The net result should be a quality review process whose focus is more clinical, which better addresses the adequacy of responses to problems, and which in the aggregate is substantially more results-oriented.

**Modified Survey and Accreditation Procedures**

The availability of clinical and organizational data suggests a future routine survey and monitoring process; this would include periodic on-site surveys during the ongoing cycle of data transmission. The current Joint Commission approach to institutional accreditation includes surveying organizational characteristics related to quality care as expressed in JCAHO standards. The compliance with which is assessed by on-site surveys and the findings lead to an accreditation decision. It is anticipated that the fundamental process will continue to be applied in the future but will utilize the streamlined standards which emerge from the review of key organizational characteristics noted earlier. To the right is illustrated the addition of an indicator-driven monitoring and feedback system. The effective use of data from this system, in contrast to the data themselves, would heavily influence the on-site survey process and ultimately the accreditation award.

Surveyors with appropriate skills will first be expected to validate the quality (reliability and validity) of the indicator data. Then, with knowledge of the organization's screening data "track record," the surveyor could zero in on the effectiveness of the institution's problem analysis and problem-solving processes. The effectiveness of actions taken to improve problematic clinical or organizational outcomes would also be assessed. In this model, emphasis is placed on the use of quantifiable screening indicators to identify problems and monitor their resolution; the performance data are not an end in themselves.

Responsibility for resolving clinical problems and for improving patient care rests with the health care organization, not the Joint Commission. Nonetheless, the Joint Commission's on-site survey process should also include consultation and education aimed at strengthening the organization's governance, management and clinical activities. That is, the surveyor could assist staff to examine how (and how well) they analyze potential performance deficits, evaluate antecedent structures and processes, and develop corrective action plans. Increased effectiveness of the organization's quality management processes should then be evidenced in subsequent transmittal of monitoring data to the Joint Commission.

A survey process utilizing clinical and organizational indicator data may lead to modification of Joint Commission accreditation decision-making procedures as well (e.g., on-site focused surveys might be triggered by indicator data). However, with several years of development, testing, and evaluation yet to unfold, it is difficult to state with any certainty how accreditation decision-making will be affected.

### Field Involvement in the Developmental Process

A developmental program as ambitious and far-reaching as that set forth above will not be accomplished in the near future, nor will the program be successful without continuous and extensive input from those involved in Joint Commission accreditation programs. Both the complexity and the importance of these quality assurance initiatives dictate that the Joint Commission move forward purposefully yet prudently through its developmental agenda.

The developmental process anticipates a measured progression from small-scale pilot tests to larger-scale field trials to incremental implementation with careful evaluation throughout. Full implementation is targeted for the early 1990s, beginning with hospitals—whose experience with indicator data is broader and whose data systems tend to be more sophisticated—and then widening to include long-term care, psychiatric, ambulatory, hospice, and home health services.

Input, guidance, and critique by health care providers will be critical to the success of the accreditation and survey process initiative of the Agenda for Change. The Joint Commission will seek to understand and to account for the field's capabilities and its perceptions in shaping the revised monitoring process. During the developmental phase, field involvement will take a variety of forms including, but not necessarily limited to, the following:

- participation in a poll of accredited organizations regarding data system capacities, clinical and organizational indicators now in use, and severity adjustment methods applied, if any
- involvement as pilot test sites

- evaluation of indicators developed by task forces
- voluntary submission of indicator data to the Joint Commission during "dry runs" of the system, with feedback of analyzed indicator data
- involvement as field trial sites
- review of proposed indicators and survey methods prior to implementation in the accreditation process
- membership in a broad-based Forum of Clinical Specialty Organizations

Throughout this engagement with the health care community, an interactive process of back-and-forth communication will be employed. These discussions will focus on assessing and evaluating the revised monitoring and survey processes from the perspectives of utility and conceptual soundness, feasibility and practicality, data validity and reliability, system flexibility and adaptability, and cost and value.

## Current and Anticipated Developments

In 1989, the clinical indicator development will expand to include four additional medical specialties: oncology care, trauma care, cardiovascular care, and general surgery. As appropriate, indicators and related risk factors will be identified that are applicable to all settings (inpatient and other) where such care is provided.

The Joint Commission will also begin to address the "nonhospital" field. Selection of the areas to be addressed were based upon such factors as prior activity related to indicator development, the existence of data systems and professional interest in such efforts. In view of this, the fields of mental health and long-term care were selected.

There is a growing demand in the mental health field for measures of clinical performance. This is demonstrated by the joint efforts of the National Association of Private Psychiatric Hospitals (NAPPH), the American Hospital Association (AHA) and the American Psychiatric Association (APA) to develop clinical indicators. The Joint Commission has actively participated in this process. Purchasers of mental health services have also expressed considerable interest in the development of clinical performance indicators in this field.

It is anticipated that the indicators for this field will cover the broad range of patient care provided in various settings (e.g., inpatient, residential, outpatient, and partial-day). Following the development of these indicators, further efforts for specialized areas of care such as forensic, substance abuse, etc., will be considered.

There has been a similar interest in the long term care field in the development of clinical indicators. There is a growing expectation that external review of nursing homes will include an evaluation of clinical performance. This is demonstrated by the institution of the "new Survey Process" which is required by the Health Care Financing Administration (HCFA) in the survey of nursing homes and which has caused considerable public interest. Related developmental activity has occurred in the field, including efforts of the Gerontological Society of America (GSA) to develop nursing indicators. A GSA-sponsored fellow recently spent several months at the Joint Commission as part of a project to develop these indicators. The Joint Commission's long-term care program is also involved in a contract with the Washington Health Care Association that includes the development of indicators in addition to the review of member nursing homes.

## Summary

The Joint Commission's "Agenda for Change" is an initiative that will launch a new era for quality assurance in health care. The centerpiece calls for developing severity-adjusted measurements of clinical care as well as organizational indicators of quality and incorporating these measurements into a modified and more relevant survey process. Recent advances in health care research methods and database developments permit more precision in monitoring and improving health care quality. Increased demands for quality data by providers, government, business, insurers, and consumers have encouraged the Joint Commission along with other organizations to focus on clinical and organizational indicators. The use of clinical and organizational indicators in the survey process will afford each institution timely feedback concerning its clinical and managerial performance. This collaborative venture between the Joint Commission and the health care organization will help the organization respond to increasing demands for quality of care documentation and data. More valid and reliable measurements of quality of care, and evidence of both good and less-than-optimal performance, will strengthen the institution's/department's ability to improve care.

There is a great opportunity here and now for the *Therapeutic Recreation* field to be proactive and join other professional organizations in defining what is a "quality and appropriate service"; how it changes over time; how does it differ by type of provider; what response is expected when care is found to be substandard; and how effective these responses are in improving care. When developing indicators, the Therapeutic Recreation professional (as will all other professionals) needs to consider different philosophies of treatment; issues of retrieval of information (thus possibly causing us to rethink current documentation practices to meet the needs of the future); sampling major disability/age/practitioner groups; those organizational and administrative factors which are necessary for quality services to be provided; covariate factors which influence the outcome of care; the accuracy of reported data; and resource utilization.

This is an excellent opportunity for Therapeutic Recreation professionals to collaborate within their organization and to reach out to other related activity and arts therapy organizations to demonstrate accountability for those services that we all have always "known" and "felt" in our hearts to be an essential component of quality care.

## References

Joint Commission on Accreditation of Healthcare Organizations (1987). "Rehabilitation Services," *Consolidated Standards Manual*, p. 143.

Joint Commission on Accreditation of Healthcare Organizations (1988). "Recreational Therapy," *Accreditation Manual for Hospitals*, p. 199.

# CHAPTER FOUR

# Quality Assurance: Advancement Opportunities For Therapeutic Recreation

CAROLYN EBGERT, RN

## Introduction

Providing consultation to patient care systems in the public and private sectors has provided me with a wealth of information regarding the application of quality assurance principles. I would like to share the information about quality assurance from an experiential viewpoint. Opportunities for the advancement of therapeutic recreation through quality assurance for the professional and manager will be discussed within a highlights and recommendations format. Hopefully, in the process, the reader will be convinced that he/she can make a difference in the quality of patient care, regardless of the system of employment.

Quality Assurance is a dynamic concept that loses its essence when it is concretely defined. An effective quality assurance program is a "gestalt." As such, the whole is more than the sum of its parts. Imagine an orchestra and the various instruments that work together in a coordinated and integrated fashion–the product is beautiful music. An effective quality assurance program will likewise integrate knowledge, behavior, and systems issues.

Quality Assurance should be viewed as a developmental process. Developing an effective quality assurance program is analogous to giving birth. It can be a very painful experience, yet the product is extremely rewarding. But just as in child rearing, the developmental process doesn't stop at birth. As raising a child through adolescence to adulthood has its trials, tribulations and benefits, so does the continued refinement of an effective quality assurance program. Paramount to the establishment of a sound quality assurance program is the level of commitment by all who are a part of the process. Each member of the health care delivery system must be involved and committed to the QA effort if the process is going to be a successful one.

## The Impact of QA

Quality Assurance is increasingly the focus of attention in both the public and private sectors of health care delivery. Because of increasing health care cost, pressure from consumers, and restrictions by payors, health care providers are searching for methods to produce effective and efficient results while reducing costs. During this process, it is important that quality patient care not be sacrificed. Quality Assurance data provides for a source of information that federal and state agencies can use to develop public policy. In periods of financial retrenchment, quality assurance data may play a major role in resource allocation.

In a hospital system, every facet of an effective quality assurance program costs money. The staff time needed to develop and implement a quality assurance program, the widespread documentation, system change in response to standards (e.g., transitioning from the Consolidated Standards Manual to the Accreditation Manual Standards), and even a regulatory agency survey visit all add up to considerable expense. However, not implementing quality assurance safeguards within health care systems can be even more costly. Direct costs can be attributed to the uncertainty in the quality of the outcome of patient care, lower staff productivity, decrease in staff morale, and consumers' uncertainty about delivery of care.

When developing and implementing a quality assurance program, it is important to take a systems approach. It is necessary to evaluate all aspects of the therapeutic process. It is necessary to examine macro as well as micro perspectives involving hospital and departmental issues. Consider using "Change Theory" (Chinn and Benne, 1976). Assess resistance to change, recognizing that even positive change is often threatening to those staff who want to maintain the status quo. Look at the driving forces, the positive energy that can be used to facilitate change. Developing and implementing a quality assurance program requires organizational and behavioral change. Complying with regulatory guidelines takes time. It is difficult to change a system overnight. Careful and considerate planning when dealing with change decreases stress and increases the effective use of the system's energy and resources.

The critical components necessary to implement an effective quality assurance program are as follows:

1. It is essential that there be enough time to develop and plan for change.
2. Resources need to be available to do the job correctly.
3. Communication is necessary to ensure that quality assurance findings reach the appropriate people.
4. A feedback loop needs to be established to allow the system to continue to monitor itself.
5. There must be a willingness to take action to resolve identified problems.

6. Accountability at each layer of the organization must be the system norm.
7. A commitment to patient quality care is essential.

All professionals want to provide quality care. However, many do not understand how quality assurance activities can help. Quality Assurance and many of its vigorous applications are just not part of their schema regarding improving patient care. Many professionals perceive quality assurance as "busywork." Some even perceive it as a waste of time. It is imperative to educate staff and to show them examples of how quality assurance can make a difference. Documented results go a long way in convincing staff of the benefits and value of implementing QA programs.

There is a widespread need for professional preparation regarding quality assurance. It is clearly an omission in many professional curriculi and often falls on the responsibility of on the job training. Regrettably, such training is usually focused on the flurry of preparation for a survey visit from an organization such as the Joint Commission or on the follow-up work needed to correct deficiencies, rather than being a routine activity coordinated by the agency quality assurance director. The subject of Quality Assurance needs to be a concurrent topic within hospital orientation programs as well as an integral part of the inservice program.

## Applications to Therapeutic Recreation

Where does the Therapeutic Recreation professional fit in the "big picture" related to quality assurance? Keep in mind that quality assurance is a systems activity. The information in the following sections will provide examples of opportunities for advancement for the Therapeutic Recreation profession, the TR manager, and the TR specialist.

## Professional Opportunities

According to Monning (1983) a professional association has four main functions:

1. To set boundary lines, including lines of demarcation between qualified and unqualified persons;
2. To define the scope of practice and maintain high standards of professional practice;
3. To raise the status of the professional group; and
4. Promote recognition by society of its practitioners as the only ones fully competent to practice its particular skills (p. 41).

All of the above functions should be addressed by therapeutic recreation professional organization(s). The outcome of these functions directly contributes to the assurance of quality patient care through the formation of standards of practice, establishment of professional credentials, and the sponsorship of educational programs to increase consumer understanding of the importance of Therapeutic Recreation.

The following are recommendations for specialists to consider in an effort to enhance the provision of quality service:

1. Be involved in your professional organization. If you are not a member, join! The professional organizations lobby for your professional interests, as well as define more clearly TR's role in health care delivery. If you are unhappy with the activities of your professional organization, get involved . . . empower yourself to make a difference.

2. Be visible. This sounds so simple. However, we frequently forget that many other health care professionals and the public have misconceived ideas regarding the Therapeutic Recreation profession. Be aware of how your behavior presents your profession to others. Are you projecting the professional image that you desire? If not, explore opportunities to change. Market your profession to the consumer and to other health care professionals.

3. Obtain certification through your professional sanctioning organization. Certification projects a message to the public that you are interested in protecting them. Adhering to certification standards assures the consumer that you possess a specific level of competence.

4. Get involved in the national, state, and local legislative process. If you do not understand the legislative process, invest time learning about it. There are many informative guides available. There may be an established program within your professional organization to educate its members regarding the legislative process. Additionally, explore ways to obtain representation on advisory boards of hospitals, schools, etc.

5. Recommend curriculum changes to ensure that graduates have a better understanding of current theories and applications reflecting therapeutic recreation service.

6. Ensure that your professional organization(s) are proactive rather than reactive regarding health care issues. Be leaders and innovators. Continue to monitor other professional organizations and allied health professionals to gain new ideas and perspectives.

7. Support and conduct research to establish a scientific theoretical base of knowledge for your profession. Research activities provide the "electrical outlet" for your professional members to "plug into" improved patient care and professional growth.

8.  Organize yourselves within the system environment in which you work (e.g., organize regional meetings to discuss mutual concerns). Network and share resources. These types of activities create visibility for your profession and increase the likelihood of improved patient care.

## Managerial Opportunities

A quality assurance program is a managerial tool. Quality Assurance data can provide information on whether staff are following policy procedures, implementing recognized standards of care, and/or providing quality care. An effective quality assurance program provides information related to staff performance that is useful in performance appraisals. It facilitates the identification of effective as well as ineffective practices.

Staff involvement in developing and implementing a quality assurance program is instrumental in creating a commitment to quality patient care. The democratic approach within a quality assurance program encourages group consensus regarding the goals and philosophy of the TR department. Quality Assurance activities work best when there is a group effort and everyone knows the "rules of the game." The attitude of managers often makes a difference. If they believe that an effective quality assurance program makes a difference, this attitude will be conveyed to their staff. It is important for managers to have the mind-set that they are in charge of organizing and maintaining a departmental program that not only ensures compliance with regulatory agency standards but also provides for the highest possible quality of care.

Highly recommended is the incorporation of a peer review mechanism within the service department. A peer review component in your department's quality assurance program leads to increased accountability. Individual accountability can also be increased by denoting quality assurance expectations in job descriptions and performance evaluations. Staff usually want to do a good job. Providing staff with standards and explicit expectations provides them with clear and identified goals. Quality Assurance expectations provide a direction for staff performance.

It is important for managers to understand that they are part of a system. However, it is equally important to realize that a departmental QA program should be gathering quality assurance information that impacts the whole system and that it is important to share this information with others. Communication is essential if the system is to profit from the department's quality assurance activities. Also, it is necessary to keep in mind that, in most hospital settings, there are departments (e.g., Therapeutic Recreation) and there are programs (e.g., a Child and Adolescent program). Therefore, quality assurance findings should provide information regarding the department's performance, as well as information regarding the performances of the staff. Communication is essential if desired outcomes are to be achieved. All departments/services/programs contribute significantly to a hospital's ability to operate successfully. When one area operates ineffectively, the entire organization is adversely affected. Value your department's contribution.

Quality Assurance tools (monitors) have the same need for systematic rigor and specification as do the implementation of treatment protocol. Keep the "tool" in good working order. Train people to use it. Sharpen or adjust the tool to ensure better results. If the tool requires subjective ratings, test the tool for inter-rater reliability. This will ensure that all staff are using the same rule of measurement when examining outcomes. It may take some spot checking on various quality assurance activities to ensure that all staff have similar standards and perceptions of quality care. It is important to look at the outcomes of quality assurance activities. Be certain that you end up with what you set out to measure.

Too many managers report that their quality assurance activities are not effective, that QA is only a paperwork exercise. Such a view usually indicates a lack of understanding regarding how to produce an effective quality assurance program. Instead of being responsible for ineffective programs, managers can just as easily be responsible for creating effective ones.

Managers should review quality assurance data to facilitate program planning, staff development, policy and procedure refinement, clarification of supervisory issues, and identification of staffing needs. Quality Assurance data provides feedback related to individual and group performance. As mentioned previously, quality assurance findings can be utilized to make changes in staff knowledge, behavior, or system issues (e.g., channels of communication, policy and procedure, and etc.). Quality Assurance data is useful in demonstrating to administrators the need for increased resources or the reasons for altering programs.

When developing a quality assurance program, consider utilizing the Ten-Step Model recommended by the Joint Commission on Accreditation of Healthcare Organizations (Joint Commission, 1987). Focus on the major aspects of care. If you are working in a psychiatric health care facility, the major aspects of care are usually assessments, treatment planning, progress note documentation, and the various treatment modalities provided by your department. Although good documentation does not necessarily mean good patient care, poor documentation is what many regulatory agencies use as an indicator of inadequate care. It is very important that your staff understand how to adequately document the provision of patient services. Frequently the provision of care across disciplines is facilitated by a written treatment plan. This document is especially important for communication between shifts in a hospital. The treatment plan should be monitored through Department QA activities.

An annual evaluation of your department's quality assurance program will ensure that your quality assurance mechanisms are fine-tuned and upgraded to provide you and your staff with usable feedback.

## Individual Practitioner Opportunities

Self-improvement opportunities for the individual practitioner are boundless. Probably the most important thing you can do to affect the quality of patient care is to BELIEVE that you can make a difference. The first step to believing you can make a difference is self-examination. Where are you in the system? Look at the big picture. Do you have a sense of powerlessness? Do you contribute to organizational malaise? Determine your role within the system and consider the possibilities of how you can be an agent for positive change.

Quality Assurance data can provide useful feedback for the individual practitioner that can improve patient care and identify areas of needed improvement. Be open to peer review. Promote and use peer review to the point that it is normalized and nonthreatening. Share new information and expectations with other staff members. Facilitate the personal and professional growth of those around you. Consider the role of the mentor: find one and/or be one. Discuss your professional role with other professionals and the public. Safeguard the importance of Therapeutic Recreation. Keep up with the literature. Be a patient advocate. Get involved. Be creative with your resources. Examine all identified possibilities.

Quality Assurance is a powerful tool/process. It can be implemented with creativity, and the outcomes can be quite revealing. Or it can be implemented with mistrust, and nonenthusiasm and the outcomes will be meaningless. The decision lies with each professional practitioner and manager. Empower yourself and believe that you can make a difference!

## References

Chinn, R. and Benne, K. (1976). General Strategies for Effecting Changes in Human Systems. *The Planning of Change*, Third Edition. Bennis, W. G. (Editor). New York, NY: Holt, Rinehart and Winston.

Joint Commission on Accreditation of Healthcare Organization (1987). *Agenda for Change.* Chicago, IL: JCAHO Publications.

Monning, R. (1983). Professional Territoriality in Nursing. *The Nursing Profession: A Time to Speak.* Chaska (Editor). New York, NY: McGraw-Hill, p. 41.

## SECTION TWO
## QUALITY ASSURANCE OUTCOME MEASURES

CHAPTER FIVE

# Quality Assessment: The Use Of Outcome Indicators

BOB RILEY, Ph.D, C.T.R.S.

### Introduction

This year, the United States will spend $550 billion on health care, approximately 11.5 percent of the gross national product. The Medicare and Medicaid programs will add another $120 billion. Such widespread expenditure has resulted in many drastic changes within the health care delivery system. Among the most notable are the prospective payment system (PPS) and the increased emphasis upon quality services and the measurement of their effectiveness.

The impact of these changes to therapeutic recreation is both immediate and long-range. The need to establish valid outcome measures and a reliable monitoring system is critical to the growth and continued acceptance of therapeutic recreation. Determining what is effective therapeutic recreation intervention depends upon examining the relationship between various program/treatment protocols for a specific illness/diagnostic category and the associated outcomes of those treatments. This is referred to as patient outcome research. On the other hand, once valid outcome measures have been established, the process of determining whether those desired outcomes are, in fact, being produced becomes equally important. This methodology is referred to as patient outcome quality assessment.

The current status of outcome measurement within therapeutic recreation is an extraordinary mix of opinion and scientific study. Unfortunately, more emphasis lies on the subjective side of the issue. While there is general agreement among therapeutic recreation professionals that patient outcome measurement needs to be developed, there exists little consensus as to what actually constitutes valid outcome measures or how we should monitor them.

This chapter addresses the critical issue of outcome measurement as it relates to the quality assessment process. A general overview of the conceptual framework of quality assessment and the need for the establishment of clinical indicators is provided. This introduction is followed by a detailed discussion of the concept of outcome measurement and its application to practice. Lastly, an overview of the utilization of outcomes in a therapeutic recreation quality assessment system is presented.

## Quality Assurance and Quality Assessment

During the past decade we have witnessed the emergence of a new science within health care, one directly brought about by the new concern for increased quality of care. Quality assurance (QA) and quality assessment have gained widespread acceptance and appeal as appropriate methodologies for both the measurement and the enhancement of quality care. Perhaps Greenfield (1989) summarizes best the reasons why QA has been so well embraced:

> The time when medicine could afford the luxury of a leisurely pace
> in identifying optimal practices at a reasonable cost has passed.
> Payers, providers, health care organizations, and more recently pa-
> tients are clamoring for ways to deliver maximally effective care
> for the fewest dollars. How to identify the practices that repre-
> sent such care is among the most pressing problems facing American
> medicine. (p. 1142).

QA represents the coordinated efforts of professional groups and healthcare agencies to provide the highest quality of care possible. It involves a wide spectrum of activities ranging from determining an appropriate definition of care to the establishment of actual standards of practice, that if implemented, will result in acceptable levels of service. The application of QA strategies in therapeutic recreation has been previously discussed elsewhere (Navar and Dunn, 1982; Reynolds and O'Morrow 1985; and Riley, 1987) and will not be reviewed here. However, the same cannot be said for quality assessment and its application to therapeutic recreation.

Quality assessment represents one of the integral components of the QA process. It involves ongoing monitoring and evaluation of professional services in an effort to determine the level of quality of care being provided. According to Donabedian ". . . Quality assessment, much of the time, is a professional rather than a research enterprise. It is the first step in obtaining information that should lead to action intended to safeguard and enhance the quality of care" (1988a, p. 173). Prior to the initiation of a quality assessment program, it is necessary to have first defined the parameters of what constitutes quality of care within the context of a specific system. Additionally, a wide range of strategic questions also need to be addressed:

- What services are to be assessed?
- What are the practices that are to be assessed?
- How are these activities supposed to be conducted?
- What are these practices supposed to accomplish?

(Donabedian, 1988)

Once the broad spectrum of services has been defined and the appropriate responses to these probing questions have been addressed, the design and implementation of a quality assessment program can commence. A critical first step in the establishment of a valid quality assessment program is the selection of clinical indicators.

A clinical indicator is defined as ". . . a quantitative measure that can be used as a guide to monitor and evaluate the quality of important patient care and support service activities" (JCAHO, 1989, p. 330). As such, clinical indicators are not direct measures of quality. They serve more as "screens" or "flags" that identify issues that may potentially require more intensive analysis. In this sense, "indicators are intended to focus each organization's internal monitoring and evaluation process on important aspects of patient care and assist in pinpointing potential quality of care problems" (JCAHO, 1986, p. 3).

The process of establishing clinical indicators is an important one and should involve all departmental staff. The selection of a clinical indicator should be made on the basis of how well it provides direct feedback about important aspects of care within the service delivery system. It should be stressed that the degree of effectiveness of the overall quality assessment process is directly related to the identification and utilization of valid clinical indicators.

Much has been written regarding the value and the use of clinical indicators in the quality assessment process and most of this information has been linked to recent efforts by the Joint Commission on Accreditation of Healthcare Organizations (JCAHO). As a result of the JCAHO strategic plan Agenda for Change (1986), the necessity for establishing clinical indicators has gained a great measure of importance among many health care providers. This is due, in part, to the fact that monitoring clinical indicators (quality assessment) has been directly linked to the Joint Commission's accreditation process. Given advances in health care technology and research methodology, it is now plausible, according to the Joint Commission, to go beyond simply asking the basic question: *"Can* this organization provide quality health care?" to a more definitive inquiry: *"Does* this organization provide quality health care?" (JCAHO, 1986, p. 2). The Joint Commission is not alone in its pursuit of progressive quality management. Other regulatory and policy setting organizations, including the Health Care Financing Administration (HCFA) and the Agency for Health Care Policy and Research (AHCPR), are actively involved in research endeavors that address the establishment of valid quality indicators.

The development of clinical indicators as part of the quality assessment process has very direct and serious implications for both health care organizations and service providers. Essentially, the goal of quality assessment is to provide feedback regarding the level of service given to patients. Through data collection and analysis, it becomes evident which organizations deliver the "best care" and which do not. Likewise within organizational settings, comparisons can be made among service departments and possibly, among individual service providers. It has been suggested that in the future, quality performance profiles will play a significant role in both accreditation (JCAHO, 1986) and in reimbursement (Brinkley, 1986; and Roper, Winkenwerder, Hackbarth & Krakaver, 1988).

### Approaches to the Measurement of Quality Care

Even when valid clinical indicators have been carefully constructed, the concept of quality care remains illusive to measurement. According to the Joint Commission: "the quality of patient care is determined by a number of factors, including accessibility, timeliness, effectiveness, efficacy, appropriateness, efficiency, continuity, privacy and confidentiality, participation of patient and patient family, and safety and supportiveness of the care environment" (JCAHO, 1989, p. 330). Clinical indicators related to the domain of therapeutic recreation can be formulated to address each of the factors listed above (although addressing all of the factors is not necessarily practical nor suggested). For example, *accessibility to care* could be monitored by establishing an indicator that measures the length of time that transpires prior to a client receiving designated therapeutic recreation services. *Safety of care environment* could involve the use of indicators to monitor the number of accidents and/or harmful incidents that occur during therapeutic recreation programming. Which of the above elements are best to monitor? The decision is dependent upon a number of factors. Further discussion regarding this topic has been presented within a general health care context by Donabedian (1980) and Steffan (1988); and within the scope of therapeutic recreation as noted in Riley (1987).

One specific area of the quality assessment domain that has gained a great deal of interest is that of measurement strategies: structure, process and outcome. It is well recognized that outcome measurement together with structure and process formulate the classic triad used to define quality of care (Donabedian, 1980). As Figure 5.1 denotes, each of these approaches addresses a specific dimension and/or time frame within the health care continuum. In spite of the fact that a great deal of information has been written regarding the need for outcome-based measures, the status quo for most QA plans has been the utilization of structure and process indicators.

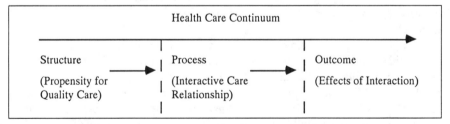

Figure 5.1–Approaches To The Assessment Of Quality Care

*Structure* measurement (from a methodological perspective) is often considered a quality assurance activity and not necessarily part of the assessment process. This view is becoming more popular given recent developments by JCAHO (1986) with respect to their accreditation strategies. Variables included under the rubric of structure would include material resources, human resources, organizational structure, and policy guidelines (Donabedian, 1988b). In essence, structure variables measure the probability or propensity for quality care. Such attributes reflect only general tendencies and expectations. Measurement at this level often provides insufficient information regarding the relationship between structure variables and the process of care, as well as between structure indicators and the outcomes of care. Historically, the use of structure variables and reliance upon the data they provide has been widespread. This is due, in part, to the emphasis placed upon structure measurement during the accreditation process in past years. This method of measurement has proven to be less expensive, less time consuming and more easily applicable than other quality assessment approaches.

The *process* approach, in contrast to structure, truly reflects direct health care intervention. In the context of therapeutic recreation, this approach addresses the interaction between client and therapeutic recreation specialist. Application of the process approach reveals what is actually done in the act of care giving. Within the therapeutic recreation context, this would include the completion of the assessment process, writing of specific program plans, implementation of intervention, and completion of both formulative and summative evaluation regarding client's progress. The major assumption here is that such practices are inherently good and necessary, and furthermore, that such intervention strategies lead to positive end results regarding clients' outcomes.

Strategies for monitoring process indicators have gained popularity because such efforts do, in fact, reflect true quality assessment. For the most part, process indicators represent the professional's perspective as to what constitutes quality care. These views are often embedded in standards of practice, operational plans, and policy and procedural manuals.

Given the volume of procedures that potentially need to be monitored, however, the process approach can become quite costly. This occurs because procedures are not researched and tested with respect to efficacy and effectiveness. The result is that the quality assessment process is mired in an overabundance of procedures to monitor, as well as having to use indicators of uncertain validity. A strict adherence to the process approach often occurs because of a lack of available data pertaining to expected outcomes of service. Therapeutic recreation serves well as an example of a service in this predicament.

The assessment of *outcomes* denotes the direct effects of service upon the well-being of both individuals and specified populations. Outcomes have been defined as ". . . the end result of medical care: what happened to the patient in terms of palliation, control of illness, cure, or rehabilitation. The concept of outcome directs attention specifically to the patient's well-being; it emphasizes individuals over groups, and the interests of unique patients over those of society" (Lohr, 1988, p. 37). The most desirable attribute of outcomes is that they are self-validating. That is, it is quite evident whether or not outcomes have occurred. Specific to a definition of outcome is the notion that it is the client/patient behavior that is being measured, not the provider's. In the context of therapeutic recreation, outcome measurement addresses the degree to which the patient has benefited from a given program or intervention. It assumes that specific strategies or protocols are implemented with the assurance that such procedures will produce certain predictable results. Outcome measurement attempts to establish the causal relationship between the processes of care and the end products of care. Ideally, as illustrated in Figure 5.1 (p. 56), the cause and effect relationship among all three approaches should be well documented. That is, sound structure variables lead to acceptable processes and subsequently, good procedures lead to predictable outcomes. In theory this relationship makes sense. In practice however, it is rarely documented.

**Understanding Outcome Measures**

The long standing debate surrounding which specific measurement approach is best to use in assessing the quality of care is well documented (Donabedian, 1980; Jonas, 1981; and Lee and Jones, 1933). Recently, there has been a mandate for the increased use of outcome measurement in quality assessment by the JCAHO (O'Leary, 1987), HCFA (Graham, 1987), and the American Medical Association (1986). It is believed that outcome measures provide the most accurate account of the level of quality that a given facility or practitioner actually provides. The move toward outcomes is directly linked to the cost containment trend that has emerged during the past decade. As Prevost remarked, "Answering the question 'Does the hospital have the capacity to provide high quality care?' is no longer sufficient. Consumers and insurance companies are much more educated now and want to know if they are getting high quality care for the dollars they are spending" (as quoted in Brinkley, 1986).

Even though researchers, accrediting organizations, and regulatory agencies have placed a great deal of emphasis on outcomes, widespread confusion and misunderstanding still exist regarding outcomes: What are they and how are they best utilized? As the call for the use of outcomes filters down from agency directors through service managers to front line staff, the message is often misconstrued and its original meaning never reaches its audience.

Outcomes are used to measure the effects of care on the health status of patients and populations (Donabedian, 1988b). In direct application to therapeutic recreation, outcomes would be defined as the measurable change in clients' health status or well being after receiving therapeutic recreation intervention. The concepts of *measurable change* and *relationship* are critical to this definition.

Outcomes need to be defined and subsequently monitored within the frame-work of applied measurement. Specific patient changes that are to be monitored and documented, need to be measured in some quantifiable manner. The use of either subjective or objective data (or a combination thereof) is acceptable as long as the observations are measurable. This is necessary in order to draw compari-sons between pre- and post stages of treatment, in determining the impact of the intervention. Likewise, altered patient behavior must also be attributable to the intervention provided under the rubric of a given service (i.e., therapeutic recrea-tion). As previously discussed, the causal relationship between the process of care (intervention) and the outcomes of care (change in patient behavior) is critical to quality assessment. The linkage between these two variables must be logically established prior to the commencement of the quality assessment process.

## Efficacy and Effectiveness

The above discussion brings to light two additional concepts that are related to the use of outcome measurement: efficacy and effectiveness. Efficacy reflects the level of benefit expected when health care services are applied under "ideal" conditions. Such intervention involves a controlled environment under which the most skilled practitioners, using the best technology, provide care to predictable patients. In essence, efficacy studies provide an understanding of what can opti-mally be achieved under ideal conditions. Effectiveness, in contrast, represents the level of service and expected outcomes derived from practice ". . . rendered under ordinary circumstances by average practitioners for typical patients" (Lohr, 1988, p. 37).

Ideally, it is important to know both the efficacy and the effectiveness of a treatment protocol or therapeutic intervention. Both approaches are important to the establishment of criteria that reflect acceptable levels of care. As Bunker states:

> In assessing the quality of care received by a population (by defini-
> tion an average), we would like to be able to compare such care with
> that achievable under optimal conditions–its *efficacy*. In assessing
> the quality of care received by an individual patient or provided by
> an individual physician, one might be willing to accept as a standard
> the average received by the other patients– its *effectiveness*.
> (Bunker, 1988, p. 52)

Unfortunately, reliable data to establish outcome measures is scant in thera-peutic recreation, regardless of whether efficacy or effectiveness studies are used. With increased pressure from a variety of sources to establish outcome indicators, the therapeutic recreation profession needs to respond to two major inquiries:

- First, what are the expected outcomes of therapeutic recreation intervention?
- Second, what are the direct contributions of these expected outcomes to the overall level of patient improvement?

As depicted in Figure 5.2, the establishment of outcome measures should be accomplished at two distinct points on the health care delivery continuum. The first point is during the intervention stage when specific programs and protocols are provided. Outcome measures established at this stage would be used to validate the causal linkage between process and outcome dimensions of care. Outcome measures used at this level could be derived from efficacy studies or consensus from within the field. In this process, quality assessment would be utilized to verify that both appropriate and quality levels of care had been rendered. As such, the quality assessment process monitors both the effectiveness and the efficiency of services provided.

The second stage for involving outcome measures occurs at the end of the health care continuum when the effects of selected interventions have hopefully contributed to the overall improvement of the patient. Establishing outcome measures at this stage involves the use of broad based generic screens (or results) that are fairly common to most patients, regardless of the nature of their disability/illness or the type of service they received. These outcomes are often derived from societal expectations of what constitutes quality health care and the desirable effects (outcomes) of such service.

The establishment of a valid link between specific intervention outcomes and the generic screens of the overall health care continuum is the most essential and critical aspect of efficacy studies. Much of the concern raised by HCFA and other regulatory agencies is directly related to this issue (Lanning and O'Connor, 1990). The determination of which services significantly contribute to the overall improvement of patients' well-being is of critical importance. At issue are both ethical and economic concerns: 1) Are patients being subjected to treatments that have no direct impact upon their overall well-being?, and 2) Are services that have the potential of significantly contributing to patient improvement being underutilized? The answers to these questions, as derived through both efficacious investigation and quality assessment, would begin to serve as justification for whether or not therapeutic recreation has a legitimate role in the health care process.

### Application of Outcomes to Quality Assessment

In concept, outcomes are the results of care as measured by changes in the health status and/or well being of patients. As discussed above, most outcomes are derived through vigorous research in an attempt to determine the efficacy of an intervention or given protocol of care. However, when such research attempts are scant or nonexistent, then efforts to monitor existing levels of care become even

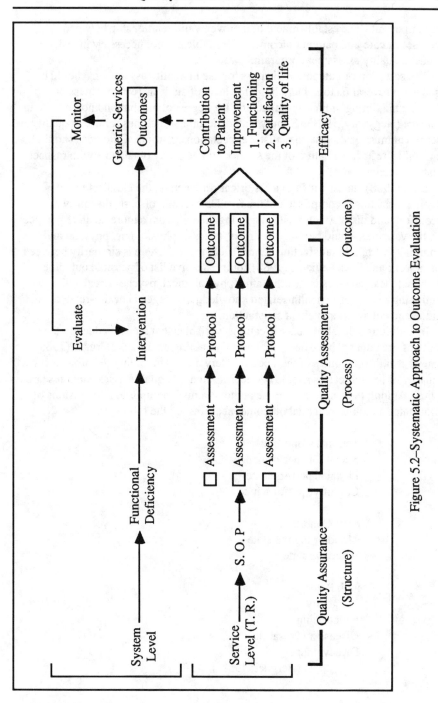

Figure 5.2–Systematic Approach to Outcome Evaluation

more important. The establishment of a proven valid relationship between processes of care and patient outcomes is desirable but not necessary in order to conduct a quality assessment program.

The selection of outcome indicators for use in quality assessment should be based upon several factors, including: the level of analysis (effectiveness or efficacy); the timing of measurement; and the degree of attribution known to be in existence (Hegyvary, 1991). Simply stated, defining outcomes for use in quality assessment must be done with realistic expectations in mind. Outcomes should be measurable, reflect the nature of the service and be easily obtainable with respect to data collection.

Lohr (1988) states that from a historical perspective, the classical list of outcome measures is comprised of "the five Ds": death, disease, disability, discomfort, and dissatisfaction. Considering this list from a more positive perspective, the variables would be: survival rates, states of physiologic, physical and emotional health, and satisfaction (Lohr, 1988, p. 39). There is similarity between Lohr's work and Donabedian's (1980) comprehensive list of possible outcomes, which includes: changes in health status (physiological, psychological and social functioning); changes in health-related knowledge; changes in health-related attitude and behavior; and client satisfaction.

In addition to the above classifications, variables that are embedded in the quality of life concept have been increasingly gaining attention. Bergner (1989) suggests that the outcomes of therapeutic interventions involving the broad array of quality of life indicators should be incorporated into quality assessment research studies. Among the variables that the author claims are important dimensions of health status and thus, potential outcome measures are the following:

- Functional Condition
    Social role performance
    Physical performance
    Cognitive performance

- Mental Condition
    Mood or feeling state
    Affective state

- Health Potential
    Longevity
    Functioning
    Disease and disability
    Disadvantage
        (Bergner, 1989, p. 150)

The variables contained in the above lists are quite comprehensive and represent the more global or generic outcomes of health care services (as depicted in Figure 5.2, p. 61). Addressing more specific variables that represent realistic outcomes of individual service interventions that can be used as part of the quality assessment process, Bergner (1989) suggests the following:

- Symptoms

- Functional Status
  Self-care
  Mobility
  Physical activity

- Role Activities
  Work
  Household management

- Social Functioning
  Personal interactions
  Intimacy
  Community interactions

- Emotional Status
  Anxiety
  Stress
  Depression
  Locus of control
  Spiritual well-being

- Cognition

- Sleep and Rest

- Energy and Vitality

- Health Perceptions

- General Life Satisfaction
                (Bergner, 1989, p. 149)

Two other types of outcome indicators that are currently used in the quality assessment process are: changes in health-related attitudes and behaviors, and patient satisfaction. Germane to the variables of health-related attitude and behavior are the issues of safety and risk management, program attendance, and patient's adherence to the treatment plan. Services of a quality nature should be risk-free and involve the patient in all decisions regarding their treatment. Client refusal to participate in either the planning or implementation of intervention programs *may* be indicative of poor service quality.

Patient satisfaction is an outcome variable that has received much attention as a viable measure of the quality of care (Riley, 1990). As Lohr suggests: "The growing attention given to consumers' views about quality makes satisfaction an increasingly important element in evaluating the end results of care. A high level of satisfaction is seen as a desirable outcome in its own right" (Lohr, 1988, p. 43). The use of patient satisfaction is not suggested without caveat. This dimension is extremely difficult to measure. Due to the intrusive nature of direct interview or written question, patients will often simply state what they think the questioner wants to hear. This is often true in therapeutic recreation if the person who provided the intervention is the same individual who administers the satisfaction instrument.

In spite of these difficulties, the monitoring of patient satisfaction still remains an important aspect of quality of care. It represents the one source of direct feedback regarding the interpersonal aspects (process) of care. Regardless of methodological limitations, this dimension of outcome measurement should be part of any department's comprehensive quality assessment program (Donabedian, 1988b).

The selection, monitoring and measurement of outcomes is a highly complex process. In therapeutic recreation, outcomes should be selected with consideration for the department's mission statement, philosophy and written plan of operation. A direct relationship should exist between the services a department purports to provide and the selection of outcome indicators. When outcomes are poorly linked to specific therapeutic recreation practices, they provide little guidance for improving quality of care.

In the therapeutic recreation process, outcome indicators must describe client responses or behaviors, not those of the practitioners. It is important to identify critical points throughout the total treatment process that designate when it is reasonable to expect that outcomes can be achieved and measured. It is also imperative that in the context of quality assessment, therapeutic recreation practitioners are willing to be held accountable for a patient's achievement (and nonachievement) of specific outcomes.

In closing, it should be restated that clinical indicators (whether they be structure, process, or outcome) address specific areas of concern and do not determine the overall quality of a given service. Care must be used in establishing outcome indicators as well as in monitoring and evaluating their results. Constant vigilance must be employed to make certain that the quality assessment process is used for the purpose it was intended . . . to improve the quality of patient care.

## Concluding Remarks

The measurement of outcomes has gained a ground swell of support in recent years. This popularity has been fueled by the conceptual appeal of outcomes as true indicators of the end results of the health care process. It is viewed that outcome measurement is the best approach to increasing both the quality and efficiency of health care.

Specific to therapeutic recreation, the emphasis upon outcome measurement is critical for two reasons. First, it places increased importance upon the urgency for initiating efficacy research within the field. It has become essential to measure the effects of therapeutic recreation intervention upon the well-being of recipients. Secondly, it is equally important to document the contribution of therapeutic recreation to the overall effectiveness and efficiency of the general health care system. Quality assessment efforts at the practitioner level can begin to provide valuable data and feedback regarding which outcomes are readily achievable given the use of specific types of intervention. These findings can then be used to further analyze the relationship between intervention outcomes and their contribution to the overall health and well-being of patients.

Assuring quality therapeutic recreation services demands dedication, commitment, and hard work. Establishing strong, valid linkages between therapeutic recreation processes and identified outcomes presents a formidable challenge. It is a complex and demanding task, but one that must be completed. In many respects this challenge resembles the attempt to assemble a multifaceted jigsaw puzzle. In the beginning, with all the pieces thrown together the task seems impossible and motivation is low. As pieces are placed together, however, and parts of the picture begin to emerge, the image becomes more evident and the motivation to complete the task more steadfast. It is in this manner that we all must begin to place the pieces of outcome strategies together, so that one day the quality picture can emerge.

## References

American Medical Association (1986). JCAHO to Review Clinical Outcomes. *American Medical News*, September 19, 1986.

Bergner, M. (1989). Quality of Life, Health Status, and Clinical Research. *Medical Care*, 27(3) 148-156.

Brinkley, J. (1986). Key Hospital Accrediting Agency to Start Weighing Mortality Rates. *New York Times*, November 4.

Bunker, J. (1988). Is Efficacy the Gold Standard for Quality Assessment? *Inquiry*, 25:511-58.

Donabedian, A. (1980). *Explorations in Quality Assessment and Monitoring*, Vols. 1-3. Ann Arbor, MI: Health Administration Press.

Donabedian, A. (1988a). "Quality Assessment and Assurance: Unity of Purpose, Diversity of Means." *Inquiry* (25) 173-192.

Donabedian, A. (1988b). "Quality of Care: How Can It Be Assessed?" *Journal of American Medical Association*, (260) 12, 1743-1748.

Graham, J. (1987). Quality Gets a Closer Look. *Modern Health Care*. February, 2, 20.

Greenfield, S. (1989). The State of Outcome Research: Are We on Target? *New England Journal of Medicine*. 320: 1142-433.

Hegyvary, S. (1991). Issues In Outcome Research. *Journal of Nursing Quality Assurance*, 5 (2) 1-6.

JCAHO (1986). *The Joint Commission's "Agenda For Change"*. Chicago, IL: JCAHO Publications.

JCAHO (1989). Characteristics of Clinical Indicators. *QRB*. (15) 9: 330-339.

Jonas, S. (1981). *Health Care Delivery In The United States*. New York, NY: Springer Publishing.

Lanning, J. and O'Connor, S. (1990). The Health Care Quality Quagmire: Some Signposts. *Hospital and Health Services Administration*. 35: (1), 39-54.

Lee, R. and Jones, L. (1933). *The Fundamentals of Good Medical Care.* Chicago, IL: University of Chicago Press.

Lohr, K. (1988). Outcome Measurement: Concepts and Questions. *Inquiry* 25: 37-50.

Navar, N. and Dunn, J. (1982). *Quality Assurance: Concerns for Therapeutic Recreation.* Champaign, IL: University of Illinois.

O'Leary, D. (1987). Quality Control Challenges in the New Competitive Market place. *Journal of Cancer Program Management,* 2 (1), Winter, 7-10.

Reynolds, R. and O'Morrow, G. (1985). *Problems, Issues, and Concepts in Therapeutic Recreation.* Englewood Cliffs, NJ: Prentice Hall.

Roper, W.; Winkenwerder, W.; Hackbarth, G.; and Krakaver. (1988). Effectiveness in Health Care. An Initiative To Evaluate And Improve Medical Practice. *New England Journal of Medicine,* 319 (18): 1197-202.

Riley, B. (1987). *Evaluation of Therapeutic Recreation Through Quality Assurance.* State College, PA: Venture Publishing.

Riley, B. (1990). Utilization of Consumer Satisfaction as Outcome Measure: Implications For Therapeutic Recreation. *Research Into Action,* 7(1). Champaign, IL: Office of Recreation and Park Resources, University of Illinois.

Steffen, G. (1988). Quality Medical Care: A Definition. *Journal of the American Medical Association,* 260 (1): 56-61.

# CHAPTER SIX

# Monitoring and Measuring Outcomes in Therapeutic Recreation

JOHN W. SHANK, Ed.D., C.T.R.S.

W.B. (TERRY) KINNEY, Ph.D., C.T.R.S.

### Introduction

Just as the therapeutic recreation discipline was getting used to the idea of monitoring and evaluating the STRUCTURE and PROCESS of service delivery, it is being rapidly pressed to monitor and evaluate OUTCOMES! This should come as no surprise, however, since the entire health care industry is very concerned about demonstrating the effects of services upon consumers. The emphasis on outcomes stems in large measure from the cost/benefit concerns of health care, which as a system is becoming much more competitive and consumer driven.

Pressure to identify outcomes emanates from many sources, all of which have some influence on the continued existence of therapeutic recreation in health care. Accreditation bodies, such as the Joint Commission on Accreditation of Healthcare Organizations (JCAHO), believe that the best way to assure quality services is to monitor the outcomes of services and to make whatever adjustments are necessary to deliver quality services on a consistent basis. Perhaps the most significant pressure comes from agencies and authorities that ultimately determine the reimbursement value of a service. That is, if therapeutic recreation wants to lay a legitimate claim to a portion of the health care dollar, it will have to demonstrate patient outcomes that are deemed valuable to third party payers. A clear example underscores this point. In 1985 the federal government's Health Care Financing Administration (HCFA) published in the *Federal Register* its proposed rules for home health care services eligible for reimbursement under Title 19 of the Social Security Act. Of course, therapeutic recreation specialists believed that their services should be reimbursable, and should be designated as a legitimate home health care service, but HCFA disagreed. In response to public comments received from therapeutic recreation advocates HCFA stated that the Secretary of Health and Human Services exercised broad discretion in determining those services that are reimbursable, especially when there existed no legal statutes to mandate the service. In those cases the Secretary used the following criteria to determine reimbursability:

- was the service a part of "active treatment" (under the direction of a physician and reasonably expected to improve the condition of the recipient);
- and was the service directly influential in decreasing the length of stay in an institution and maintaining the individual in the community and out of the institution?

Without evidence of patient outcomes that are important to the federal government (i.e., HCFA), therapeutic recreation can expect to be continually rejected as a reimbursable service.

This single point (and there are many others) clearly illustrates the necessity for therapeutic recreation to begin to monitor and evaluate outcomes. This should be initiated not only to verify appropriate and quality services, but also to demonstrate the contributions the service can make to lower health care cost. Embedded in these pressures brought to bear on the discipline is the overriding question regarding the contributions therapeutic recreation makes to health care and rehabilitation. If not directly through the measurement of patient outcomes, how will the discipline demonstrate its unique or complimentary contributions?

One of the expected standard of any discipline is a strong research agenda designed to develop and test knowledge and to enhance understanding related to the theory and practice of that discipline. As has been made clear throughout this text, quality assurance is concerned with the quality and appropriateness of service. However, quality health care is dependent on the integrity of the health care practitioner's individual judgments in the context of clinical practice. A critical element in this judgment is the evidence one has that particular interventions have demonstrated desirable consequences in controlled research environments. Obviously, there is a direct relationship between research and quality assurance. Research tests the assumptions that guide practice and demonstrates the efficacy (or lack thereof) of particular interventions. In the ideal sense, the research process should preceed the incorporation of these interventions into practice and subsequent monitoring. Thus, by doing so the research-practice link becomes the foundation and purest sense of ensuring quality and appropriate care.

## Efficacy Research and Therapeutic Recreation Outcomes

The therapeutic recreation discipline has extremely little empirical data to address issues of its efficacy. It is time for the discipline to address the relationship between outcome monitoring and efficacy research, and recognize that both processes must occur simultaneously. As discussed above, the ideal procedure would be if efficacy research demonstrated that a particular treatment protocol was most effective with a certain population. This would then allow the protocol to be implemented and monitored through quality assurance mechanisms to make sure the consumers were receiving the most appropriate service available and at a desired quality level of care. Unfortunately, we are a far distance from this ideal. Nevertheless, a simultaneous effort on both the research and quality assurance fronts would be mutually beneficial to the discipline of therapeutic recreation. Dennis O'Leary, the President of the JCAHO echoed this point: "Sound efficacy studies, on a broad scale, require an understanding of the meaning and use of outcome information, which in turn requires the development of valid clinical indicators, which in turn requires basic experiential information . . . ." (1988, p. 31). While therapeutic recreation has little to show in terms of efficacy research, a small comfort can be taken in that very few of the other health care disciplines can point to any significant data bases for efficacy evaluation.

Recently the therapeutic recreation discipline has been given the opportunity to demonstrate its contributions to the field of rehabilitation. This opportunity came as a result of an initiative by the National Institute on Disability and Rehabilitation Research (NIDRR) to sponsor a three-year grant to "assess definitely the merits of therapeutic recreation and to measure its impact on the rehabilitation of disabled persons" (*Federal Register*, 1987). The NIDRR established specific research priorities to direct this project. These priorities lend to the TR discipline some insight into what the federal government views as relevant and worthwhile service outcomes associated with therapeutic recreation. These specific research priorities of NIDRR are:

- determine the correlation between TR and successful rehabilitation outcomes to establish its effectiveness in rehabilitation;
- investigate the impact on physiology (heart rate, oxygen intake, ventilatory volume, blood pressure);
- investigate the impact on psychological well-being (self-esteem, emotional stability, internal control, interpersonal adjustment);
- assess the effectiveness in reducing and preventing secondary disability and readmittance to medical/rehab facilities;
- assess the impact on length of stay;
- investigate the comparative effects of psychological well-being between those individuals engaged in integrated vs. segregated recreation programs.

While each of these priority areas require further operationalization from a research perspective, they also have direct relevance to the practitioner. That is, if a federal agency as influential as NIDRR feels these areas are a priority for research, then the direct implication is that they should be (at least from NIDRR's perspective) a priority for practice. A sound research agenda could begin with practitioners and researchers reviewing these outlined categories and selecting site-specific outcomes that are germane to these specific areas. In many cases data sources for these outcomes are readily available or can easily be incorporated into ongoing documentation. Such data sources include existing service records of the program, the program staff, participants, and persons outside the program who are knowledgeable about the service participants. Once data sources and collection techniques are identified, the foundation has been established for determining efficacy of specific treatment interventions.

## Models For The Conduct of Efficacy Research

It is important to note that the mere gathering of data, in and of itself, is not worthwhile unless it is used to scientifically document the effect of a unique and controlled intervention. The NIDRR grant was awarded to Temple University, and although the results of this research will not be determined until some time in the future, valuable lessons have been learned about conducting efficacy research in multiple field sites. One of the more valuable lessons is the identification of a number of data gathering designs that are particularly relevant to the unique constraints of carrying out research in a field setting. Moving away from laboratory settings that provide maximal control and into actual clinical settings presents a myriad of problems that mire the ability to determine causal attribution.

Although efficacy research is complicated by real life constraints present in clinical environments, there are several designs that can be used effectively to gather empirical data on therapeutic recreation efficacy.

**Ex Post Facto Evaluation.** If medical records are kept accurately, it is possible to conduct a correlation analysis between the time spent in therapeutic recreation and certain rehabilitation outcomes. The type of TR service (e.g., leisure education, community reintegration, etc.) can also be monitored for analysis. This design does not intrude on day to day treatment at all, since it is conducted "after the fact" (ex post facto), and merely involves looking back through medical records. This design assumes that TR staff accurately monitor the amount of time (usually recorded as 15 minute units) and type of service delivered to each client. The Temple University study is looking at diversional participation, individual and group TR treatment, and self-initiated participation. The choice of outcomes is dependent on what is routinely documented in the client's charts. Some typical outcome indicators might be: requests for pain medication, social interaction, length of stay, compliance issues, and a variety of functional indicators gathered from the various therapies within the agency.

From a pure research stand point, this is considered a weak design since it does not account for many of the variables that could have influenced the relationship between TR involvement and client outcomes (if any exists). However, as researchers have increasingly discovered, it is virtually impossible to conduct pure research in field settings. Given this fact, if combined with other supportive evidence and arguments, ex post facto data takes on increased value.

**Two Unit Design.** When two units exist that are very similar in nature (i.e., same type of clients, staff, scheduling, and environment), it is possible to simulate a quasi-experimental design. The quasi-experimental design gathers data regarding a unique intervention while it is occurring or in the planning stages rather than after the intervention has occurred, as in the ex post facto design. This makes the quasi-experimental design somewhat stronger since the unique intervention can be isolated and controlled and, thus, studied in a more rigorous and scientific sense.

In the two unit design, the experimental unit (subjects) would receive some type of unique intervention (the focus of the efficacy research). This unique intervention might be a specifically designed leisure education program or some other service that is thought to be effective. The control unit would not receive the experimental treatment but does receive the standard services that otherwise would be provided (e.g., diversional programming). The difference between the experimental subjects and control subjects as measured against the outcome indicators testifies to the effect of the particular experimental intervention. While this design, too, lacks certain scientific strengths, it still blends well with the realities and demands of field settings. The results could be strengthened by the extent to which the researcher insures that the clients, staff, scheduling, and environment are similar in both settings. Figure 6.1 depicts this research design.

It should be noted that practitioners do not have to feel that every person on each unit becomes part of the efficacy study. In fact, individuals can be screened to meet certain criteria, and only those who meet the criteria are included in the data gathering. An example of screening criteria for an efficacy study on community reintegration techniques might be: 1) right sphere CVA; 2) below the age of 70; 3) evidence of family support; and 4) likelihood of discharge to home. Only those clients who meet the established criteria become experimental or control subjects. This approach serves to maximize staff energy in that the gathering of time consuming outcome indicators is limited to a select population.

Also, the above example should serve to remind the reader of earlier comments about the "ideal type" of efficacy research that demonstrates whether a particular treatment protocol was effective with a certain population. Within this ideal approach specific intervention is designed for a certain type of client to achieve specific outcomes. The extent to which these outcomes are achieved in an effective and efficient manner reflects true efficacy research.

**Single Unit Design.** A research design that is more scientifically vigorous, as well as more demanding is depicted in Figure 6.2 (p. 75). In using the single unit design, clients admitted to the same unit are screened for appropriateness for the

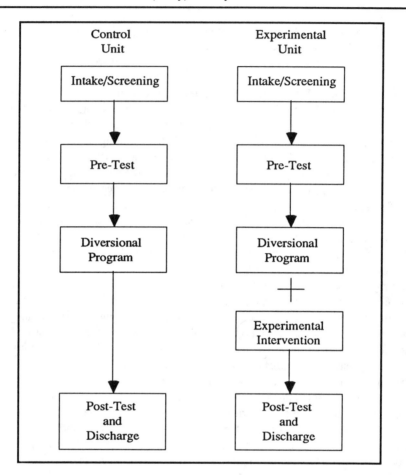

Figure 6.1–Two Unit Design

study and then placed on a waiting list. The therapist responsible for implementing the experimental treatment carries a limited case load of clients who are *randomly* selected from the waiting list. This ensures an equal chance for any eligible client to become either a treatment or control subject. When a client is discharged, the therapist returns to the waiting list and randomly selects another client to fill the caseload. The therapist conducts the treatment with his/her selected case load only and those individuals who do not get picked up from the waiting list serve as the control subjects.

While it is best if outcome data is gathered twice, as indicated in Figure 6.2, the actual data gathering process may be extremely lengthy or inconvenient for the clients or agency. An alternative is to eliminate the first instance of data gathering and simply rely on the second set of data. The fact that subjects are randomly

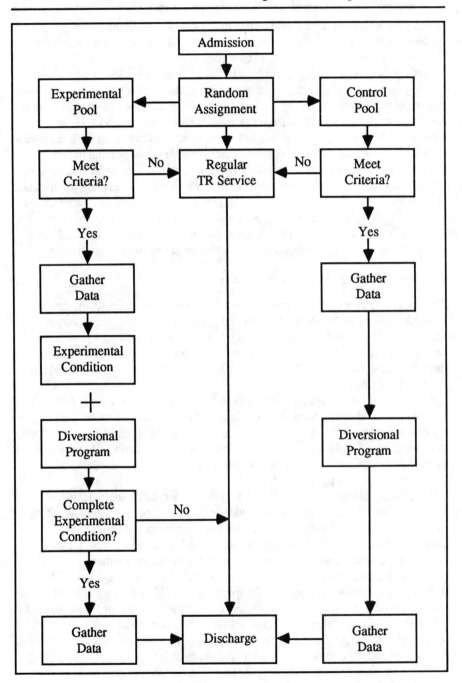

Figure 6.2–Single Unit Design

selected from the waiting list allows this modification. Since the argument can be made that eliminating the first set of data scientifically weakens the results, this modification should be viewed as a last resort.

Not providing a particular intervention also raises a question of ethics withholding treatment. The justification for not providing the intervention to all clients who meet the criteria should be obvious in this design. It is standard procedure in nearly all therapies that provide specialized services to utilize a waiting list. Very simply, some clients get the service and some do not depending on the availability of personnel resources (case loads). Another logical rationale is that there is no evidence that the treatment in fact does any good at all, and the whole purpose of the efficacy research is to determine that fact. There is little argument in providing a service to every client when we do not know if that service actually contributes anything to the rehabilitation process as well as to the individual client's progress. If the treatment can be proved efficacious, then the justification is established to expand resources to insure that everyone who is appropriate receives the service.

## Selecting Outcomes To Measure Efficacy

Each time that therapeutic recreation specialists work with their clients, they make critical decisions in the course of providing care. Usually these decisions are based on and relevant to pre-determined goals. These decisions can have positive or negative consequences, and are essentially the outcomes that ought to be monitored and evaluated at the indicators for continued care and for determining the quality of that care.

Outcomes are the observed changes in a client's status as a result of our interventions and interactions, whether intended or not. Outcomes are the complications, adverse events, or short- or long-term changes experienced by our clients, and represent the end result of our care. Outcomes can be attributed to the process of providing care, and this should enable us to determine if we are doing for our clients that which we purport to do.

Outcomes are generally measured as change in a client's health status, change in their health-related knowledge, attitudes or behavior, and ultimately their level of satisfaction with the care received. Outcomes represent those behaviors, attitudes, or knowledge that we can control and influence, and which, for the benefit of our clients, need to be changed in one direction or another.

Selecting outcomes for the purpose of research/documentation need not be a difficult task. As discussed above, TR specialists provide their services with client target behaviors in mind. These behaviors are essentially outcomes. However, the selection of outcomes should be made with consideration given to other factors besides immediate program direction. Selection criteria should include effectiveness and efficiency of outcomes, logical and reasonable expectation of achieving the outcome, time frame for viewing the outcome, and the political and personal value of the outcome.

**Effectiveness and Efficiency.** Care providers have a wealth of potential outcome indicators readily available to them. Outcome indicators should be selected and analyzed in terms of effectiveness and efficiency. Services are effective to the extent that their performance is congruent with expectation, and efficient in terms of cost-benefit relationships (Fuhrer, 1987). As implied earlier, in this time of health care cost containment, their concern is not just with whether the program works, but that it works with less expense. Thus, if the therapeutic recreation discipline can demonstrate that it effectively and efficiently provides beneficial changes in clients, then there exists evidence for the enhanced support of the discipline.

**Reasonable Expectation.** As indicated above, outcomes are directly implied in the goals and behavioral objectives specified in the systematic and individualized service delivery plans that TR Specialists routinely produce. However, these outcome expectations are often clouded with idealism and frequently buried in charts or files, rarely to be reviewed during actual service delivery. Also, goals tend to be written exclusively in terms of benefits to service recipients. To avoid these pitfalls, outcomes should be selected based on a consensus view of service providers utilizing a selection criterion of reasonable expectation. Thus, the outcomes of programs in short-term acute psychiatry would not be monitored and evaluated in the same fashion as those in day treatment programs. Indeed, outcomes need to be identified and selected relative to specific treatment protocols and specific diagnostic categories. Another way to have reasonable expectations is to have programs conceptually modeled so that outcome expectations can be deduced in a way that reveals both positive and negative impacts.

**Short- Vs. Long-Term Expectation.** Program outcomes can be identified and selected for monitoring according to whether they are susceptible to short- or long-term realization (Fuhrer, 1987). This consideration is important because it is quite likely that a service could produce short-term outcomes but have minimal long-term impact. Likewise, it is quite possible that an intervention might not have any noticeable impact until months after the client has been discharged. It would be a serious mistake to select an outcome if your time frame for data collection (monitoring) is not compatible with the expected appearance of the outcome.

**Impact Beyond The Client.** According to Fuhrer (1987), it is also important to consider outcomes that impact others besides the immediate service recipient. For instance, the increased community independent living skills of a client may enable greater interaction with a nondisabled population, and as a consequence contribute to the improvement of attitudes toward disabled persons. Another example might be the implications of services for hospitalized children which reduces the stress on family members and subsequently results in fewer demands that the parents place on medical staff. This is an especially important criterion for the therapeutic recreation discipline. We need to be attuned to the benefits that occur in other service areas as a result of the specialized service that we deliver.

Long-term consequences and the impact on persons other than the clients can actually reflect outcomes we did not anticipate or are unfamiliar with. Typically our research begins with certain assumptions that result in a selection of particular tests and scales to measure outcome. An equally valid approach, especially when one wants to leave open the possibilities for new perspectives, is to utilize qualitative methodology. Qualitative methods, such as in-depth, open-ended interviews, enable an uncovering of impact or outcomes of services as uniquely experienced by the clients and their families. To illustrate this point, consider the commonly expected outcomes of a community reintegration program: awareness of community leisure resources. In-depth interviews conducted at the point of discharge may uncover many other unrelated benefits that were more important to the client—opportunities to be in the presence of relatively healthy patients and subsequently less conscious of illness and disability. If other interviews revealed similar benefits, these outcomes could be monitored more closely and routinely.

**Relevance and Value Perspective.** It is also useful to consider the varying value perspectives that operate in determining outcomes or the consequences of care. For instance, service recipients might value recreation services mostly in terms of the distance it provides from the stress of illness and hospitalization. Administrators might place premium value on reducing the total costs, whereas the societal concern is for productive (i.e., employable) citizenry. Finally the service provider (therapeutic recreation specialist) values above all else the client's acknowledgement of the importance of recreation and leisure in this person's life. "Important potential benefits of a program may be overlooked if only some of these value perspectives are considered" (Fuhrer, 1987:7).

There is even a further level of consideration when one selects outcomes for quality assurance purposes. This consideration has to do with the issue of relevance. Certain outcomes, such as a client's attendance at programs (an indication of service utilization), or the number of injuries or registered complaints against the service providers, are rather apparent and easily monitored. Certainly they are attractive because of this ease. Another set of outcomes, such as "awareness of leisure resources," or recreation activity skill acquisition may be of concern to the TR specialist, especially since these outcomes appear to isolate our services as "unique." However, in all instances these outcomes have questionable value or relevance to the treatment team or the larger health care and rehabilitation community. The question raised here is the extent to which therapeutic recreation outcomes should be complimentary with other service providers and evidence contribution to the outcomes most highly regarded by the health care rehabilitation system.

Figure 6.3 depicts the value levels at which outcomes can be considered. The first level indicates outcomes that are specific and unique to the service. In our case, these might be improved leisure skills or changes in attitudes and leisure behaviors. The second level indicates outcomes specific and immediate to the client. These might be reduction of pain, improved mobility, better coping, etc. The third level indicates outcomes of concern to the broad health care bureaucracy. These are things such as reduced in-patient days, reduced recidivism, improved employability, reduced dependence on social service systems, etc.

In the case of therapeutic recreation and its relationship to outcomes, a simple maxim works well:  one is good, two is better, and all three is best.  While research that shows efficacy in only the first level is beneficial, the extent to which we can demonstrate an impact on levels two and three can only lend strong argument for the enhanced support of our discipline.

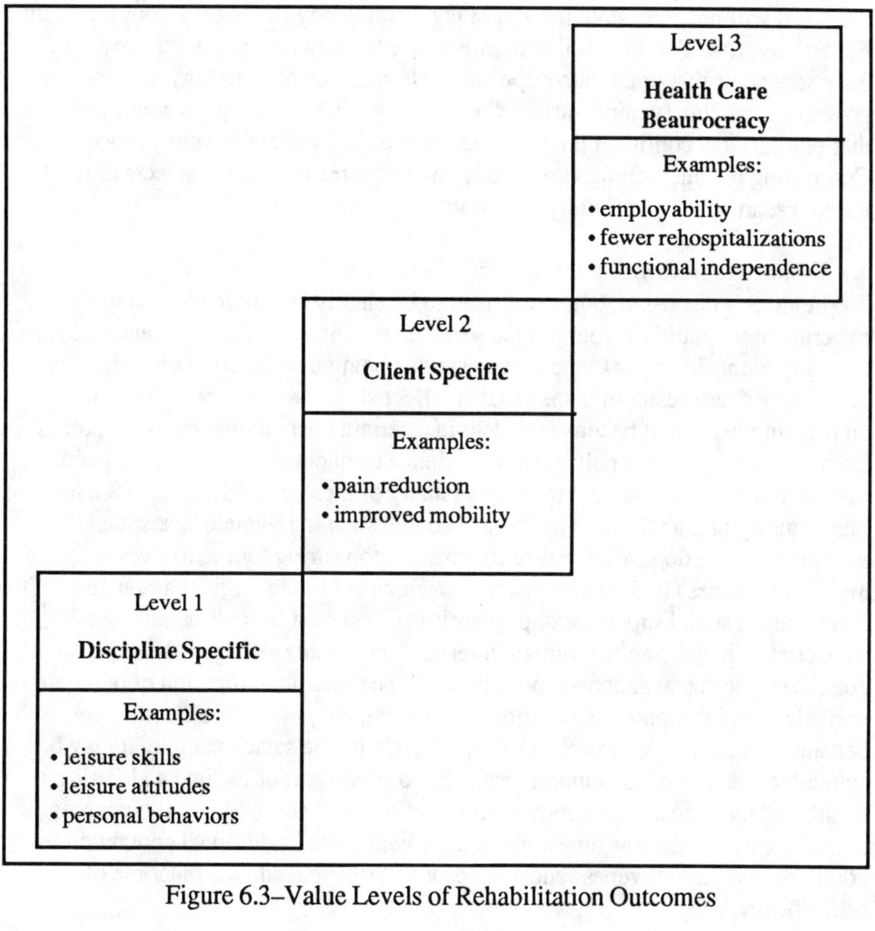

Level 3

**Health Care Beaurocracy**

Examples:

• employability
• fewer rehospitalizations
• functional independence

Level 2

**Client Specific**

Examples:

• pain reduction
• improved mobility

Level 1

**Discipline Specific**

Examples:

• leisure skills
• leisure attitudes
• personal behaviors

Figure 6.3–Value Levels of Rehabilitation Outcomes

## Steps To Implementing Efficacy Research

A series of relatively simple questions can guide the development and implementation of efficacy research in field settings. In each of these, ideas can be exchanged with colleagues to refine thoughts and eliminate or control weaknesses. Good research is rarely done alone; research is one of those phenomena where team work significantly contributes to success.

### 1.) What specific service do you contribute or could you contribute that is not provided by anyone else?

The issue of uniqueness is of strict importance here–not from a sense of being unique as a discipline, but from a research methods perspective. If you select community reintegration as a unique focus to research and then find that a nurse specialist is conducting pre-discharge counseling and education with the same clients, it will be impossible for you to lay claim to any findings of your research. Essentially, it will be impossible to prove whether any changes were a result of your service or that of the nurse specialist. In research terminology, the nurse's program is an "intervening variable" which must, in some way, be controlled so that you can feel confident that any change was, in fact, due to your service. Controlling for intervening variables is one of the most difficult aspects of field based research, but is infinitely important.

### 2.) What outcomes will your service affect?

As previously discussed, outcomes need to be clearly and logically tied to the experimental condition, your unique service. In point of fact, many outcomes are typically identified prior to the unique service being developed; that is, the service is developed as a result of a need that is reflected by the outcomes. As an example, suppose that it becomes evident in a certain hospital that many amputees from an inner-city, blue collar area experience frequent rehospitalizations and further amputation. Inquiry reveals that many of these individuals do not have many family or friends. It is hypothesized that such individuals lack social support, become depressed or disenfrachised, stop caring for themselves properly, and finally regress to their abusive habits which led to the original amputation. If this is true, a social support group specifically designed for individuals meeting such criteria may be an appropriate intervention. In this example, the experimental condition (the social support group) is developed after identification of outcome variables (social support, depression, recidivism, etc.). Other outcomes may become evident as the research is designed. Using the same example, it may be suggested that the social support group could spend part of its time addressing health and hygiene and promoting physical fitness. Thus, additional outcomes could be cardio-vascular fitness and health awareness. Additional content areas could focus on assertiveness and self-responsibility and add the outcome of self-efficacy.

### 3.) Are the outcomes relevant?

It is easy to become carried away with the process of identifying outcomes as described above. Such frivolity can seriously endanger the research by "watering down" the focus of the experimental condition. To avoid this problem, practitioner/researchers need to continually return to the relevancy of the outcomes as described in the previous section on "Selecting Outcomes To Measure Efficacy."

### 4.) How are you going to measure the outcomes?

This issue, like intervening variables, is very critical to the integrity of research. What is at the heart of the concern is measurement reliability and validity. All research needs to be conducted in consultation with other knowledgeable individuals to avoid hidden pitfalls. Nowhere is this more evident than in research methodology and measurement. It is clearly beyond the scope of this chapter to discuss issues of reliability and validity except to inculcate the notion that consultation on this issue is highly desirable.

Reliability and validity aside, most rehabilitation agencies routinely collect a wealth of potential outcome measures. Psychological tests, functional indicators, and periodic progress notes constitute possible measures. Many hospitals conduct routine follow-up interviews and those results can be beneficial. In the case of measuring new outcomes it becomes necessary to find a way to build such measurement into routine data collection. If measures are not treated as routine they stand the chance of not being completed. One note of caution is imperative– the measuring of outcomes can be time consuming and thus, time consideration should be one of the criteria by which outcomes and their measures are selected.

### 5.) How are you going to implement the experimental condition?

The answer to this question returns full circle to question #1: the identification of unique services. As with measurement, research methodology requires expert consultation and is better done before, rather than after the fact. The manner in which the experimental condition is implemented and conducted represents the integrity of the research design and the extent to which you can lay claim to any results. Even once the research design is identified, the researcher must maintain vigilant watch over the research process for possible problems. Nearly every professor who supervises graduate student research has a drawer full of horror stories of well designed research going awry as a result of some well-intentioned but uninformed individual.

## Conclusion

The intent of this chapter was to draw attention to, and greater understanding of, the relationship between quality assurance and research. Simply put, the most appropriate standard for quality assurance is that aspect of practice that has been shown to be efficacious. Efficacy research can provide a sound and reasonable basis for monitoring the quality and appropriateness of routine care.

Efficacy research and quality assurance have more in common than the focus on outcomes of service. Both require a discernable level of professionalism and a real commitment of time and energy. Neither procedure is easy or convenient, but both offer the therapeutic recreation discipline the opportunity to demonstrate, preserve and promote the best that it can offer the fields of health care and human services.

## References

*Federal Register*, 52 (217), November 10, 1987.

*Federal Register*, 50 (49), March 13, 1985.

Fuhrer, M. (1987). *Rehabilitation Outcomes: Analysis and Measurement.* Baltimore, MD: Brookes Publishers.

O'Leary, D. (1988). The need for clinical standards of care. *QRB*, February, 31-32.

CHAPTER SEVEN

# The Use of Patient Satisfaction Data as an Outcome Monitor in Therapeutic Recreation Quality Assurance

MICHAEL RHODES, C.T.R.S.

## Introduction

As efforts to measure the quality of health care intervention continue to dominate the medical market, it is important to recognize the role of consumer satisfaction. Consumer satisfaction measurement regarding services or products is not a new concept in our society. *Consumer Guide* has been in publication since 1966; *Consumer Digest* since 1959; *Consumer Reports* since 1936 and the first publication designed to address consumer satisfaction, *Consumer Research Magazine*, was established in 1928. As a matter of fact, interest in consumer satisfaction with health care services is not a new concept either. As early as 1966, Donabedian argued that the "quality of care is determined by its effectiveness in achieving or producing both patient health and satisfaction" (Petersen, 1988, p. 25). In 1973, at the American Psychiatric Association's Annual Meeting in Hawaii, Michigan's Northville State Hospital presented a paper entitled "The Patient Satisfaction Scale as a Management Tool" (LINK, 1974, p. 1).

Outcome monitoring in therapeutic recreation quality assurance programs is a new concept. As this concept evolves, so will the methods used to gather data. What existing outcome monitoring used in therapeutic recreation centers on is the practitioner's expectations or standards and whether or not such standards are being met. But as societal values change, practitioners are now discovering that they also need to be concerned with the consumer's expectations. This is not to suggest that the traditional absolutist approach is invalid. Quite the contrary. Practitioners now realize that they must provide the consumer with information about therapeutic recreation services and work with consumers regarding service expectations. In monitoring the expectations of our consumers, we need to monitor both our direct consumers and our indirect consumers. Our indirect consumers include our referral sources such as the physician and other members of our treatment team. Also included are third parties such as insurance carriers, workers' compensation reviewers, and employee assistance programs. The indirect consumers of therapeutic recreation service have been addressed elsewhere (West, 1988). This chapter will concentrate on the direct consumer (the patient), and the subsequent use of patient satisfaction data as an outcome monitor in the therapeutic recreation quality assurance process.

## The Use of Patient Satisfaction as a QA Data Source

There are many sound reasons why we would want to use patient satisfaction data as a method of improving patient care. Ultimately, Schroeder (1988) may have stated the most important reason in stating: "In today's age of competition in health care, those agencies that do not attempt to deliver excellence as defined by consumers may not survive" (p. IX). Consumers feel that they can identify with hospitals which provide high quality care. Studies by the National Research Corporation found that between 54 and 78 percent of consumers feel that they can tell which hospitals provide quality care (Peterson, 1988). A second reason for the attention given to consumer satisfaction is that facility marketing has burst onto the scene in health care competition. Predictions for marketing include a trend toward the marketing of "quality." According to a survey by Professional Research Consultants, Inc. (Powills, 1987), quality, in the mind of the consumer, is of greater importance than price. The greatest source of health care advertising is television, with newspapers a close second. Clearly, practitioners must begin to listen to their consumers within such a highly competitive market. Practitioners must realize that they are in a competitive business, one in which survival is not guaranteed.

While we strive for financial survival, we should also strive for excellence in the delivery of service. We should monitor our ability to provide excellence through our quality assurance programs. The ultimate purpose of QA monitoring is to look at outcomes and identify trends of service in an effort to correct problems before they emerge. We need to monitor both the positive and the negative results regarding consumers. The Technical Assistance Research Programs (Peterson, 1988) identified that one known patient complaint represented six to ten serious unknown incidents of dissatisfaction and twenty to fifty less serious unknown incidents of dissatisfaction. Data gained from monitoring patient satisfaction within therapeutic recreation services can be used in a multitude of ways, including: the marketing of TR services, identifying problems and improving care, identifying employees who patients feel are outstanding or problematic, and ultimately improving programming to better meet the needs of the patients. If we know what patients expect, then we can better meet their appropriate expectations.

There are a variety of reasons, both for and against, using patient satisfaction as a quality assurance monitor. Ware and Davies (1988) identified four common arguments against using consumer data as well as four common arguments for

**The Arguments Against Using Consumers' Data:**

1. Data reveal more about the consumer than about the quality of care.
   - Consumers' ratings of medical care correlate with individuals' attitudes toward the community, satisfaction with life, health status, educational level, age, . . . .

2. The data will reflect how much was done, not how well it was done.
   - The evidence does suggest that consumers' ratings of care do reflect, at least in part, how many services they received.

3. The data will disagree with physicians' judgement regarding quality.
   - Physicians' judgements should be the criteria against which all other evaluations of quality of care should be validated.

4. Consumers' data simply reflect whether the provider was nice to them.
   - The higher the interpersonal scores, the higher the technical scores by the consumer.

**The Arguments For Using Consumers' Data:**

1. Consumers' assessments of quality predict their behavior in the marketplace.
   - Satisfied consumers are less likely to change physicians.

2. Consumers need not necessarily be qualified judges to provide accurate information about quality.
   - Most of the arguments against using consumers' data in QA voice skepticism about ratings. However, consumer reports may be much more accurate.

3. Data from patients are less expensive than other QA data sources.
   - In 1987, HCFA awarded $300 million to PRO's to assess quality of care for 25 percent of the anticipated 22 million Medicare hospital admissions over the next two years.

4. Data from consumers provide information not otherwise available.
   - With the shift to outpatient services, many of the traditional sources of data are not available.

Figure 7.1– The Pros and Cons of Using Consumer Data

**The Arguments Against Using Consumers' Data:**

1. Bias from personal characteristics is not so strong as to invalidate consumers' ratings of the interpersonal or technical quality of their care.

2. Consumers' ratings of technical quality do reflect, at least in part, how many services they received.

3. For common problems, consumers can distinguish between the technical aspects of care judged good and less than good by physicians.

4. Interpersonal features of care do not obscure consumers' ability to distinguish levels of technical process for common outpatient problems.

**The Arguments For Using Consumers' Data:**

1. Whatever "quality" means to consumers, their perceptions of quality affect their choices among health care alternatives.

2. Consumers' reports (as distinct from ratings) hold considerable promise as a data source for quality assurance activities.

3. The costs of obtaining data from consumers are not higher, and are probably lower, than those for obtaining data from more traditional sources such as record audits.

4. Consumers are the best source for obtaining data on the interpersonal aspects of care; moreover, consumers can provide some of the data on technical quality of outpatient care not available from traditional sources such as claims or records.

Figure 7.2– Ware and Davies Conclusions

using consumer data (See Figure 7.1). The authors reviewed and evaluated existing research that has been reported in support of each of the arguments using consumer data. Figure 7.2 details their conclusions for each of these arguments. In summary, the authors state that consumer ratings of interpersonal aspects of patient care provides useful and valid information for quality assurance monitoring. However, they also state that consumer data should only be used as a supplement to more traditional data sources.

## Patient Satisfaction and Data Collection

There are a variety of methods that can be used to obtain data from consumers in an attempt to monitor satisfaction with health care services. But prior to the collection of data the following question must be answered: What specific information do I want to obtain? In most cases, data is obtained based upon the practitioner's expectations of service delivery. Peterson (1988) suggests that practitioners survey consumers' views and design monitoring systems around their expectations. An accepted way to obtain the consumer's expectations is through the use of a technique called the focus group. The focus group is led by a group facilitator, and patients are asked to respond to open-ended questions pertaining to their expectations of their hospitalization and what is important to them in terms of quality service.

Another common approach to collect patient views is to use a written pre-admission survey. Expectations can be then marked as to their importance to the consumer. Regardless of the approach adopted, it is important to involve the consumer in the development of the instrument. Pilot the instrument with an adequate number of consumers to obtain feedback on the types of questions asked and the importance of the questions. Be certain to find out if any of the questions are confusing, poorly worded, or if any additional questions are needed before survey implementation. Do not forget to involve your staff in the design of the tool. Allow staff to complete and provide feedback. Finally, with whatever approach chosen in the development of the satisfaction instrument, be sure to leave room for open comment from the patient.

The two most common approaches used to obtain consumer satisfaction data are questionnaires and telephone surveys. Since telephone surveys are considered more costly than printed questionnaires, most agencies have opted to use printed questionnaires. However, telephone surveys do have some advantages, including the ability of the investigator to further probe client-stated dissatisfaction or satisfaction. Other approaches that can be used include personal interviews and group interviews. Regardless of whether you interview directly an individual, a group, or use a printed questionnaire, you must decide how to ask the questions in your tool. Ware and Davies (1988) divide questions into two types; ratings and reports. The authors state that *ratings*, (a five-point Likert scale that asks the consumer to evaluate the response from excellent to poor) are inherently more subjective than reports. *Reports* the consumers to indicate with a yes or no their evaluation of a statement. They deal with what did or did not occur. They are thus more objective as they can be confirmed by an outside source. Figure 7.3 provides an example of Ware and Davies Ratings and Reports questions for both a technical area and an interpersonal area. Figure 7.4 (p. 89) offers the application to thera-peutic recreation, using examples of ratings and reports for both technical and

Ware and Davies' sample of the distinction between consumer ratings and consumer reports from "Involving Consumers in Quality of Care Assessment," *Health Affairs*, Spring, 1988.

|  | Technical | Interpersonal |
|---|---|---|
| **Rating** | Evaluation (excellent-poor) of doctor's thoroughness. | Evaluation (excellent-poor) of courtesy and respect shown by the doctor. |
| **Report** | Indication (yes-no) of whether the doctor checked blood pressure. | Indication (yes-no) of whether the doctor introduced himself/ herself. |

Figure 7.3– Comparison of Consumer Ratings and Consumer Reports

interpersonal services. Mail surveys are encouraged for use over telephone surveys because of a lower chance of a biased response and a more complete assurance of confidentiality.

Another technique that many evaluators recommend in the development of survey is to state half of the questions positively and half of the questions negatively to prevent acquiescent response set (ARS). ARS is the tendency to agree with statements of opinion regardless of content. Petersen (1988) suggests that questions should be arranged in chronological order, beginning with the initial contact and proceeding through service delivery and discharge. If you decide to use a printed survey, make sure that it is professional in appearance, protects the confidentiality of the respondent, and is acceptable in length. If the instrument is a mail survey, be sure to use a self-addressed, stamped envelope. Consider using a cover letter that encourages patients to respond and that thanks them for their time. You may also want to send a follow-up post card to improve your response rate. Again, Petersen (1988) suggests that if you use a mail survey, send it two to three days after discharge since research indicates that the return rate is less than 50 percent for surveys sent after one week past discharge. Another technique that Petersen offers is the capitalization of key words to emphasize the main idea of each question. For example, "MY THERAPEUTIC RECREATION SPECIALIST was always COURTEOUS to me."

Now that you have decided on your format and determined that your questions are objective and clear, criteria must be set for what percentage of the population will actually be surveyed. Decide whether to survey all patients who used therapeutic recreation services or a percentage of the total. You must decide how often

|  | Technical | Interpersonal |
|---|---|---|
| **Rating** | Evaluation (excellent-poor) of of information given to me by the therapeutic recreation staff to help me plan my free time post-discharge. | Evaluation (excellent-poor) of courtesy and respect shown by the therapeutic recreation staff member assigned to me. |
| **Report** | Indication (yes-no) of whether the therapeutic recreation staff provided me with information to help me plan my free time post-discharge. | Indication (yes-no) of whether the therapeutic recreation specialist introduced himself/herself on my day of admission. |

Figure 7.4–Application of Consumer Measurement to Therapeutic Recreation

to collect and analyze the data. The gathered information must be timely, and it is suggested that you review the data no less than once monthly to keep the monitor from being too retrospective.

**Application of Consumer Satisfaction Questionnaires in Health Care**

A review of literature identified several types of questionnaires currently in use. There are general health care questionnaires, such as the Hulka and the Ware (see Roberts and Tugwell, 1987); there are population specific questionnaires, such as the Michigan Department of Mental Health Client Satisfaction Scale (Link, 1974). there are discipline specific questionnaires, such as the Occupational Therapy Satisfaction Questionnaire (Stanfield, Rowland and Moore, 1988); and there are program specific questionnaires, such as the West Bloomfield Day Hospital Discharge Survey (Boe and Dudley, 1986). Each type seems to have its advantages and disadvantages for application in a specific setting.

The first type of questionnaire is the general health care model. Although there were many to choose from, the two most prevalent in the literature are the Hulka and the Ware Questionnaires. The Hulka questionnaire was designed to assess patient satisfaction as an outcome. It was constructed using three sections: Professional Competence, Personal Qualities, and Cost/Convenience. Each section has 12 to 14 statements. To avoid ARS, there are some statements that are worded in a positive way and some in a negative way. It is commonly implemented by using a five-point Likert scale with a range of strongly agree to strongly disagree. Appendix 7A contains examples of questions contained within each of the three sections (Roberts and Tugwell, 1987).

The Ware Questionnaire (1988) is also outcome-oriented and divides patient satisfaction issues into eight sections; Access/Convenience, Finances, Availability of Resources, Continuity of Care, Quality/Competence of Physician, Humaneness of Physician, General Satisfaction and Efficacy of Care. Each section has three to ten statements that the patient rates using a Likert scale. Examples of questions found under each of the eight sections is provided in Appendix 7B. Like the Hulka, the Ware avoids ARS in the wording of the questions. (Some questions worded in a positive way and some in a negative way.)

Roberts and Tugwell (1987) suggest that Ware's eight sections could be placed under the three more general sections that Hulka used. Questions on the Ware that fell under the sections of Access/Convenience, Finances, Availability of Resources and Continuity of Care are similar to Hulka's section on Cost/Convenience. Ware's sections on Quality/Competence of Physician, General Satisfaction and Efficacy of Care are related to Hulka's section on Professional Competence. Finally, the Ware section on Humaneness of Physician is much aligned with Hulka's section on Personal Qualities. The authors concluded that both the Hulka and the Ware Questionnaires are reliable and valid patient satisfaction instruments. They felt that they were easy to administer, easy to interpret, and provided comparable results.

The second type of questionnaire identified was the population specific model. One of the oldest health care patient satisfaction surveys in existence is the Michigan Department of Mental Health's Client Satisfaction Scale (LINK, 1974). This is a highly objective rating scale that asks patients to answer yes or no to a series of questions related to their health care services. The questions are divided into three sections: Community and State Hospital Patients; Community Residents; and State Hospital Patients. Examples of questions within each of the three categories appear in Appendix 7C. The Client Satisfaction Scale has been used in other states besides Michigan and contains some questions that are specific to therapeutic recreation. It is the oldest of the surveys, yet it is objective and it is outcome-oriented.

The third type of satisfaction tool that appears in the literature was the discipline specific model. In an issue of the *O.T. WEEK*, Stanfield, Rowland and Moore (1988) presented a discipline-specific questionnaire for occupational therapy. The Occupational Therapy Satisfaction Questionnaire was developed by the Occupational Therapy Department of the Psychiatric Pavillion at the Medical Center of Central Georgia. It consists of 19 statements that request the client to answer "yes," "sometimes," or "no," with space for comments after each statement. Examples of the types of statements used by this instrument appear in Appendix 7D. The published results were very positive in terms of outcome, but even the authors recognize that the tool has not been tested for validity or reliability and that the return rate of 52 percent would need to be improved upon before drawing any major conclusions. It should be noted that, of the 152 respondents to the survey, 100 percent were completely satisfied with OT Services. Beyond the flaws in the survey, this positive type of outcome is something that can be used to market services.

The fourth and final type of survey that was developed was the program specific instrument. The West Bloomfield Day Hospital Discharge Survey (1986) was developed by Jan Boe, RN, Cal Dudley, M.D., and the psychiatric staff at the Sinai Hospital of Detroit. The instrument combines may of the styles that were previously discussed, including: ratings questions using a Likert scale; discipline-specific questions; program-specific questions; and open-ended questions. Practitioners working in psychiatric day treatment can most easily conceptualize the rationale for this type of survey because settings go beyond the traditional roles of therapeutic recreation and often ask the CTRS to provide services beyond that of therapeutic recreation. At Sinai Hospital of Detroit's Day Treatment Programs, the CTRS is asked to wear the hat of a CTRS; a co-leader of group therapy; a leader of educational seminars that do not directly deal with leisure issues; and a patient-care coordinator to meet the individual needs of the patients. Because of the complex roles that all staff assume, it is felt that a program-oriented rather than a discipline-specific survey would be better. The West Bloomfield Day Hospital Discharge Survey appears in Appendix 7E.

Like the other surveys that were previously discussed, the Day Hospital Discharge Survey can and does provide valuable outcome information. This survey has been used as an ongoing quality assurance monitor since September of 1986. For the two year period of 1986-1988, we had 109 completed surveys out of 155 admissions for a return rate of 70 percent. Unlike the mail surveys, this survey is given to the patient on the day of discharge. Transferred patients, patients who did not receive a survey, and patients who refused to complete the survey were sent one through the mail. However, we are still working on ways to improve the return rate. Additionally, we have not identified how to handle patients who are unable to complete the survey due to their illness or their inability to read or write. We have considered developing a family survey to address this issue.

Among the outcomes that we have been able to identify through the survey were:

- 84 percent of the patients serviced who completed the survey felt that their problems had improved;
- 96 percent of the patients knew what medication they were taking and how to take it;
- 96 percent of the respondents felt that their discharge plans were at least partially clear; and
- 95 percent felt that occupational therapy, recreational therapy, group therapy, educational seminars, patient coordinator and the community meetings were at least somewhat helpful.

One of the most significant outcomes from the survey thus far has been our ability to change the program to meet the changing needs of the patients. Like most day hospitals, the West Bloomfield Day Hospital is a group-oriented program. However, many of the patients (noted under the open comment section) liked the "one-to-one" attention that the program offered on a limited basis. We have since adjusted the program to allow for more one-to-one contact by the patient coordinator and the various disciplines. Another significant outcome involves our policy that all patients should receive the same services. With respect to our community adjustment (trips) portion of the program, the majority of the patients surveyed felt that the trips were helpful, but this was not a unanimous position. But for years we had been involving everyone in the community trips. Each portion of the program is now individually tailored for each patient's specific needs. If a patient does not need community reintegration, there are now other options available.

Other areas of the program have also been adjusted to allow for more individualized attention. We will continue to use this survey in an attempt to identify outcome and improve patient care. However, this is not to say that this survey should not be improved. After an extensive review of the literature, is is clear that the survey has its flaws. All of the questions are worded in a positive manner, most of the questions are ratings rather than more objective reports, and the survey tool is given on the day of discharge, which may bias the results as patients are less likely to give an honest response. Finally, we have had a return rate of 70 percent and would like to improve upon this.

## Summary

This article has attempted to explore the use of patient satisfaction data as an outcome monitor in therapeutic recreation quality assurance. It has identified reasons why you would want to use patient data, has discussed how to develop a survey tool and has given examples of various types of questionnaires that have already been developed. It is the hope of the author that this chapter will assist the reader in developing a tool to evaluate patient satisfaction data in their agency. The written questionnaire is only one type of instrument to obtain the data. Each agency will need to assess all of the methods available and find the way that will allow it to identify outcome and improve patient care in the most cost efficient manner. Although patient satisfaction data has been proven to be a way to obtain outcome data, it needs to be used with more traditional methods and not as the only source of monitoring. If predictions that quality will be more important to the consumer than price are accurate, then outcome data from the consumer will be essential to our survival. As quality assurance monitoring evolves, so will the ways to obtain the data. As has often been stated, "If you are not part of the solution, then you are part of the problem." Share your innovations with others so that this evolutionary process can be as smooth and painless as possible. If you are using patient-satisfaction data and outcome monitors in QA, please consider publishing your results.

## References

Boe, J. and Dudley, C. (9186). The West Bloomfield Day Hospital Discharge Survey, Unpublished Report, Detroit, Michigan.

*LINK*, (1974). Michigan Department of Mental Health Newsletter, 4:11.

Petersen, M. (1988). Measuring Patient Satisfaction: Collecting Useful Data, *Journal of Nursing Quality Assurance*, 2:3, 25-35.

Powills, S. 1987. Winds of Change Hit Hospital Marketing, *Hospitals*, 61:29.

Roberts, J. and Tugwell, P. (1987). Comparison of Questionnaires Determining Patient Satisfaction with Medical Care, *Health Services Research*, 22:5, 637-654.

Schroeder, P. (1988). From the Editor, *Journal of Nursing Quality Assurance*, 2:3, ix.

Stanfield, D., Rowland, S., and Moore, N. (1988). Study Looks at OT Through the Eyes of its Clients, *O.T. Week*, February 25, 3-4.

Ware, J., and Davies, A. (1988). Involving Consumers in Quality of Care Assessment, *Health Affairs*, Spring, 33-48.

West, R. (1988). Definition of Therapeutic Recreation: A Prospective From Key Publics, *ATRA Newsletter*, 4:3, 3-5.

## Appendix 7A
## Hulka Questionnaire

### I. Professional Competence

1. People do not know how many mistakes doctors really make.
2. Today's doctors are better trained than ever before.
3. Doctors rely on drugs and pills too much.
4. Given a choice between using an old reliable drug and a new experimental one, many doctors will choose the new one.
5. No two doctors will agree on what is wrong with a person.
6. Doctors will not admit it when they do not know what is wrong with you.
7. When doctors do not cure mildly ill patients, it is because the patients do not cooperate.
8. Doctors will do everything they can to keep from making a mistake.
9. Many doctors just do not know what they are doing.
10. Doctors spend more time trying to cure an illness you already have than preventing one from developing.
11. Doctors are put in the position of needing to know more than they possibly could.
12. Even if a doctor cannot cure you right away, he/she can make you more comfortable.
13. Doctors help you both in health and in sickness.
14. Doctors sometimes fail because patients do not call them in time.

### II. Personal Qualities

1. You cannot expect any one doctor to be perfect.
2. Doctors make you feel like everything will be all right.
3. A doctor's job is to make people feel better.
4. Too many doctors think you cannot understand the medical explanation of your illness, so they do not bother explaining.
5. Doctors act like they are doing you a favor by treating you during the examination.
6. A lot of doctors do not care whether or not they hurt you during the examination.
7. Many doctors treat the disease but have no feeling for the patient.
8. Doctors should be a little more friendly than they are.
9. Most doctors let you talk out your problem.
10. Doctors do their best to keep you from worrying.
11. Doctors are devoted to their patients.
12. With so many patients to see, doctors cannot get to know them all.
13. Most doctors have no feeling for their patients.
14. Most doctors take a real interest in their patients.

## III. Cost/Convenience

1. Nowadays you really cannot get a doctor to come out during the night.
2. You may have to wait a little, but you can always get a doctor.
3. It is easier to go to the drugstore for medicine than to bother with a doctor.
4. In an emergency, you can always get a doctor.
5. There just are not enough doctors to go around.
6. Doctors try to have their offices and clinics in convenient locations.
7. More and more doctors are refusing to make house calls.
8. People complain too much about how hard it is to see a doctor.
9. It is hard to get a quick appointment to see a doctor.
10. Doctors should have evening office hours for working people.
11. Most doctors are willing to treat patients with low incomes.
12. A doctor's main interest is in making as much money as he can.

Comparison of Questionnaires Determining Patient Satisfaction with Medical Care, Roberts and Tugwell, *Health Services Research*, December, 1987.

## Appendix 7B
## Ware Questionnaire

I.  **Access/Convenience (CC)***

1.  Parking is a problem when you have to get medical care.
2.  If I have a medical question, I can reach someone for help without any problem.
3.  In an emergency, it's very hard to get medical care quickly.
4.  It's hard to get an appointment for medical care right away.
5.  It takes me a long time to get to the place where I receive medical care.
6.  Places where you get medical care are very conveniently located.
7.  Office hours when you get medical care are good for most people.
8.  People are usually kept waiting a long time when they are at the doctor's office.

II.  **Finances (CC)***

1.  Medical insurance coverage should pay for more expenses than it does.
2.  I think you can get medical care easily even if you don't have money with you.
3.  I am happy with the coverage provided by medical insurance plans.

III.  **Availability of Resources (CC)***

1.  More hospitals are needed in this area.
2.  There are enough family doctors around here.
3.  There are enough doctors in this area that specialize.
4.  There are enough hospitals in this area.
5.  There is a big shortage of family doctors around here.

IV.  **Continuity of Care (CC)***

1.  I hardly ever see the same doctor when I go for medical care.
2.  If more than one family member needs medical care, we have to go to different doctors.
3.  I see the same doctor just about every time I go for medical care.

## V.  Quality/Competence of Physician (PC)*

1.  Doctors aren't as thorough as they should be.
2.  Most people are encouraged to get a yearly exam when they go for medical care.
3.  Sometimes doctors take unnecessary risks in treating their patients.
4.  Doctors are very careful to check everything needed to provide complete medical care.
5.  I think my doctor's office has everything needed to provide complete medical care.
6.  Doctors ask what foods patients eat and explain why certain foods are best.
7.  My doctor's office lacks some things needed to provide complete medical care.
8.  The medical problems I've had in the past are ignored when I seek care for new medical problems.
9.  Doctors don't advise patients about ways to avoid illness or injury.

## VI.  Humaneness of Physician (PQ)*

1.  Doctors always do their best to keep the patient from worrying.
2.  Doctors always treat their patients with respect.
3.  Sometimes doctors make the patient feel foolish.
4.  Doctors always avoid unnecessary patient expenses.
5.  Doctors cause people to worry a lot because they don't explain medical problems to patients.
6.  Doctors respect their patients' feelings.
7.  Doctors never recommend surgery (an operation) unless there is no other way to solve the problem.
8.  Doctors hardly ever explain the patient's medical problems to him (her).

## VII. General Satisfaction (PC)*

1.  I'm very satisfied with the medical care I receive.
2.  The care I have received from doctors in the last few years is just about perfect.
3.  Most people receive medical care that could be better.
4.  There are things about the medical care I receive that could be better.

## VIII. Efficacy of Care (PC)*

1. If you wait long enough, you can get over almost any illness without seeing a doctor.
2. Most sick people are helped a great deal when they go to a doctor.
3. Good personal health depends more on a person's strong willpower than on vaccinations, shots and vitamins.
4. Some home remedies are as good as the drugs that doctors give for curing illness.
5. Doctors can almost always help a person to feel better.
6. People understand their own health better than most doctors do.
7. Recovery from illness requires good medical care more than anything else.
8. Doctors make a great many mistakes that people never hear about.
9. Doctors are able to revive or cure most medical problems that people have.
10. Whether or not people get well is sometimes a matter of chance.

Comparison of Questionnaires Determining Patient Satisfaction with Medical Care, Roberts and Tugwell, *Health Services Research*, December, 1987.

# Appendix 7C
# Client Satisfaction Scale

## Michigan Department of Mental Health

### Community and State Hospital Patients

- Is there a quiet place to be alone?
- Do you think the food is satisfactory?
- Are you treated respectfully?
- Are there enough social and recreational activities?
- Is your social worker helping you?
- Are you afraid of some of the residents?
- Are your religious needs satisfied at the hospital?

### Community Residents

- Do you prefer living in the home to living in the hospital?
- Is there adequate transportation available in the community?
- Can you have visitors in the home?
- Is a phone available to you for local calls?
- Is the lighting at the home satisfactory for reading?

### Special for State Hospital Patients

- I would go home tomorrow if I could.
- I talk with my doctor at least once a month.
- I have a good doctor.
- Would you recommend this hospital to a friend that needs help?

**Appendix 7D**
**Discipline Specific Model**

**Occupational Therapy Satisfaction Questionnaire**
**(for 152 responders out of a total of 295)**

| Behavior | Yes | ST | NO | Comments |
|---|---|---|---|---|
| 1.  Introduces Self | | | | |
| 2.  Listens when I talk | | | | |
| 3.  Cares about me | | | | |
| 4.  Is kind and gentle | | | | |
| 5.  Is polite and courteous | | | | |
| 6.  Is friendly | | | | |
| 7.  Explains what they are going to do to me | | | | |
| 8.  Gives adequate instructions on how to do projects | | | | |
| 9.  Informs me about the actual program | | | | |
| 10.  Gives me an adequate orientation to the crafts area | | | | |
| 11.  Answers my questions within a reasonable amount of time | | | | |
| 12.  Asks me how I am feeling | | | | |
| 13.  Was helpful towards my getting better | | | | |
| 14.  Assists me to plan for my needs after discharge | | | | |
| 15.  Offers an adequate amount of therapeutic activities | | | | |

| Behavior | Yes | ST | NO | Comments |
|---|---|---|---|---|
| 16. Explains the need for activity and allows me to help plan my activity | | | | |
| 17. Knows what he or she is doing | | | | |
| 18. Is willing to help me as I need it | | | | |
| 19. I am completely satisfied with the occupational therapeutic services I received | | | | |

*O.T. Week*, February 25, 1988
Dee Stanfield, OTR/L; Sylvia Rowland, OTA;
and Norman Moore, MD

\* There was a comment section beside each statement, as well as at the end of the questionnaire.

## Appendix 7E
## West Bloomfield Day Hospital Discharge Survey

The West Bloomfield Day Hospital staff would appreciate your responses to the following questions in order that we can continue to evaluate and improve the Day Hospital program!

1.  **The problem(s) that I was experiencing on admission which *could be* addressed at the Day Hospital are now:**

    solved            improved            the same            worse

2.  **The Day Hospital program and staff assisted me in exploring ways to cope with my problems:**

    totally      frequently     sometimes      infrequently      not at all

3.  **My plans after discharge are:**

    clear      mostly clear      partially clear      never been discussed

Please rate the following components of the Day Hospital program regarding their perceived value in assisting you with your problems:

   6.  Not applicable
   5.  All of the time/very helpful
   4.  Usually/quite helpful
   3.  Some of the time/somewhat helpful
   2.  Rarely helpful
   1.  Never/not helpful

4.  **Occupational Therapy**

   A.  Was helpful in learning new skills     1  2  3  4  5  6
       and building self confidence.

   B.  Provided an atmosphere where            1  2  3  4  5  6
       I felt comfortable working in the
       groups and interacting with others.

C.  Helped me identify problem areas          1   2   3   4   5   6
and recognize behaviors which
interfere with doing tasks or activities.

D.  Has helped me recognize progress          1   2   3   4   5   6
as I worked towards reaching my
goals.

E.  Gave me ideas for new activities to       1   2   3   4   5   6
structure my time after discharge.

5.  **Recreational Therapy**

A.  Was helpful in learning new skills.        1   2   3   4   5   6

B.  Gave me the opportunity to try             1   2   3   4   5   6
games/activities/sports I hadn't done
in a long time.

C.  Gave me ideas for new activities to        1   2   3   4   5   6
use after discharge.

D.  I enjoyed having fun in a group.           1   2   3   4   5   6

E.  Helped me look at problem areas in         1   2   3   4   5   6
how I use my leisure time.

F.  We visited new community resources         1   2   3   4   5   6
that may prove useful after discharge.

6.  **The Seminars and Discussion Groups**

A.  Were helpful in assisting me in explor-    1   2   3   4   5   6
ing or thinking about my problems.

B.  Provided an atmosphere for discussion/     1   2   3   4   5   6
questions/comments related to a variety
of topics.

C.  Helped me learn new things.                1   2   3   4   5   6

7.    **Group Therapy**

    A.    Provided an atmosphere where I felt    1  2  3  4  5  6
        comfortable sharing and examining
        personal problems.

    B.    Was helpful in exploring ways to cope    1  2  3  4  5  6
        with my problems.

8.    **Coordinator/Staff Member Assigned to Me**

    A.    Was available to discuss my    1  2  3  4  5  6
        problems and progress when I
        needed to.

    B.    Was helpful in exploring problems    1  2  3  4  5  6
        and feelings and future plans.

9.    **Community Meeting**

    A.    Allowed me the opportunity to make    1  2  3  4  5  6
        suggestions/requests/complaints
        regarding the Day Hospital program.

10.    **If you are being discharged on medication, do you know what
medication you are taking and when you are to take it?**

        yes          no          not applicable

11.    **The most helpful part of the Day Hospital program was:**

_____

_____

_____

_____

_____

_____

_____

**12.**   **Please feel free to offer any other suggestions for improvement of the program:**

_____

_____

_____

_____

_____

_____

Thank you,

The Day Hospital Staff

(Developed by Jan Boe, R.N., Program Manager, West Bloomfield Day Hospital and Staff)

# CHAPTER EIGHT

# Outcome Measures: Monitoring Patient Progress

JULIA KENNON DUNN, Ph.D., C.T.R.S.

JANIECE J. SNEEGAS, Ph.D., C.T.R.S.

CYNTHIA CARRUTHERS, Ph.D., C.T.R.S.

## Introduction

In therapeutic recreation we are facing a continuing demand for accountability. This demand comes from several fronts– from consumers, from our own ongoing desire for professionalization, as well as from external accrediting organizations. One such group, the Joint Commission on Accreditation of Healthcare Organization (JCAHO) has taken the lead and is actively moving toward the incorporation of outcome measures to strengthen accountability. Fortunately, outcome measures are not a new concept in therapeutic recreation. Some therapeutic recreation professionals have been incorporating outcome measures as a component of the program planning process for some time now. In addition, curriculum outcome measures have been used by the educational systems for over a decade, providing guidelines form which therapeutic recreation can draw. This chapter will examine the current demand for accountability through outcome measures, illustrate the ways it can be documented in therapeutic recreation, and provide guidelines for the evaluation of written outcome measures.

## Current Demand for Quality Assurance

Within the health services arena, quality assurance (QA) has become an increasingly important requirement in the search for accountability. Wells and Brook (1988) have identified five general social trends which have influenced the growth and increasing sophistication of quality assurance procedures. The first is the dramatic increase in technology within the medical sciences. Specialization has become the rule rather than the exception, which has brought about a need for demonstrating competence within a given discipline. (The development of an exam by the National Council on Certification of Therapeutic Recreation is in response to this need within the field of therapeutic recreation.)

The second trend is third-party reimbursement. The need now exists to demonstrate eligibility for third-party payment in order to secure funding and inclusion of services. Third-party payers are more likely to reimburse professional services that have identified what it is that they do to address client needs and who further can document that they have met those needs through outcome-oriented data.

The third trend affecting quality assurance, according to Wells and Brooks, is the "increasing sense of social responsibility, as reflected in the development of public work employment programs and federal entitlement programs" (p. 43). Independent of external pressures, public institutions are assuming increased responsibility for providing quality and appropriate services. The development of programs to assist individuals with chemical dependency may be an example of this trend reflected within our profession.

The rising cost of medical care has also affected quality assurance. Consumers place greater emphasis on knowing their dollar is well-spent. The development of cost containment programs, such as diagnostic-related groups (DRG's) has also limited the amount or scope of care which may be provided and paid for. Thus, various disciplines are scrambling to verify the importance and, thereby, inclusion, of their services.

The fifth, and final general trend is the consumer movement. "Increasing malpractice suits and legislation supporting consumer's rights attest to the increasing role of the consumer in health care transaction" (p. 43). Consumers are holding professionals and health care organization more responsible for the quality and appropriateness of the services they provide.

In response to these trends, accrediting agencies have stepped up their efforts to monitor quality care more closely. The Joint Commission of Accreditation of Healthcare Organizations (JCAHO) has moved progressively from a position of inquiring as to whether quality health care CAN be provided, given adequate structures and processes, to a position of *IS* quality care being provided. Recent attention has therefore been directed toward the development of outcome measures.

## Defining Outcome Measures

Outcome measures may be classified as either program outcomes or client outcomes. For the purpose of this chapter, the focus will be on client outcomes. Client outcomes refer to the results of processes carried out by therapeutic recreation practitioners. The outcomes pertain to changes in client health status, attitudes, and knowledge which are directly related to the care received. Health status defined within therapeutic recreation includes improvement in physical or psychological status, as well as increases in leisure related knowledge, skills, and awareness.

Although the focus on outcome measures has come more recently from the health care field, outcomes have been present in other contexts for a significant period of time. Within the educational arena, Morris and Fitz-Gibbon (1978) define outcome objectives as those which "describe the behavior that the program's target group should evidence at its conclusion as proof that they learned something" (p. 17-18). Performance objectives have been defined within a recreational context by Russell (1982) as "the behavior or attitude that the program's target constituency should demonstrate at its conclusion–some skill, attitude, or knowledge they did not have before . . . what happened to the partici- pant as a result of experiencing this program?" (p. 113). In fact, a variety of terms have been used to define what we are now calling outcome measures: objectives, behavioral objectives, educational objectives and performance measures.

Although it may be challenging for practitioners to specify and measure client outcomes related to involvement in their programs, there is recommended action which can be taken, which has proven to be successful, within therapeutic recrea- tion to utilize outcome measures in quality assurance programs. First, it is important to review the difficulties and issues surrounding the specification and measurement of client outcomes.

## Issues in Outcome Specification and Measurement

One of the major tasks involved in specifying outcomes involves establishing a direct relationship between the services provided and client outcomes. Thus, one of the primary concerns is to define the scope of care and thoroughly specify what services are being provided by therapeutic recreation personnel in a particular agency. This level of specification is often absent in therapeutic recreation. Many programs are not documented sufficiently to enable a clear understanding of what actually occurs within the program. Program content, as well as the processes which are utilized by the staff, must be clearly identified. The staff must clearly delineate the nature of the program and the expectant results to the client.

Another important issue concerning the specification of outcome measures is identified by Cohen (1988). An integral step in the specification of outcomes is the "consensual judgement of achievable benefits of care". What are the benefits of involvement in therapeutic recreation programs? A key to finding the answers to this question is without a doubt efficacy research. As a profession, therapeutic recreation needs research to support its claims that it provides a service that changes clients in both positive and predictable ways. Organized data in each facility will do much to support our claims. Research on a larger scale is also essential. Encouraging, however, is Cohen's statement supporting the use of professional judgement in defining our services. Although sufficient research does not exist, there is value in obtaining professional consensus as to the obtainable benefits of involvement in therapeutic recreation services. While some important work already exists within this area for therapeutic recreation, most is in general, global terms and is not related directly to specific therapeutic interventions. A good deal remains to be done to obtain professional consensus, and even more to validate that consensus through research.

Cohen (1988) addresses an additional concern in the measurement of outcomes. It is important to determine the most valid point in time when outcomes should be assessed. This is particularly problematic within the therapeutic recreation process, especially as the length of client stay decreases. Often, the effects of treatment may not be evident until some time after client discharge. Given that follow-up measurement within our profession is in the infant stage of development, little is known about the effects of treatment over time.

The issues outlined above are at first glance overwhelming. However, if viewed systematically, all that is required is that we first, define our services in measurable forms; second, identify the consequences of our involvement; and third, establish feasible timelines for the measurement of outcome attainment. In fact, outcome measures currently exist within therapeutic recreation. The systems approach described by Peterson and Gunn (1984) incorporates outcome measures as performance measures. Educational objectives also offer examples applicable to therapeutic recreation. Both of these sources offer invaluable assistance to professionals seeking to incorporate outcome measures.

Professionals in therapeutic recreation are being challenged to improve their skills in writing and utilizing outcome measures in an effort to evaluate their programmatic interventions. The first step toward addressing this challenge is understanding the techniques involved in writing outcome measures.

### Writing Outcome Measures

Anderson, Ball and Murphy (1975) provide six points to consider as the foundation for writing objectives (outcome measures). First, outcome measures should be used in the measurement of basic knowledge and abilities obtained in programs with defined content. This suggests that programs should be written in a systematic format that clearly outlines the purpose for client involvement in the program. Second, outcome measures should be written to an appropriate level of specificity and not reduced to trivial detail. "The degree of specificity may vary [based on the program and the client population] and should relate to the purpose of instruction and the understanding of the students and instructors" (pp. 182-183). Outcome measures should be reviewed to determine both the appropriate level of specificity, as well as their representativeness to the intervention. Outcome measures for a specific program should be viewed as a collective group to assure that all program objectives are represented by an outcome monitor and that such monitors are equal in their level of specificity. Third, outcome measures should allow for individual differences of clients participating in a group program. Clients vary in their ability levels. Both programs and outcome measures should be developed to allow for the flexibility needed to accommodate the range of clients' abilities in the group. Fourth, though long-term or complex objectives may not be as specific as short-term ones, they nevertheless should be included in a client's program. This is particularly important when dealing with clients within long-term or residential settings. Fifth, outcome measures "must be appropriate to the social milieu at a given time" (p. 183), and clients should participate in the development of outcome measures. In other words, outcome measures should be relevant to the behaviors needed by clients to succeed in their environment or the environment to which they will be discharged. Sixth, outcome measures should be adaptable to varied situations and circumstances to allow for differentiation of skills and abilities.

Additionally, outcome measures should generate data by which the quality of a program can be assessed. Outcome data are collected for each client involved in a specific program (e.g., leisure awareness or fitness). However, cumulative data for all clients participating in that program should be used to determine the degree to which the clients within the program have attained the intended benefits of the program. It would be desirable to establish a level of acceptability prior to the client involvement; for example, "90 percent of the clients will be able to identify five leisure resources upon conclusion of the Leisure Resources program."

In order to be useful, outcome measures must be developed and monitored by the professionals responsible for evaluating client progress. In order for this process to occur, the outcome measure should contain a statement of the intended result of the program and communicate it in such a way that it excludes the greatest possible number of other interpretations of the intent (Mager, 1962). To maximize effective communication of the intent of outcome measures, they should be written in a specific format.

The commonly accepted format for writing outcome measures includes three elements: a statement of the performance or behavior that is expected of the client, a statement of the conditions under which the behavior will be observed, and the criterion or standard of quality that the behavior should fulfill to demonstrate that the outcome measure has been achieved. Each of these elements should be specific enough to communicate the intent of the outcome measure and yet not be so detailed that it becomes trivial.

The statement of performance or behavior should identify a measurable behavior that indicates the main intent of the outcome measure. Peterson and Gunn (1984) suggest that the "least amount of behavior that is still representative of the intent" of the outcome measure be used as the performance statement. This requires professionals to determine the minimum level of performance that would be accepted as an indicator of achievement of a particular outcome measure.

In therapeutic recreation we are frequently dealing with two forms of behavior, overt and covert. Overt behaviors are those that can be observed. Such behaviors would logically be illustrated in the realm of physical and social skills and abilities. Behavioral statements for overt outcome measures would include action verbs such as: run, jump, walk, draw, shake hands, say "hello," or stand. However, we also are concerned with covert behaviors. These behaviors are those behaviors which cannot be observed, that are cognitive, emotional or attitudinal (e.g., attitude toward leisure, playfulness, knowledge of leisure resources). For those behaviors which are covert, the performance statement should "add an indicator behavior" (Mager, 1962, p. 44) to the outcome measure. Indicator behaviors are representative overt behaviors which would illustrate the change in covert behaviors. In the example of a leisure resource outcome intended to result in clients being able to identify resources in their home, the concept of *identify* is a covert behavior (unobservable). Therefore, a performance statement might include an indicator behavior for *identify* such as, write a list of leisure resources in the home. In this case the act of writing a list is observable and can therefore be measured. Thus, whether we are dealing with outcomes that are overt or covert, the outcome measure should indicate a behavior which can be observed to indicate that the clients in the program have achieved the desired change. These behavioral statements describe what the clients will be doing to demonstrate achievement of the measure (Mager, 1962).

In therapeutic recreation we also deal with both simple and complex behaviors. In writing an outcome measure for a simple behavior, the desired behavior is indicated in the performance statement; such as, "clients will write a list of five activities that they have attended." For complex behaviors, "qualifiers" or more simple behaviors can be added to help define the more complex outcome. Peterson and Gunn (1984) refer to this form of objective as abstract or indirect. As such, they recommend that the designed program attempt to "select an observable and measurable action that captures the essence of the . . . objective content" (p. 105). Here, we might be dealing with complex behaviors such as conversation skills or team membership. For these behaviors, simple representative behaviors would be selected to define the intent of the complex behavior as in the following example:

"... conducting a minimum of two conversations during the meal as characterized by the following:
1.  initiates conversation with another resident
2.  listens to the other resident's response
3.  continues conversation on an appropriate topic
4.  speaks in acceptable tone and at an appropriate volume
5.  maintains appropriate eye contact and body positioning throughout
6.  concludes the conversation in an appropriate manner . . . "
    (Peterson and Gunn, 1984, p. 109)

The first element of outcome measures has been described as the behavior that will be displayed by the client. The second element is the condition under which that behavior will be displayed. The outcome measure should include any relevant conditions that would assist the observer in determining whether the behavior occurred as intended by the outcome statement. Peterson and Gunn (1984) describe the statement of condition as one which "sets the stage, by identifying necessary equipment, activities, time lines or other events that are essential to the performance of the desired behavior" (p. 104). They further advise that the behavior should be observed "in the most natural environment or setting possible" (p. 103). Examples of statements used as conditions include: "upon request," "in a conversation," "after program participation," "at the end of the session," "during the dance," "after one week," and "when given a choice." Multiple condition statements can be used in a single outcome measure. However, it is important that all of those conditions be considered for the client's behavior to be measured.

The third element in an outcome measure is the criterion or standard of quality that is expected of the performance or behavior. The criteria selected must be logically related to the nature of the outcome specified. Peterson and Gunn (1984) describe six forms of criteria statements: 1) number of trials, commonly written as "x out of y attempts" (p. 106); 2) level of accuracy, as in "putting the golf ball to within two feet of the hole"; 3) amount of time for the behavior to occur, as in "converse for 15 minutes"; 4) percentage of fractions, the percentage of time the client will demonstrate the behavior within a specified condition, such as "partici- pate in a self-selected activity within one week of admission"; 5) form of the performance as in that required of certain physical performances in sport or dance, as in "swim the backstroke using the form described in the Red Cross Manual," and 6) procedures or characteristics which specify a series of simple behaviors which will demonstrate the achievement of a more complex behavior. An example of procedures would be: "Take own pulse rate as characterized by the following: 1) Placing second and third fingers on neck; 2) Finding pulse and maintaining finger position; 3) Counting number of beats for thirty seconds; 4) Doubling that number to get heart rate" (Peterson and Gunn, 1984, p. 109).

All criteria do not necessarily need to be described in detail in the outcome measure. Mager (1962) refers to the concept of "pointing to the criterion." This implies that existing characteristics are available to evaluate the quality of per- formance. In therapeutic recreation this may mean to refer to such criteria for swimming form as indicated in the Red Cross Manual. In the case of particular projects, the outcome measure may present the criterion as "following the proce- dures as listed in the craft kit directions."

Mager (1962) provides an excellent summary to review the process of writing behavioral objectives which can be applied to this concept of outcome measures. He states·

1. An instructional objective describes an intended outcome of instruction rather than the process of instruction itself.
2. An objective always states a performance describing what the learner will be *doing* when demonstrating achievement of the objective.
3. To prepare an objective:
   a. Write a statement that describes the main intent or performance expected of the student.
   b. If the performance happens to be covert, add an indicator behavior through which the main intent can be known.
   c. Describe relevant or important conditions under which the performance is expected to occur, . . . Add as much description as needed to communicate the intent to others (p. 69).

In addition to this, it is necessary to specify the extent to which successful performance is expected. What standard of quality should the displayed behavior exhibit to be considered as an achievement of the designated outcome?

### The Place of the Outcome Measure in the Context of a Quality Assurance Plan

One of the primary concerns of quality assurance is the guarantee that quality and appropriate services are being provided. We in therapeutic recreation need to demonstrate that our clients are achieving positive and appropriate benefit from their involvement in our programs. Williams (as cited in Cohen, 1988) who developed the approach to quality assurance based on outcomes, presents the concept of "achievable benefits not achieved." This concept is operationalized through a quality assurance program which compares actual outcome data with "consensual judgements of achievable benefits of care." For this to occur we need to have a structure in place which demonstrates the measurable intent (i.e., achievable benefits) of the programs that we offer. Outcome measures can be that structure. By utilizing outcome measures, there can be clear communication of the program's intent to all concerned with therapeutic recreation services. Furthermore in evaluating the overall effectiveness of the therapeutic recreation service and each of the specific programs, outcome measures can be used in the evaluation of client change through a systematic analysis of cumulative data regarding the achievement of the specified outcomes. Therefore, the use of outcome measures can benefit therapeutic recreation in demonstrating the level of quality and appropriateness of services that clients receive, and provide valuable data for the future improvement of programs.

## References

Anderson, S. B., Ball, S., Murphy, R. T. and Associates (1975). *Encyclopedia of Educational Evaluation*. San Francisco, CA: Jossey-Bass.

Cohen, L. H. (1988). Research on mental health quality assurance. In G. Strickner & A. R. Rodriguez, *Handbook of Quality Assurance in Mental Health*. New York, NY: Plenum.

Mager, R. (1962). *Preparing Instructional Objectives*. Belmont, CA: Pitman.

Morris, L. L. and Fitz-Gibbon, C. T. (1978). *How to Deal with Goals and Objectives*. Beverly Hills, CA: Sage.

Peterson, C. A. and Gunn, S. L. (1984). *Therapeutic Recreation Program Design: Principles and Procedures*. Englewood Cliffs, NJ: Prentice-Hall.

Russell, R. V. (1982). *Planning Programs in Recreation*. St. Louis, MO: Mosby.

Wells, K. B. and Brook, R. H. (1988). Historical trends in quality assurance in mental health services. In G. Strickner & A. R. Rodriguez, *Handbook of uality Assurance in Mental Health*. New York, NY: Plenum.

# CHAPTER NINE

# The Development and Use of Intervention Protocols in Therapeutic Recreation: Documenting Field-Based Practices

PEG CONNOLLY, Ph.D., C.T.R.S.

MARY ANN KEOGH-HOSS, Ed.D., C.T.R.S.

## Introduction

Quality assurance has become a dominant theme within the field of therapeutic recreation. Efforts to determine the accountability of therapeutic recreation services are underway on many avenues within the profession. Often mentioned within our literature during the past five to ten years are the issues of client assessment and program evaluation. It seems that these have become the alpha and omega of service delivery: that is, finding better ways of determining, documenting, and addressing client needs (i.e., assessment concerns) and finding better ways of evaluating and documenting program effect (i.e., program evaluation concerns).

While both issues are critical and in need of investigation, there seems to be a part of the puzzle we have ignored or inadvertently missed in our concerns for improving quality. This missing link is the lack of documented program interventions, or, perhaps better stated, the lack of documented service delivery or practice of therapeutic recreation that takes us from assessed need to evaluation of service delivery effect.

Until we begin to define and examine the "common practice" of therapeutic recreation, we may be remiss in attempting to probe any service effect. Until we begin to document common practice patterns or interventions in therapeutic recreation, we may very well be probing the black box rather than any specific or identified therapeutic recreation services. Further, while we recognize the desire and need to document the outcomes and efficacy of therapeutic recreation, it is virtually impossible to determine such efficacy without first documenting and evaluating the content and process of the service being evaluated.

The purpose of this paper is to present concerns surrounding the need to define and document field-based practices in therapeutic recreation. The approach we have taken is to examine the concept of protocol for therapeutic recreation service delivery.

### Defining Common Practice As Related To Monitoring Outcomes

Most professions hold claim to specific purpose, definition and interventions. In fact, most professions would state that their definition and interventions are unique when compared to other professions yet common amongst practitioners within their own profession. This seems to be a hallmark with professions to indicate both uniqueness and utility to their service recipients. Therapeutic recreation demonstrates this by claiming to be unique when compared to other health-related professions. But what has recently become apparent in the field of therapeutic recreation is the need to define what is common practice amongst therapeutic recreation professionals.

This challenge to the field of therapeutic recreation has come largely from outside our field, from external accrediting bodies, healthcare reimbursement authorities, and from such federal sources as the Health Care Financing Administration (HCFA). As health care financing resources become stretched, a need emerges in all health care arenas to investigate the extent to which professions meet patient need. This is accomplished by monitoring whether the necessary and efficient services are delivered to improve the patient's health condition, remediate illness, and/or rehabilitate to the highest level of functional ability.

Since professions themselves have promoted their unique interventions to improve, remediate, and rehabilitate, external authorities have come back with the demand to the professions to define both the relationship and level of effectiveness of such service intervention to patient diagnostic need. The effort here is to define consistency in health service delivery in order to arrive at necessary patient outcomes. A logical inference exists that intervention is both based on identified patient need and delivered (somewhat consistently) to arrive at a desired patient outcome in relation to alleviating diagnostic need or, at the very least, stabilizing the patient's condition. In other words, professions are being asked to prove the cause and effect relationship between their interventions and outcomes within the context of patient diagnostic needs.

This concern with defining cause and effect relationships within the health care professions underscores the need for the documentation and analysis of common practice or proven interventions within each profession. Claiming to have a specific effect without being able to identify specific interventions that lead to that effect is no longer accepted as justifiable evidence toward the effectiveness of a profession. Further, it is not only important that the profession can document common practices that are effective, but there must also be evidence that these common practices are in fact used consistently by the profession's practitioners in similar patient diagnostic settings.

The true sign of a profession is not only consistency in definition and purpose of the professional arena, nor is it just documented evidence of consistent preparation for entry into the profession. The validity of a profession lies in the common practices instituted by its practitioners based on client diagnostic need. Herein lies the major challenge for the field of therapeutic recreation.

The effort here is not to perpetuate the profession, but to assure the public that involvement with a therapeutic recreation practitioner will encompass at least minimally standard practices. We need to assure the public of this consistency of intervention and outcome to includes the patient, the agency, external accrediting bodies, and funding sources. The motivation for these efforts should be to assure quality of care.

## The Concept of Protocol

Some definitions will help clarify the use of the term "protocol" in this paper. First, "practice" is defined as: a repeated or customary action, the usual way of doing something, the continuous exercise of a profession or a professional business. "Practitioner," then is defined as one who practices a profession. If we refer these definitions to therapeutic recreation, the question or focus of inquiry within this discussion is: what is common practice in therapeutic recreation? Once we are able to define common practice, we may begin to seriously investigate areas of common practice in need of improvement and the outcomes of therapeutic recreation services.

"Protocol," on the other hand, usually relates to a more rigorous type of action or group of procedures that are instituted in specific situations. We often hear of diplomatic protocol or military protocol which relates to specific procedures set into play under specific circumstances. The concept of protocol can also be applied to the professions as they define common practices in relation to specific diagnostic needs.

In other words, given a specific diagnostic need or problem, a particular protocol may be developed and tested and used with consistency to lead to a particular pre-determined outcome that is defined as alleviating or remediating the identified diagnostic related need or problem. Protocol, then, becomes a means of responding in consistent practice patterns to commonly identified patient needs.

## Protocol As Examined In Other Health Fields

Although the concept of protocol has been mentioned as being used extensively in other health care professions, a literature search did not yield any sources which documented either the development or content of service delivery protocol related to other professions, except for one article from the field of nursing. In this instance, Marker (1987) presented her model for a hierarchy for nursing standards. Within this article, the author discussed the process of developing standards for nursing care, differentiating between standards of practice and standards of care.

Within this discussion, Marker recommends the development of nursing protocol. The author defines such protocol as being beyond procedures and states that "protocols outline the specific care and management of broad patient care problems or issues" (p. 14). According to Marker, "procedures are viewed as a minor aspect of professional nursing in terms of time consumed, expertise required, and degree of sophistication of practice involved" (p. 14). Other salient aspects of protocol according to Marker are that:

> "Protocols . . . constitute a major portion of professional practice. They continue over hours to days and deal with issues requiring sophisticated judgement and decision making . . . Protocols focus on nursing process of assessment, intervention, and evaluation. They may be written to define dependent, independent, or inter-dependent aspects of nursing practice . . . " (p. 15).

Marker goes on to state:

> "Protocols are put into practice when the nurse selects from a manual or computer file the protocols that a particular patient requires. The practitioner then integrates the protocols into the patient's plan of care . . . Because continuity, consistency, an expediency are all important factors, the use of protocols in this manner facilitates all three considerations . . . " (p. 15).

According to Marker, the five broad areas of nursing care for which protocol are proposed are:

1. Management of patients on noninvasive equipment;
2. Management of patients on invasive equipment;
3. Management of patients undergoing diagnostic, therapeutic and prophylactic measures;
4. Management of problematic physiological and psychological states; and
5. Selected nursing diagnoses.

Some of the examples of protocol issues described by Marker are:  post-op management, IV therapy, blood transfusion management, seizures, suicide, immobility, pain, just to name a few.

A closely related concept to protocol development was found in an article by Clough and Hall (1987) on developing institutional criteria sets for nursing diagnosis. The purpose of these criteria sets is to define patient/client populations by diagnostic information and to develop process and outcome criteria specific to this diagnostic information within a specific professional care model. This concept, given the ongoing mandate to establish cause-effect relationships in professional practice, has far reaching implications and applications for the field of therapeutic recreation. Further, it is conceivable that this concept of institutional criteria sets can be used as a model for the development and definition of protocol relevant to therapeutic recreation practice.

It is important to note that Clough and Hall suggest the development of these criteria sets within a peer committee structure and to include a peer review process. The function of the institutional criteria sets is to document and evaluate service delivery and to document, evaluate and measure quality of care.

The institutional criteria sets can accomplish several goals according to Clough and Hall: "to serve as references when planning and documenting care, to serve as instructional tools to reinforce specific care, and to encourage and promote the use of consistent practice" (p. 33). According to Clough and Hall, the criteria sets should include information on:

1. Major etiologies or causes for diagnostic needs relevant to professional practice (i.e., therapeutic recreation forms the basis of our concerns)
2. One or more outcomes reflecting client status relative to assessment criteria
3. Interventions designed to accomplish stated outcomes

Clough and Hall stress the concept of etiology or causes for diagnostic needs and emphasize this as the critical starting point for development of criteria sets. This information on etiology is based upon a broad perspective of medical, psychological, and/or other documented reference information. The information on etiology should be delineated to specific areas relevant to the practice area, or from our concerns, to the field of therapeutic recreation and its respective service interventions. Additionally, information relevant to independent therapeutic recreation intervention as opposed to team focused intervention should be delineated.

The concept of intervention process and the development of process criteria should focus on the nature, sequence of events, and strategies or procedures employed in the delivery of therapeutic recreation services. This information should answer questions of what strategies and procedures therapeutic recreation employs within the therapeutic recreation practice process.

The concept of outcome criteria defines the end result of care. Outcome criteria should focus on measurable change in health status of the diagnostic-related client population. Three main questions should be answered via the establishment of outcome criteria according to Clough and Hall: "(a) what outcome is expected; (b) when the outcome will occur; and (c) how the outcome can be detected" (p. 36). Outcome criteria are established to indicate the overall resolution of the client diagnostic-related problem rather than the end result of any specific intervention process (i.e., "client will demonstrate a reduction or reversal of _____ " or "client will demonstrate an increase or improvement of _____ ").

Clough and Hall emphasize the importance of peer evaluation of developed institutional criteria sets. The authors suggest that the following questions be addressed within this peer evaluation system: "(a) Do these process criteria describe the care delivery system related to the defined diagnostic grouping? (b) Are any process criteria missing? (c) Are these outcomes expected if the care related to the diagnostic grouping is administered effectively?" (p. 37).

### Documentation Of Common Therapeutic Recreation Practice Approaches: A Critical Step Toward The Development of Protocol

If the Clough and Hall model is applied to therapeutic recreation practice, it is apparent that the starting point for development of protocol is the study of the diagnostic groups served by the field of therapeutic recreation. In regard to the application of therapeutic recreation practice for specific diagnostic groups, very little information exists in the professional literature. It can easily be stated that more information exists on the adaptation of recreation activities by broad-based disability populations than on specific therapeutic recreation interventions used with specific diagnostic groups.

Therapeutic recreation practitioners are cautioned here to avoid the pitfall of using the Clough and Hall model to define recreation programs. The concept of protocol throughout this paper is designed to address specific diagnostic needs and not as another means of defining adapted recreation activities.

By using the Clough and Hall model within a peer review system, field-based examples of therapeutic recreation practice procedures applied to specific diagnostic needs can be documented. Continuing with the peer review model on a broader scale of state or national level review, these criteria sets can be filtered and refined via the judgement of the professional collective. The preliminary documentation will not result in fully embraced "protocol" examples, nor will the singular ideas or conceptualizations of any one professional result in fully accepted protocol. However, these preliminary descriptions are a step in the process of documenting and developing acceptable diagnostic-based protocol for the field. As a starting point, all in the profession should be cautioned to examine each presented protocol cautiously until evidence of the peer review model within its development is discerned.

## Sample Protocol Design

The purpose of the proposed protocol design is to write, process and outcome criteria for specific diagnoses which: (a) serve as quality assurance tools to measure and evaluate independent therapeutic recreation practice; (b) serve as references when planning and documenting care; (c) are utilized as instructional tools when reinforcing therapeutic recreation practice.

The following provides a discussion of the sections of the protocol design worksheet which is shown in Figure 9.1. The first two components on the worksheet refer to diagnostic information. The grouping and specific diagnosis chosen by professionals for development should be defined and referenced as they appear in such recognized reference materials as the DIAGNOSTIC AND STATISTIC MANUAL III R (DSM-III-R) or the ICD 9CM.

1. Diagnostic Grouping _____

   _____

   _____

   _____

2. Specific Diagnosis _____

   _____

   _____

3. Specific Problems (relevant to therapeutic recreation intervention)

   _____

   _____

4. Assessment Criteria _____

   _____

   _____

   _____

5. Overall Objectives _____

   _____

   _____

Figure 9.1–Protocol Design Worksheet*–Page 1

| 6. Etiology/ Specific | 7. Process Criteria (Interventions) | 8. Outcome Criteria |
|---|---|---|
| (Focus on broad perspective of medical psychological, and/or other documented reference info; needs to be delineated with specific areas/problems relevant to T.R.) | (Focus on nature, sequence of events and activities in the delivery of T.R. services–not recreation or leisure activities per se) | (Describe the end result of care; measurable change in health status; what outcome is expected? When will it occur? How will it be detected?) |

9.  References _____

_____

_____

10.  Cross-References _____

_____

11.  Signatures and Titles of Committee Members and Date:

Signature _____ Title _____
Date _____

Signature _____ Title _____
Date _____

Signature _____ Title _____
Date _____

Figure 9.1–Protocol Design Worksheet* –Page 2

* Adapted from Clough, J.G. and Hall, K. (1987). Writing institutional criteria sets for nursing diagnosis. *Journal of Nursing Quality Assurance*; 1:2, 31-42.

The third component on the worksheet refers to problems traditionally associated with the diagnostic information which are relevant to therapeutic recreation practice/intervention. Included in this section might be the signs, symptoms, and characteristics of the diagnosis. It must be emphasized here that only those problems which pertain to therapeutic recreation should be listed. Not all of the problems associated with a specific diagnosis can nor should be addressed by therapeutic recreation.

The fourth component of the worksheet is assessment criteria. This component refers to the overall functional areas addressed by the therapist assessing the patient/client. Whenever possible, give information on standardized instruments which may be used in assessing a patient/client. The fifth component of the worksheet refers to the overall objectives of care for a patient/client in this particular diagnostic area. This concept of overall objectives should address services provided when a patient/client is referred for treatment to therapeutic recreation services.

The sixth component of the worksheet is the etiology section. The etiology or cause of a specific diagnosis is delineated here. Again, only information on etiology which is relevant to therapeutic recreation should be listed. Considering the emphasis on the total person in therapeutic recreation intervention, it may be helpful to consider information from etiology in the categories of physical, mental/ emotional, and social functioning. This section should also provide general information on a specific diagnosis. Any documented information listed in this section should be referenced in the ninth (reference) section of the worksheet.

The seventh component of the worksheet overviews the process criteria. Process criteria focus on the nature, sequence of events, and the strategies or procedures employed in the delivery of therapeutic recreation services (treatment). These criteria are to answer the question of what strategies or procedures a Certified Therapeutic Recreation Specialist (C.T.R.S.) performs within the therapy process. Treatment, in most cases, is directed toward the alleviation and reversal of identified problems.

The eighth component of the worksheet lists the outcome criteria. Outcome criteria describe the end result of the therapeutic recreation treatment. In this section, identify the measurable change in the status of the selected patient/client population. These criteria must answer three (3) questions: (a) What outcome is expected as a specific result of the therapeutic recreation intervention; (b) when will the outcome occur; and (c) how can the outcome be observed and measured. Outcome criteria are written to reflect problem resolution and should relate to the overall problems rather than the end result of individual interventions. Outcome criteria should demonstrate a reduction or reversal of identified problems. Measurable outcomes for each problem listed should be stated, if possible.

The ninth component of the protocol design worksheet is the reference section. It is crucial to the development of the protocol for the field of therapeutic recreation that legitimate and accepted reference documents are used in their development. The tenth component provides a cross-reference section. As protocols are developed and standardized, this section can be utilized when problems and/or etiologies are similar to others developed.

The eleventh component is the part of the worksheet which states the name of the committee, its members, and the date completed. Here, information about the developers is provided.

As a profession following a protocol, therapeutic recreation professionals are gathering data, engaging in treatment, and assuming the responsibility for providing accountable services. The development of protocols for specific diagnostic areas served is vital to documenting practice and to establishing accountability of service delivery for our profession.

For the purpose of our discussion, two protocols have been developed using the Clough and Hall model for developing institutional criteria sets (see Figure 9.1). Mary Ann Keogh-Hoss has developed a preliminary paper on Dementia/Alzheimer Type (Appendix 9A) and Carmen Russionello has developed a preliminary paper on Depression/Major Depressive Episode (Appendix 9B). It is important to note that these two models represent preliminary conceptualizations. They have not been subjected to peer evaluation nor testing at this point.

## Conclusions and Future Needs For Development

We must begin to document common practices in therapeutic recreation in order to be able to meet our quality assurance needs and to effectively document the outcomes of therapeutic recreation services. At this time, there appears to be much more in our literature regarding recreation activity adaptation than in regard to therapeutic recreation interventions relative to diagnostic needs. This imbalance presents a major credibility gap in our field as external authorities are demanding to know the cause and effect of therapeutic recreation services. Documenting intervention protocol will aid in the effort to provide accountable health care services.

In order to accomplish the above outlined task, it is imperative that we begin to collect information from a variety of therapeutic recreation practice settings. Then, through a peer review system, we can begin the much needed development of documented field-based practices in therapeutic recreation.

As has been previously discussed, peer review is the key towards defining current common therapeutic recreation practices. It is suggested that peer review start at the local level, be continued at the state level, and be submitted at the national level for review and approval.

Peer review at the local level, in determining current common practice for a specific diagnostic group, can be facilitated by chart review. A certain perception by the group of what is common may or may not be proven by a comprehensive chart review. Charts for review should be for a specific diagnostic group receiving therapeutic recreation services within a time period of six months. A minimum of twenty charts should be reviewed. These charts should be from a variety of local facilities, not just one facility, whenever possible.

The peer review group should be made up of therapeutic recreation professionals from a variety of facilities offering therapeutic recreation services to the specific diagnostic group being reviewed. Before the review is conducted, the elements to be reviewed must be agreed upon.

As this area is very new to the field, more sophisticated techniques will be developed. To start with, the following elements are suggested for review in defining common therapeutic recreation practice:

1. Length of time service is provided
2. Average time of sessions
3. Number of sessions
4. Assessment criteria
5. Specific areas/problems relevant to therapeutic recreation
6. Interventions–nature, sequence of events and activities in the delivery of service (not specific recreation/leisure activities)
7. Outcome criteria–describe the end result of care in measurable terms
8. Define overall objectives
9. Evaluate outcome criteria–met or unmet

This provides a starting point for peer review to define common therapeutic recreation practice at the local level. It should be noted that, initially, inconsistencies and inadequacies may be seen in this process. This should serve not to terminate the process but to ignite those involved to clarify what it is that truly comprises therapeutic recreation treatment.

Once peer review has occurred at the local level, through a comprehensive chart review process, this information should then be reviewed at the state level through the existing therapeutic recreation state organizations. After state review has taken place, information should be submitted at the national level through the therapeutic recreation associations for review and approval. Should enough states initiate this process, the current task facing therapeutic recreation professionals at the national level of defining common therapeutic recreation practice would be reduced from an overwhelming task to one of consensus across the states, with considerable local, grassroots representation.

## References

Clough, J. G. and Hall, D. (1987). Writing institutional criteria sets for nursing diagnosis: From idea to implementation. *Journal of Nursing Quality Assurance*; 1:2, 31-42.

Marker, C. G. (1987). The Marker model: A hierarchy for nursing standards. *Journal of Nursing Quality Assurance*; 1:2, 7-20.

# Appendix 9A
## Sample Protocol For Therapeutic Recreation:  Dementia/Alzheimer Type

1. *Diagnostic Grouping*: Dementia

2. *Specific Diagnosis*: Alzheimer Type

3. *Specific Problems* (relevant to therapeutic recreation):
   (a) loss of recent memory;
   (b) confusion/disorientation/forgetfulness;
   (c) loss of judgement and ability to abstract;
   (d) possible loss of skills in any life area.

4. *Assessment Criteria*: Assess fine and gross motor skills, receptive and expressive communication skills, cognitive and social skills. Request results of SPECT & PET scans (look at brain activity) [can be done at any hospital with a radiology department] for confirmation of diagnosis.

5. *Overall Objectives*: to provide an assessment that allows for the development and implementation of an individualized treatment plan; provide information to others working with the individual; identify skills intact; identify skills lost; and to focus on tasks which provide positive experiences.

6. *Etiology/Specific:* Progressive Brain Disorder with no known cure. Rate of progression unique to the individual. Seven causes under investigtion:
   (1) Genetic
   (2) Abnormal protein
   (3) Infectious agent-virus
   (4) Toxin-salts of aluminum
   (5) Blood flow reduction
   (6) Acetylcholine-biochemical disturbance
   (7) Elephant combination of above

7. *Process Criteria* (Interventions):
   • Communicate the need for activities and a consistent structured environment to all persons involved with care.
   • Review background information and assessments.
   • Conduct an assessment.

- Develop an activity calendar listind time, place and activity. Have calendars promptly posted and availible for all.
- Provide points of orientation in the environment (i.e., clocks, calendars, current magazines and newspapers). Reality Orientation Classroom techniques not recommended.
- Provide range of activities for physical, mental and social stimulation. Activities for mental stimulation should focus on reminiscence, remote memory and matching skills. Where possible incorporate discussion sessions on common past experiences. Mandatory to provide many opportunities and encourage verbalization.
- Limit the size of a group on mental stimulation to no more than six persons. Ensure that other groups are of a manageable size. Four is the ideal number.
- Provide a structured environment for activities, (Free of distraction with comfortable furniture and pleasant surroundings.)
- Monitor responses to activities at least weekly using the ACTIVTY OBSERVATION CHECKLIST.
- Should an individual exhibit inactivity, request an evaluation of themedication regimen with the prescribing physician, pharmacist and other professionals.
- Follow any behavior programs developed for the individual. Institute behavior programs with the team if needed.
- Follow established bowel and bladder routines.
- Eliminate the use of restraints where possible.
- Use cue-response-consequence when providing instruction for the extremely confused.
- Provide opportunities for nutritious snacks with activities keeping special diets in mind.

8. *Outcome Criteria:*
   - Maintenence of skills in as many life skill areas as possible.
   - Responses to different types of activities measured with the ACTIVITY OBSERVATION CHECKLIST.
   - Identification of the activities the individual can do.
   - Demonstration of a  reduction in identified behavior problems.
   - Demonstration of a reduction in signs and symptoms of agitation and wandering, if present.
   - Identification of medications that sedate individuals and promote confusion, disorientation and falling.

9. Resources:

Aronson, M. K. (1988). *Understanding Alzheimer's Disease*. New York,NY: Macmilan Publishing Company.

Heston, L. L. and White, J. A. (1983). *Dementia*. New York, NY: W. H. Freeman and Company.

Hoss, M. A. K. (1986). *Recreation Activities and An Examination of the Effects of Activity Programming on Persons with Alzheimer's Disease*. Doctoral dissertation.

Kalicki, A. E. (Ed.) (1987). *Confronting Alzheimer's Disease*. Maryland: Rynd Communications.

Restak, R. M. (1984). *The Brain*. New York, NY: Bantam Books.

Wurtman, R. J. (1985). Alzheimer's Disease. *Scientific America*, 252:1, 62-74.

10. Cross-References_____

_____

_____

11. Signatures and Titles of Committee Members and Date: *Figure 2 was developed by Mary Ann Keogh-Hoss, Ed.D., C.T.R.S., Executive Director, Creative Leisure Services, Spokane, Washington.

**Appendix 9B**
**Sample Protocol for Therapeutic Recreation:**
**Depression/Major Depressive Episode**

1. *Diagnostic Grouping:* Depression

2. *Specific Diagnosis:* Major Depressive Episode

3. *Specific Problems* (relevant to therapeutic recreation): As indicated by
   DSM-III-R (1987)– (a) loss of interest or pleasure in all, or almost all,
   activities; (b) low self-esteem; (c) feelings of hopelessness; (d) insomnia
   or hypersomnia; (e) psychomotor agitation and retardation; (f) poor
   appetite or overeating; (g) low energy or fatigue; (h) poor concentration
   or difficulty making decisions.

4. *Assessment Criteria*: Potential assessments should possess the following
   capabilities– the ability to assess levels of motivation, functional independence skills, cognitive, psychological and psychomotor abilities and
   disabilities, self-esteem, physical fitness level, focus of control, perceived
   freedom in leisure, barriers to activity participation.

5. *Overall Objectives:* To provide an assessment that allows for the
   development and implementation of an individualized treatment plan; to
   convey assessment information to other health care practitioners; to
   increase functional skills concomitant to maximizing independence; to
   develop research based on individual and group programs designed to
   treat the depressive disorders and their resulting symptomotologies (i.e.,
   reduce hopelessness, increase self-esteem, ameliorate sleep and eating
   disorders, etc.); to provide a comprehensive discharge plan.

6. *Etiology/Specific:* It is stated that Learned Helplessness is both a common symptom and sometimes a cause of depression, and that it is
   sometimes on the opposite end of the spectrum from percieved freedom.
   Since other research tends to support this claim, it is imperative TR
   Specialists assess for this pathology and devise treatment strategies that
   allow the individual to move along the continuum toward perceived
   freedom and independence.
       According to Kuiper (1987), depressives internalize more failures
   than normal and, interestingly, they also appear to internalize abnormal
   amounts of successes. This incongruence in casual attribution runs
   parallel with the notion that distorted perceptions of personal control can
   cause withdrawl and perhaps even apathy and depression.

Those who support these claims through their research argue that "when recreation participation was decreased, opportunities for exercising control over the envionment decrease and increased depression therefore followed." Therapeutically designed exercise programs can treat some types of depression as well as a host of the symptoms associated with the illness.

Psychologically these programs can ameliorate self-concept and a greater perceived locus of control and mastery over the environment. The psychological benefits may be intertwined with the physiological benefits.

7.  *Process Criteria* (Interventions): The choice of treatment is based on the acquisition and analysis of as much information on the individual as posibly can be gathered. Past and present, subjective and/or objective evidence ascertained through the written assessment and behavioral observations are some of the methods employed.

The Recreation Therapist is competent to assess and refer patients to the following therapeutic groups or individual process as indicated:

(a) stress management– to increase the individual's awareness of individual stressors and methods to cope and maintain a healthy lifestyle.

(b) physical fitness– to increase cardio-pulmonary conditioning and decrease depression, increase appetite and sleep.

(c) leisure education–to increase perceived freedom in leisure, identify and clarify leisure interest; to provide opportunity to break down barriers associated with decreased participation in recreation and leisure act.

(d) relaxation therapy groups– to increase the individual's ability to use his/her own inner resources to combat some of the symptoms and etiologies of depression.

(e) mixed media groups.

(f) psychomotor agitation and retardation programs.

[other information available]

8.  *Outcome Criteria:* The patient can expect the following outcomes after actively participating in Recreation Therapy for the amount of time indicated by the related treatment:

(a) decreased depression

(b) increased perception of control over the environment

(c) increased sleep

(d) increased appetite

(e) increased energy

(f) increased cardio-respiratory fitness

    (g)  increased self-esteem

    (h)  increased psychomotor abilites

    (i)  increased awareness of healthy lifestyle approaches

    (j)  increased amounts of "pleasant" activites engaged in

    (k)  increased decision making abilities

9.  Resources:

American Psychiatric Association (1987). *Diagnostic and Statistical Manual of Mental Disorders*. Third Edition Revised. Washington, DC: American Psychiatric Association.

Bregha, F. J. (1980). Leisure and freedom re-examined. In Goodale, T. L. and Witt, P. A. (Eds.) *Recreation and Leisure: Issues in and Era of Change*. State College, PA: Venture Publishing, Inc.

Conway, R. W.; Smith, K.; Alexander, E.; Felthous, A.; Scholl, R.; and Levy, R. (1981). Total fitness as a psychiatric hospital program. *Bulletin of the Menniger Clinic*, 45:1, 65-71.

Ellis, G. D. and Niles, S. (1985). Development, reliability, and preliminary validation of a brief leisure rating scale. *Therapeutic Recreation Journal*, 19:1, 51-57.

Ellis, G. D. and Witt, P. A. (1984). The measurement of perceived freedom in leisure. *Journal of Leisure Research*, 16:2, 110-123.

Geist, J. H., Klein, M., and Eischens, R. R. (1979). Running as treatment for depression. *Comprehensive Psychiatry*, 20:1, 41-54.

Iso-Ahola, S. (1980). *The Social Psychology of Leisure and Recreation*. Dubuque, IA: William C. Brown.

Kuiper, N. (1978). Depression and casual attributions for success and failure. *Journal of Personality and Social Psychology*, 36:3, 236-246.

Lewinsohn, P. M. and Libet, J. (1972). Pleasant events, activity schedules, and depressions. *Journal of Abnormal Psychology*, 79:3, 291-295.

Lewinsohn, P. M. and Graf, M. (1973). Pleasant activities and depression. *Journal of Consulting and Clinical Psychology*, 41F:2, 261-268.

Lobstein, D. D., Mosbacher, B. J., and Ismail, A. H. (1983).  Depression as a pow
erful discriminator between physically active and sedentary middle-aged men.
*Journal of Psychosomatic Research*, 27:1.

Master, A. M. (1944).  Electrocardiogram and "two step" exercise:  Test of cardiac
function and coronary insufficiency.  *American Journal of Medical Science*,
207, 435.

National Institute for Mental Health (1984).  Physical fitness and mental\health.
*United States Department of Health and Human Services*, Washington, DC:
DSHS Publication No. (ADM) 84-1364.

Ragheb, M. G. and Beard, J. G. (1982).  Measuring leisure attitude.  *Journal of
Leisure Research*, 14:2, 155-167.

Rotter, J. B. (1966).  Generalized expectancies for internal versus external control
of reinforcement.  *Psychological Monographs*, 60:1.

Russioniello, C. V. (1987).  *A Comparison of Perceived Freedom in Leisure and
Depression*.  Unpublished Master's Thesis, Eastern Washington University.
Cheney, WA.

Seligman, M. E. P. (1975).  *Helplessness–On Depression, Development, and
Dying*.  New York, NY:  Charles Schribner's Sons.

Wassman, K. B. and Iso-Ahola, S. E. (1985).  The relationship between recreation
and depression in psychiatric patients.  *Therapeutic Recreation Journal*, 19,
63-70.

Witt, P. A.; Compton, D. M.; Ellis, G.; Howard, G.; Aguilar, T.; Forsyth, P.; Niles,
S.; and Costillo, A. *The Leisure Diagnostic Battery*.  Denton, TX:  North
Texas State University.

Witt, P. A. and Ellis, G. D. (1985).  Development of a short form to assess perceived freedom in leisure.  *Journal of Leisure Research*, 17:3, 223-233.

10.     Cross-References _____

_____

_____

_____

11. Signatures and Titles of Committee Members and Date: *Appendix 9B was developed by Carmen Russionello, C.T.R.S., Sacred Heart Medical Center, Spokane, WA.

# CHAPTER TEN

# Therapeutic Recreation Protocols: Client Problem Centered Approach

LANNY KNIGHT, C.T.R.S.

DAN JOHNSON, C.T.R.S.

## Introduction

For an occupation to be considered a profession it must meet an extensive list of criteria. Reynolds and O'Morrow (1985) summarized criteria from a variety of sources with which a vocation must compare itself. They include specialized knowledge, lengthy study, individual competence, an organization, standards of professional competence, and a responsiveness to the public. The common thread among these requirements is standardization. Standardization that assures consumers of the service that they can expect a safe and effective product.

As Therapeutic Recreation has furthered its development as a profession, many issues have been dealt with concerning standardization. Standards of Practice, defining quality of care in Quality Assurance (QA), development of testing for certification, and defining therapeutic recreation are all examples of standardization efforts. The development of therapeutic recreation protocols is another piece of the standardization puzzle; that is, the standardization of interventions.

## Protocols As Standard Interventions

Protocols are a group of strategies or actions initiated in response to a problem, an issue, or a symptom of a client. They are not programs or program descriptions that typically describe Therapeutic Recreation, but are approaches or techniques that will lead to expected treatment outcomes. These strategies or actions are used to define the therapeutic recreation intervention. They describe what we do to achieve outcomes or desired states. Protocols distinguish therapeutic recreation's role in treatment and the uniqueness of our services.

The validation of therapeutic recreation protocols will develop the standard treatment strategies for the profession. As standard interventions are developed, they become a basis for an evaluation of the quality of care of therapeutic recreation.

Within therapeutic recreation QA programs, we can no longer evaluate just the structure and outcomes of our services. We must define our process also. Historically, because of lack of standardization, it has been difficult for this to be accomplished.

With standards of practice providing the basis for structure, protocols can be the basis for both the process and the evaluation of outcomes in quality assurance programs.

Protocols are closely intertwined with standards of practice and efficacy research. Standards of practice provide an overview of structure, process, and outcomes of what is expected from staff and the department in the delivery of professional services. Efficacy research measures the effectiveness of those services. The validation of protocols, in turn, will affect how we define our standards of practice.

## Protocols In Other Professions

A review of the literature of protocols in other professions reveals that, with the exception of nursing, little information exists. And despite volumes of standards, criteria sets, and nursing diagnoses, Marker (1987) states:

> "The nursing profession continues to struggle with identity crises, internal fragmentation, and disjointed attempts to define itself, justify its existence, and spell out its contribution to consumer health care."

Clearly, as a brief review of the literature suggests, if therapeutic recreation professionals can aggressively pursue protocol development, then they can be among the leaders in this aspect of health care delivery.

The nursing profession suggests many formats that can be applied to the development of therapeutic recreation protocols. The first is derived from the work of Carolyn Marker (1988) and her Marker Model pyramid of nursing standards. The Marker Model specifies formats outlining the process for job descriptions, performance standards, procedures, protocols, guidelines, and standards. Noteworthy in her approach is the differentiating of procedures and protocols. Standards of practice, protocols, and procedures represent differing levels of specificity for therapeutic recreation. Standards of practice guides what the profession does. It provides the framework for globally defining services.

Protocols guide treatment and the ongoing management of patient care problems. Protocols require professional judgement and expertise to articulate protocols into specific treatment plans.

Procedures guide the practitioner to complete psychomotor tasks via step-by-step instructions. Procedures are more specific than standards of practice or protocols, and can often be accomplished by lesser-trained personnel.

The work of Clough and Hall (1987) can also be applied to the Therapeutic Recreation protocol formats. Clough and Hall developed institutional criteria sets according to nursing diagnosis and have stated:

> "By categorizing patients according to nursing diagnoses, nurses can write process and outcome criteria that are nursing specific; then the quality of nursing care can be measured against standards specific for nursing" (p. 33).

Clough and Hall's Criteria Sets utilize a diagnosis taxonomy originating from the North American Nursing Diagnosis Association (NANDA). It incorporates the philosophy of human response patterns to define nursing diagnosis and nursing service. The criteria set is completed by specifying, among other items, etiology, process criteria, outcome criteria, and references.

The author's criteria sets are useful in that they structure protocols based on specific problems, outline nursing interventions, and utilize a review of the literature. The disadvantages of the criteria set format is that they are limited to accepted nursing diagnoses and that the interventions and outcomes tend to be general.

The American Nurses' Association and the Association of Rehabilitation Nurses (1988) have published a document entitled *Rehabilitation Nursing: Scope of Practice*. Their diagnostic and criteria sets "provide a general framework by which the quality of care (outcomes) in rehabilitation nursing can be evaluated" (p. 12). The format includes diagnostic categories, NANDA classification categories, nursing diagnosis, a definition, defining characteristics, related factors/ etiologies, process criteria (general), and outcome criteria (general). This format emphasized a symptom-based approach to intervention that facilitates the making of protocols that are more definable, specific, and useful to practitioners. The use of a symptom-based approach is further reinforced by studying the Symptom Index Appendix of the DSM-III-R.

It is interesting to note that the DSM-III, the diagnositic and statistical manual of the American Psychiatric Association, was developed partly through dissatisfaction and lack of reliabililty of the DSM-II. The DSM-II was diagnosis based, whereas the DSM-III and DSM-III-R use clinical indicators at the symptom level. Of primary importance is the use of symptoms as clinical indicators, as opposed to the use of diagnoses as the most common demoninator (Barlow, 1981).

The authors believe that a diagnosis-related approach to protocols is too general to be useful to therapists because clients exhibit varying symptoms within the same diagnosis and because many diagnoses contain the same symptoms that are treated similarly. By developing protocols according to symptoms, a therapist can choose treatment protocols related to problems that are based on validated assessment.

In developing the model for protocols, a number of issues were investigated. A format was developed that combined both nursing diagnoses and criteria sets that will be used throughout this chapter as the structural foundation for protocol development.

The format for protocol development is as follows:

1. The treatment problem–the client problem that is being addressed by the therapeutic recreation specialist.
2. The defining characteristics–the observations, symptoms and manifestations that tell us when the problem is present.
3. Related factors and etiologies–the internal and external elements that have an impact on the clients and contribute to the existenceof their problems.
4. Outcome criteria–the expected changes in client status after and as a result of therapeutic recreation interventions.
5. Process criteria–what the therapeutic recreation specialist will do to facilitate the client achieving the desired outcome.

Each step of protocol development is interrelated and, in total, provides a basis for directed and effective therapeutic recreation service. Examples of the protocol process are contained in Appendix 10A Examples of  Protocol for Therapeutic Recreation .

To understand the protocol more clearly, each element has been explained in further detail:

**Problem**

There are three types of problems that are addressed in therapeutic recreation. First is the actual problem. This problem is present; it is validated by the observation of major signs and symptoms. We know it is there because we can observe it or test for it, etc. On the basis of an assessment, there is little argument whether the problem is real or not. For example, the problem of anxiety manifests itself in specific signs and symptoms that are readily identifiable through observation. Trembling, restlessness, shortness of breath, sweating, dry mouth, complaints of feeling keyed up or exaggerated startle response, trouble falling asleep or staying asleep, and overall irritability are all signs of anxiety.

The second type of problem is a nondefined/or observed problem. This problem may be present and is highly suspected to be present, but there are not enough confirming data to substantiate an actual problem. However, usually there is substantial circumstantial evidence to confirm that a possible problem may be present. For example, a possible problem may be binge-eating. While the behavior has not been directly observed, there is enough circumstantial evidence to suspect that a problem exists. For instance, very little is eaten at meals, yet there is a progressive weight gain. There is a sour smell to the client's breath that might be consistent with purging. After meals the client disappears quickly to the bathroom, where suspected purging is taking place. All these are suspicion indicators, but not a confirmation of binge-eating.

The third type is that of potential problem. This is a problem that may happen because there is a presence of high risk factors. These might be termed prodromal signs, those behaviors or symptoms that are usually observed prior to a problem manifestation. An example may be self-mutilating behavior. Whereas not yet observed, the presence of denial of anger, lack of insight into emotional responses and a previous history are all prodromal signs to self-mutilating behavior; hence it is labeled as a potential problem (Carpenito, 1987).

Basically, the problem area can be divided into two major categories. First, is an independent problem. This is where the responsibility for the problem is solely that of the therapeutic recreation specialist and requires no other medical supervision or shared responsibility with other treatment team members.

Nurses, because of their scope practice, are licensed to diagnose and treat independent problems. In fact, the entire nursing diagnoses classification system is one built on independent nursing practice (Carpenito, 1983). An example in therapeutic recreation of where independent problems would be observed would be in community therapeutic recreation settings where there is the opportunity to work with clients without medical supervision.

The second and most typical category is collaborative problems. This is where the responsibility of the problem is shared with others on the treatment team and requires medical order and/or supervision. This shared responsibility occurs both within the assessment of the problem and in the treatment of the problem. Collaborative problems may be shared only with the physician in terms of responsibilities, or may be shared and distributed among the other treatment team professionals. For instance, a problem with impaired affective response, a difficulty in recognizing or expressing feelings, may be dealt with by the individual physician or psychologist, art therapist, nurse, or be the responsibility of the TRS. Another example may be impaired decision making, which may be first recognized by the TRS and delegated to the TRS by the primary clinician or treatment team. This is still a collaborative problem in that there is medical supervision. The rest of the treatment team is aware of the problem and is delegating the responsibility of the problem to therapeutic recreation services.

### Defining Characteristics

The defining characteristics are derived from assessment data. These characteristics are subjective and objective in nature and provide documentation of specific problems. The gathering of the assessment data to support the defining characteristics can be attained in two ways:

1. Informal process, which may be through interview, observation, record searching, discussions with family, etc.
2. Standardized assessment, such as the Leisure Diagnostic Battery (LDB) or the Comprehensive Evaluation in Recreation Therapy (CERT).

Regardless of the assessment process used, the assessment needs to be validated and deemed reliable. The essential steps in the assessment process are 1) collecting information; 2) interpreting the information whereby the TRS determines the significance of the data collected and assigns meaning to it; 3) clustering the data to determine specific conclusion; and 4) identifying the problems or symptoms that are to be worked on by the TRS.

### Related Factors And Etiologies

Related factors and etiologies may be internal or external. The problem may be the result of a systemic disease, or it may be the result of an environmental factor. For instance, impaired mobilization of upper extremities may be the result of multiple sclerosis, or it may be the result of an external factor of being in traction after a major traumatic injury. Both are etiologies of impaired mobilization of the upper extremities. Since the protocols are not diagnosis-specific, but more problem- or symptom-based, there are many problems that will cross diagnostic lines and have several potential etiologies. For instance, impaired decision making is a symptom of schizophrenia as it is with depression, with dysthymia, with some personality disorders and more. All possible related factors and etiologies of the problem should be listed to put in context where the problem source may be.

### Outcome Criteria

Outcome criteria may also be stated as client goals. These are the expected changes in the status of the client after he/she has received therapeutic recreation intervention. The outcome criteria are written in terms of what the client is expected to do and can reflect any of the following areas:

1. Demonstration of remediation or rehabilitation of the problem area or a demonstrated improvement in health status through increased comfort and/or coping strategies,
2. The maintenance of the present optimal level of health,
3. Optimal levels of coping with significant others,
4. Optimal adaptation to terminal illness,
5. Collaboration and satisfaction with health care providers.

## Process Criteria

Process criteria are written in terms of what the therapeutic recreation specialist will do to have the client achieve the desired outcomes as listed in the outcome criteria.

Therapeutic recreation interventions can be directed toward any of the following:

1. Assessment of causative and contributing factors
2. Reduction or elimination of the factors
3. Promotion of selected activities
4. Teaching of health related skills
5. Referrals to identify the needed services

Lines four and five are examples of therapeutic recreation protocols developed for specific problems (McFarland and McFarlane, 1989).

## Conclusion

Imagine, if you will, the year 1992. A client is admitted to a treatment unit. The TR Specialist conducts a comprehensive assessment on the client, from standardized and/or validated assessments. Data collected from the assessment are entered into a computer, whereby the computer yields a potential problem list. The problem list is reentered into the computer, and validated treatment protocols are produced. The validated protocols are now used in the formulation of an individual treatment plan that is specific to the agency and the resources available to the specialist and the client. Comfort is taken by the TR Specialist, knowing that the treatment protocols used to develop the specific treatment plan have been validated and reflect state of the art treatment strategies in therapeutic recreation services.

This vision is attainable; however, the profession must adhere to a careful and systematic plan to assure that protocols are validated and reflect, not only state of the art treatment strategies, but also strategies that are within the scope of practice of therapeutic recreation. Protocols need to be well-grounded on evidence and should be able to withstand the criticism of other professionals (Fehring, 1987).

The plan for developing protocols for TR should not, and cannot, reflect only a consensus among practicing professionals. A comprehensive plan in the development of protocols for theapeutic recreation must contain two stages. The first stage involves gathering a consensus of what is the scope of practice currently initiated by TR professionals. Further steps during this stage would be comparing and contrasting results to current standards of practice, and conducting literature review to substantiate the appropriateness of services. Refinement of the protocols and consensus by top clinicians and educators would complete this phase.

The second phase would involve further validation through field-testing trials, and ultimately, research conducted on the efficacy of the protocols.

The development and validation of therapetic recreation protocols has the potential to place therapeutic recreation practice, research and education on a common path. It is a process that will firmly establish the domain of therapeutic recreation. A commitment to the process of protocol development will require openness on the part of practitioners and educators. It is a commitment that involves accountability and change. It is only with this commitment that we can remain a profession and remain calling ourselves professionals.

### References

American Nurses Association and Association of Rehabilitation Nurses (1988). *Rehabilitation Nursing: Scope of Practice.* American Nurses Association, Kansas City, MO.

Barlow, D. H. (1981). *Behavioral Assessment of Adult Disorders.* Guilford Press: New York, NY.

Carpenito, L. J. (1987). Nursing Diagnosis in Critical Care: Impact on Practice and Outcomes. *Heart & Lung,* 16:6, 595-600.

Carpenito, L. J. (1983). *Nursing Diagnosis: Application to Clinical Practice.* Lippincott: Philadelphia, PA.

Clough, J. G. and Hall, K. (1987). Writing Institutional Criteria Sets for Nursing Diagnosis: From Idea to Implementation. *Journal of Nursing Quality Assurance,* 1:2, 31-42.

Fehring, R. J. (1987). Methods to Validate Nursing Diagnoses. *Heart & Lung,* 16:6, 625-629.

Marker, C. G. (1987). The Marker Model: A Hierarchy for Nursing Standards. *Journal of Nursing Quality Assurance,* 1:2, 7-20.

McFarland, G. K. and McFarlane, E. (1989). *Nursing Diagnosis: Diagnosis and Intervention, Planning for Patient Care.* C. V. Mosley: St. Louis, MO.

Reynold, R. P. and O'Morrow, G. S. (1985). *Problems, Issues and Concepts in Therapeutic Recreation.* Prentice-Hall, Inc.: Englewood Cliffs, NJ.

## Appendix 10A
### Examples of Protocol Development For Therapeutic Recreation

Therapeutic Recreation Protocol (a)

1. **Problem**
   Indecisiveness

2. **Definition**
   A marked inability to make decisions or a faulty decision-making process.

3. **Defining Characteristics**
   - Vacillation or ambivalence regarding routine or other decisions.
   - Lack of attention or concentration to effectively enact decision-making process.
   - Lets others unduly influence personal decisions.

4. **Outcome Criteria (client will . . . )**
   - Be able to make routine decisions involving daily life activities.
   - Employ decision making process in important life decisions.
   - Gain a greater sense of perceived control through improved decision-making skills.

5. **Process Criteria (TRS will . . . )**
   - Provide opportunities that stress the need to make simple decisions. (i.e., choose red or blue)
   - Gradually increase the significance of decision-making correspondent to the client's abilities.
   - Teach client element of decision-making process.
   - Relate decision-making process to increased perceived control and self-determination.

6. **Related Factors/Etiologies**
   Associated with depressed mood in such diagnostic groupings as:
   - Major Depression
   - Dysthymis
   - Adjustment Disorders
   - Alzheimer's

Therapeutic Recreation Protocol (b)

1. **Problem**
   Impaired physical mobility of upper extremities.

2. **Defining Characteristics**
   Subjective Data:
   - Client c/o pain, fatigue, loss of sensation, or weakness in one or both upper extremities.

   Objective Data:
   - inability to move one or both upper extremities
   - impaired grasp
   - limited range of motion (ROM) of one or both extremities
   - mechanical devices preventing full ROM
   - inability to perform self-care activities
   - neglect of one or both upper extremities
   - partial or total loss of one or both upper extremities
   - impaired coordination of upper limbs

3. **Outcome Criteria (client will . . . )**
   - Maintain or increase mobility, strength and endurance of upper limbs
   - Demonstrate skills necessary for participation in desired leisure activities
   - Demonstrate improved quality of purposeful movement of upper extremity

4. **Process Criteria (TRS will . . . )**
   - Increase upper extremity mobility, strength and endurance if possible by:
     –using activities that assist prescribed ROM exercises
     –emphasizing use of affected arm in activity
     –placing objects to affected side to reinforce use of affected arm
     –instruct use of unaffected arm to exercise affected arm
   - Teach adaptive skills necessary for participation in activities of desired leisure lifestyle.
   - Teach safety precautions re: heat, cold and sharp objects.
   - Provide reinforcement of collaborative team efforts in treatment.

5.  **Related Factors/Etiologies**
    - Trauma (e.g., fractures, crushing injuries, lacerations, amputation)
    - Surgical Procedure (e.g., joint replacement, reduction of fractures, removal of tumors, mastectomy)
    - Systemic Disease (e.g., multiple sclerosis, CVA Guillain Barre, rheumatoid arthritis, Parkinson's, Lupus)

## SECTION THREE
## QUALITY ASSURANCE MANAGEMENT APPLICATION

CHAPTER ELEVEN

# Clinical Privileging: Assuring Quality Performance in Therapeutic Recreation

PEG CONNOLLY, Ph.D., C.T.R.S.

## Introduction

Clinical privileging is a concept which is gaining more and more attention in the field of therapeutic recreation. It is a concept that has more familiarity to those who work in clinical or health care settings than in other therapeutic recreation employment settings. And, it is a concept that for some sounds as unfamiliar as Hindu Sanskrit. But, nevertheless, it is a concept which the therapeutic recreation professional needs to embrace in an effort to assure quality care.

In this analysis of clinical privileging, the author has applied the concept to a concern for outcomes measures related to the delivery of therapeutic recreation, and, thus, to the concern of quality assurance. This approach will afford the macro view of the concept of clinical privileging involving general indications of this concept and exploring its meaning and interpretation to our field in a broad sense. Based on knowledge of the profession as a whole, the concept of clinical privileging in therapeutic recreation will be related to clinical privileging as it has been defined in the health care professions via both regulatory authorities and professional literature.

Hopefully, through this analysis and discussion of the privileging concerns and needs of this field, we will come a step closer to addressing quality assurance issues and to emphasizing a greater awareness of the importance of clinical competence and performance to outcome measures and quality assurance in therapeutic recreation.

## Credentialing and Clinical Privileging: General Terms and Concepts

Credentialing is a process that grants recognition for various levels of competence related to the practice in a particular professional area. The credentialing process may include certification, licensure, active membership in professional associations or societies, the award of a professional degree, or recognition of competence by virtue of performing a job for a number of years in a particular field. Depending on the field and the area of service, any one or a combination of the above methods may be used to determine an individual's competence.

Certification is the form of national credentialing program currently available through the National Council for Therapeutic Recreation Certification (NCTRC) which recognizes the minimum competence of therapeutic recreation personnel. Through the NCTRC certification plan, minimally acceptable standards for therapeutic recreation personnel have been established at the professional and paraprofessional levels. Through this voluntary program, therapeutic recreation personnel have their educational and experiential qualifications evaluated through a formal peer review process. Based on this evaluation, the individual may be awarded either the Therapeutic Recreation Specialist, the Provisional Therapeutic Recreation Specialist, or the Therapeutic Recreation Assistant certificate.

The concept of credentialing is common among most established professions. Certification's function in the practice arena represents one step in a continuum that is intended to assure the public that an individual practitioner has demonstrated mastery of certain knowledge, skills, and abilities as established by the professional community in which he or she practices.

In 1977, the United States Department of Health, Education and Welfare referred to the processes of certification and licensure as the formal identification of professional and technical competence (USDHEW, 1977). Certification was differentiated from licensure in that it was provided via a nongovernmental agency or association to individuals who met certain standards and qualifications. Licensure, on the other hand, was provided by an agency of government and grants an individual permission to engage in an occupation based on evaluation that the individual possesses minimal competency for practice in the particular occupational area. The purpose of this licensure is to protect the public health, safety, and welfare (USDHEW, 1977).

The advantages of credentialing within therapeutic recreation are numerous. The first advantage is the recognition that an individual meets the minimum qualifications for practice in the field. The second advantage relates to credibility of practitioners within the agency where the individual is employed. Many agencies and governmental units across the country have incorporated NCTRC certification standards into their job descriptions and requirements for employment or for advancement within the employing agency.

Further, since we work in health care and human service arenas, we consistently interface with other established professions such as Social Work, Psychology, Occupational Therapy, Physical Therapy, and others. These established professions also have national credentialing programs. Therefore, as a means of demonstrating professional credibility to our colleagues from these other disciplines, we should be credentialed using similar patterns and procedures as they, with personnel standards and criteria for recognition applied from our own profession. Many accrediting bodies, such as the Joint Commission on Accreditation of Healthcare Organizations (JCAHO) and the Commission for the Accreditation of Rehabilitation Facilities (CARF), may require the examination of an individual's professional credentials as minimum evidence of qualification to practice. Finally, insurance carriers and prospective payment systems dictate possession of certain recognized credentials before fees for services are reimbursed.

Certification is necessary but not sufficient for clinical privileging. The Joint Commission for the Accreditation of Healthcare Organizations (JCAHO) defines clinical privileges as "permission to provide medical or other patient care services in the granting institution, within well-defined limits, based on the individual's professional license and his experience, competence, ability, and judgement" (JCAHO, 1987, p. 109). While credentialing covers a wide scope of methods for providing recognition of an individual's competence as established by professions at the national level, clinical privileging systems are established by individual governing boards of hospitals using set criteria established by each individual hospital or agency. For an in-depth examination of how clinical privileging is viewed by the JCAHO, it is suggested that the reader review the "Medical Staff" Chapter of the *ACCREDITATION MANUAL FOR HOSPITALS* (JCAHO, 1987, pp. 109-127).

While much of the content of the chapter on "Medical Staff" deals with the physician staff member, mention is also made of "other licensed individuals permitted by law and by the hospital to provide patient care services independently in the hospital" (JCAHO, *AMH*, 1987, p. 109). According to JCAHO, some of the salient characteristics of a clinical privileging plan or system include: an established hospital level governing mechanism, staff bylaws/rules/regulations/policies, criteria established for hospital staff to insure quality care to patients, a specified application procedure, provision for peer input and recommendation, provision for an appeal process regarding adverse decisions to the applicant, initial provisional appointment of staff, time-limited appointment staff (not to exceed two years), procedures for evaluation and monitoring of clinical performance during appointment, as well as other aspects.

According to JCAHO, "Specialty board certification is an excellent benchmark for the delineation of clinical privileges" (JCAHO, *AMH*, 1987, p. 118). In the case of therapeutic recreation, where state licensure plans exist in only three U.S. states at this time, certification has become the major "benchmark" for attesting to an individual's qualifications to practice.

Credentialing and clinical privileging, then, are intricately intertwined, both with unique systems for control and application, and both with similar overall intent: to protect the consumer of services and insure quality care delivery to the service recipient. While certification programs evaluate minimally acceptable qualifications for recognition in a given profession, clinical privileging goes a step further and examines credentials as well as past and present clinical performance.

Clinical performance has a direct relationship to the delivery of quality care to patients and is referenced consistently in quality assurance literature as such. Through the quality assurance process, the delivery of quality care to patients is examined and refined. As O'Leary (1987), President of the Joint Commission has recently indicated:

> "In the past, JCAHO has used standards to assess four areas of structure and function: the facilities, or the bricks and mortar; the equipment (for general operations and for patients); the people; and the 'system'. The two main groups of people are the medical staff and the hospital staff, or employees; for both group, qualifications must be reviewed and performance monitored . . . The true unit of measure for quality is the patient outcome, not the facility. Did the patient get well? Return to work? Return to optimal function? . . . Those of us in the health professions are under considerable pressure to define and measure quality of care. If we do not do it, plenty of people would be happy to do it for us . . . It seems to me that the real key to defining quality of care, in the foreseeable future, is clinical performance. Not that other issues, such as access, will not be considered, but clinical performance will be the critical factor" (p. 8).

It is time that therapeutic recreation take a stance on its own, on its credentials for practice, on the service delivery needs of its consumers, on the establishment of the criteria for clinical privileging in practicing agencies, and, therefore, take the professional responsibility to monitor professional behavior and practice to insure quality of care to the service recipients.

## A Brief History on Credentialing in Therapeutic Recreation

Credentialing of therapeutic recreation personnel is not a new concept. In fact, there has been a formalized credentialing program for therapeutic recreation personnel for over thirty years. However, it has been during the last seven years, since the formulation of the National Council for Therapeutic Recreation Certification, that the number of credentialed therapeutic recreation personnel, as well as the strength and quality of the credentialing plan, has grown so tremendously.

In 1986, the field of therapeutic recreation celebrated the 30th anniversary of national personnel standards (Folkerth, 1986). Historically, three professional organizations (the Hospital Recreation Section of the American Recreation Society, the Recreation Therapy Section of the American Association of Health, Physical Education and Recreation, and the National Association for Recreation Therapy) were concerned about the advancement of "hospital recreation" and, in 1953, these three organizations joined forces to create the *Council for the Advancement of Hospital Recreation* (CAHR).

The major task of CAHR was to develop personnel standards for the field and, as a result, in 1956, the first set of national personnel standards was established. During the first CAHR review of hospital recreation registration, 68 individuals were granted registration (Folkerth, 1986).

In 1968, the National Therapeutic Recreation Society adopted the VOLUN-TARY REGISTRATION PLAN FOR THERAPEUTIC RECREATION PER-SONNEL, revised personnel standards, and registered under the new plan approximately 265 individuals who had been previously registered by CAHR. The terminology at this time changed from "hospital recreation" to therapeutic recreation to reflect a broadened scope beyond the arena of hospital recreation (Folkerth, 1986).

During the late 1970s, the NTRS registration plan was examined with an interest in refining and upgrading the credentialing plan. The guidelines of the National Commission for Health Certifying Agencies were reviewed and it was determined that significant changes needed to be made in the NTRS plan to improve it. Part of the change was to separate the voluntary registration program from the professional membership organization (i.e., NTRS) and to allow the credentialing program to operate as an independent certifying group in order to meet the national standards set for certifying agencies.

From 1980 to 1981, the NTRS Board of Directors adopted a massive revision of the credentialing standards for therapeutic recreation personnel, reducing six levels of registration to a two-level certification plan (professional and paraprofessional) (Carter, 1981; Folkerth, 1986). This two-level plan was instituted in the fall of 1981 along with the formation of the National Council for Therapeutic Recreation Certification (NCTRC). Since the formation of NCTRC, the therapeutic recreation certification standards have not changed significantly during the past seven years.

In 1981, the bylaws for NCTRC were adopted by the National Therapeutic Recreation Society Board of Directors and the National Recreation and Park Association Board of Trustees, thus establishing the first independent organization devoted to the credentialing of therapeutic recreation personnel.

The purpose of the NCTRC is to: (a) establish national evaluative standards for the certification and recertification of individuals who attest to the competencies of the therapeutic recreation profession; (b) to grant recognition to individuals who voluntarily apply and meet the established standards for certification in therapeutic recreation; and (c) to monitor the adherence to the standards by the certified therapeutic recreation personnel (NCTRC, 1986).

At the time NCTRC was established in 1981, it certified under its new plan approximately 3,000 individuals previously registered under the old NTRS Voluntary Registration Plan. Today, there are over 10,000 certified individuals recognized by NCTRC with an increase of about 2,000 newly certified members each year. From 68 registered "hospital recreation personnel" with CAHR in 1957, to 265 at the beginning of the NTRS Voluntary Registration Plan in 1968, to

3,000 at the beginning of NCTRC in 1981, to 10,000 certified in 1988, the growth has been tremendous and projections are that there are still many more practitioners yet to be certified.

## Issues and Trends in Credentialing

NCTRC was formed as an independent certifying agency because of the national guidelines for health certifying agencies. There are some 43 criteria that the National Organization for Competency Assurance (formerly the National Commission for Health Certifying Agencies) follow to examine the credibility of credentialing programs (NOCA, 1986). Some of the dominant concerns set forth by these national guidelines are:

1. The purpose of the certifying agency must be specifically certification and the structure must be as an independent certifying agency and not a component of a professional membership organization nor of the profession's accrediting organization;
2. There is a concern for how the personnel standards are established in that they must relate to the skill and knowledge required to function in the health profession;
3. There must be public participation in the development and monitoring of credentialing standards from consumers and employers;
4. There must be direct liaison positions with representation from the professional membership organizations;
5. There is concern regarding the evaluation mechanism in terms of it being fair and objective, reliable and valid;
6. There must be a process for individuals to appeal both eligibility requirements as well as certification decisions;
7. The certifying agency must disseminate information on an annual basis about the scope and content of its certification procedure as well as the numbers of individuals who apply for certification, the numbers certified, and the numbers who are not certified;
8. There must be plans for a recertification process to assure continued professional competence for individuals;
9. There must be a formal policy and procedures for discipline of certificants including sanction of revocation of the certificate, for conduct which clearly indicates incompetence, unethical behavior and physical or mental impairment affecting performance (NOCA, 1986).

Certainly, upon review of the above points, it is apparent that NCTRC separated from its parent organization, the National Therapeutic Recreation Society, in order to meet national guidelines for certifying agencies. The guidelines of the National Organization for Competency Assurance assist the certifying agency in developing along sound and respected principles in regard to its purpose, structure, resources, evaluation mechanism, public information, responsibilities to certification applicants, responsibilities to the public and to employers of certified personnel, recertification, and responsibilities to the National Organization for Competency Assurance.

## State Licensure of Therapeutic Recreation Personnel

Three states currently have licensure bills for therapeutic recreation: Utah (1974), Georgia (1975), and, recently, North Carolina (1986). Three state licensure laws add strength as well as governmental regulation to the practice of therapeutic recreation on the state level. This trend toward attainment of licensure on the state level is continuing with several other states actively pursuing state regulation of therapeutic recreation.

The future advancement of this profession may be affected by its ability to justify state licensure plans or some alternative method of gaining state regulatory status for the practice of therapeutic recreation. Licensure, via legal mandate, establishes job and/or title protection to therapeutic recreation personnel. The purpose of these regulatory actions is to protect the consumer from nonqualified persons practicing an area in which they do not have proven skills and knowledge. In order for therapeutic recreation to be successful with state licensure or regulatory efforts, it must be proven that the purpose of the regulation is to "insure that the public health, safety, and welfare will be reasonably well protected. Questions to be addressed in assuring public protection include: "Can anyone provide therapeutic recreation services or is specific knowledge and skill necessary?"; "Are therapeutic recreation services the same as recreation services?"; "What are the minimal skills necessary to practice before harm is caused the consumer?"; "What is 'common practice' or consistent practice in therapeutic recreation?" It is essential in examining these issues that we expand the definition of the "consumer" to include not only the direct recipient of services, but the agency/employer as a consumer of the professional's services.

The relationship between a national certification plan and a state licensure plan needs to be carefully constructed. This issue is currently being discussed by not only the therapeutic recreation profession but by other professions as well. There are some that lead us to believe there will be no need for an NCTRC if all 50 states have licensure plans. As previously stated, certification and licensure go hand in hand, and both will need to exist in the future for the advancement of this profession. For those professions who have both licensure authority and a certification plan, the license allows individuals to practice based upon an evaluation of their minimum competence, whereas their certification represents a higher level of competence that is awarded only after these individuals demonstrate a certain level of quality in practice over a period of time (usually no less than two years in practice).

### Status of Clinical Privileging in Health Care and Therapeutic Recreation Concerns

There is a debate going on in health care regarding the basic issue of clinical privileging. By tradition, clinical privileging has been directed primarily at medical staff and not at nonphysician staff. In many agencies, this practice continues. Thus, the concept of developing a clinical privileging system for therapeutic recreation may not seem relevant to some because the local hospital or health agency would not recognize such a plan even if it were developed. So why, one might ask, should therapeutic recreation practitioners worry about developing a clinical privileging plan if the local agency only monitors clinical privileges of physicians?

Additionally, even if a therapeutic recreation clinical privileging system could by incorporated at the local hospital level, there may still be questions about the consistency of the service delivered, the value and outcome of educational opportunities currently available for therapeutic recreation personnel, or the apparent lack of structured peer review systems in the field. All of these issues are necessary when considering clinical privileging systems and the absence of appropriate answers to these questions would raise concerns about the consistency of our professional field.

### Justification for Developing Clinical Privileging Plans for Therapeutic Recreation

The major impetus for developing clinical privileging plans and systems for the profession is to assure quality of care to the service recipient. It is the profession's responsibility to establish minimally acceptable levels of care to the service recipient and to monitor its clinical performance in delivering such services. It is the responsibility of therapeutic recreation personnel, whether recognized or incorporated by the hospital governing board, to self-regulate its own profession with the intent of assuring quality care to our clients. Thus far, this article has addressed very general issues in therapeutic recreation and has not begun to approach the issues of specialty skills necessary for service delivery in today's high technology health care market. What emerges are some difficult questions to be answered by the profession of therapeutic recreation: "What skills are necessary to work with various diagnostic groups?"; "How do we evaluate the basic competence necessary for the privilege to practice in these arenas?"; "How do we monitor the quality of that practice?"

As Dennis O'Leary has stated regarding the measurement of quality of care: "If we do not do it, plenty of people would be happy to do it for us." (O'Leary, 1987, p. 8). Why is the establishment of clinical privileging plans for therapeutic recreation necessary? What must be considered in its development? What are the pros and cons of actually developing such a plan? It is hoped that there will be a great deal more discussion of the topic of clinical privileging for therapeutic recreation in the literature and a substantial update of the concepts reported by Eliopoulos and Donovan in their 1980 article on developing a clinical privileging model for therapeutic recreation (Eliopoulos & Donovan, 1980).

**Measuring Professional Competence and Developing Outcome Measures**

Clinical privileging plans for therapeutic recreation today might very well rely on certification as one part of the documentation of competence to practice. But, such plans will need to go much further to assure clinical competence in practice. The quality assurance standards of the Joint Commission very clearly indicate that clinical performance is tied to the concerns for quality of care to patients. And as the President of the Joint Commission has indicated, the key to defining quality of care is clinical performance. So, based upon the above, how do we examine the relationship between competence of therapeutic recreation personnel and expected outcome measures contained within our quality assurance programs?

This must truly be the profession's ultimate goal in documenting clinical performance and quality care. The monitoring and measurement issues we will face in the very near future are certainly going to be critical ones. And, certainly, we are not alone in our confusion and/or frustration about what the key indicators and criteria of service delivery are or should be.

Through specifying clinical privileges for therapeutic recreation, there will be the establishment of criteria for the scope and limitations of practice in specific agencies. Additionally, a certain level of quality of care expectations will have been established for the profession. Through monitoring actual performance, therapeutic recreation practitioners may come closer to examining outcome measures than is currently being done.

The need to define clinical performance expectations based clearly on patient diagnostic needs is imperative. Failure to do so will place therapeutic recreation in a precarious situation as a service deliverer in the health care arena. It is possible to define appropriate quality of care and to perform quality services and, yet, still not benefit the service recipient if there is not an effort to address professional skills in direct relationship to client needs.

So while progress is being made toward examining outcomes more succinctly, caution must be taken to not get caught in the "black box" approach to service delivery evaluation (Connolly, 1984). That is, as the profession of therapeutic recreation begins to approach the examination of the outcome measures, a continuous examination of the intervention processes must be made to determine the true value of any derived outcomes. It is not only an issue of service recipients meeting outcome expectations, but also of whether or not they arrived at these outcomes based on calculated and diagnostic-related interventions.

### Conclusions: Where Do We Go From Here and What Can We Do On the Local Level?

How does professional competence relate to quality of care? This can be viewed as our greatest task to probe and prove over the next few years. Additionally, we must address the issue of whether our present level of professional competence gives assurance to the necessary outcome expectations for the patients we serve.

Therapeutic recreation must begin to recognize both professional privileging and responsibility in providing services to clients. Efforts must begin to examine the basic knowledge and skills necessary for practice and to determine the advanced skills necessary to address specialty areas of care.

The future of credentialing and the future of therapeutic recreation are intricately linked. Our strength as a profession may very well depend on our willingness to regulate ourselves. This premise must be carried on most strongly at the local level and should be evidenced in the ability to articulate and monitor justifiable clinical privileging plans in assuring quality of care to the clients served.

Therapeutic recreation is growing and learning as a profession. There has been dramatic growth in the credentialing program for therapeutic recreation personnel and, hopefully, there will be continued growth in the future. It is anticipated that as the scope and practice of therapeutic recreation continue to be defined and refined, practitioners will continue to refine and advance the necessary knowledge and skills for practice. In doing so, the profession will gain strength and receive appropriate recognition as a bona fide health profession.

Each individual in therapeutic recreation has a stake in the continued development of our credentialing program, the ongoing examination of quality in service delivery technique, the establishment of local level clinical privileging plans, the development of quality peer review systems, and the continued advancement of the overall profession. Each individual should be an example of what therapeutic recreation is and exemplify the competence we need on a daily basis in our work with the people we serve. Each practitioner should share in the responsibility for demonstrating excellence in professional practice and for helping their colleagues to do the same. Together, these individual acts will shape the future for the profession of therapeutic recreation.

# References

Carter, M. J. (1981). Registration of Therapeutic Recreators: Standards from 1956 to Present. *Therapeutic Recreation Journal*, 15:2, 17-22.

Connolly, P. (1984). Analyzing Cause As Well As Effect: A Method of Program Analysis. *Therapeutic Recreation Journal*, 18:1.

Eliopoulos, E. and Donovan, G. (1980). A Conceptual Model for Clinical Privileging in Therapeutic Recreation. In Navar, N. and Dunn, J. (Eds) *Quality Assurance: Concerns for Therapeutic Recreation.* Champaign, IL: University of Illinois, pp. 90-102.

Folkerth, J. (1986). Certification–Historical Perspectives: The First Thirty Years, 1956-1986. *National Therapeutic Recreation Society 20th Anniversary Program.* Alexandria, VA: National Recreation and Park Association.

Joint Commission for the Accreditation of Healthcare Organization (1987). *Accreditation Manual for Hospitals.* Chicago, IL: Joint Commission for the Accreditation of Healthcare Organizations.

National Council for Therapeutic Recreation Certification (1986). National Council For Therapeutic Recreation Certification Bylaws, as amended. Spring Valley, NY: NCTRC.

National Organization for Competency Assurance (1986). Sourcebook on Health Occupations: A Direction of Certification, Accreditation, and Associations, in 185 Health Fields. Washington, DC: National Organization for Competency Assurance.

O'Leary, D. (1987). Quality Control Challenges in the New Competitive Marketplace. *The Journal of Cancer Program Management.* Winter, 1987; 2:1; 6-10.

United States Department of Health, Education, and Welfare (1976). A Proposal for Credentialing Health Manpower. Washington, DC.

CHAPTER TWELVE

# Credentialing and Privileging in Therapeutic Recreation: Practical Professional Necessities

RICHARD HATFIELD, C.T.R.S.

## Introduction

Rapid developments in the American health care industry are forcing changes in that industry and its accountability systems. Legal, resource and economic issues are at the heart of these changes. While it is considered the hospital governing board's responsibility to grant staff membership and privileges, historically, the medical staff have made their recommendations which were subsequently rubber-stamped by the governing board. In this system, power was centered in the physician, including the powers of privilege delineation. When cost pressures were less intense, there was little reason to question the physician's or medical staff's powers in this area. Two factors helped foster this situation: first, it was a "seller's market" with physicians being the sellers; secondly, our society has "defined" the physician and has been reluctant to challenge the physician's position or views. Several forces have developed which have created a shift in the entire health care system. This resulting shift has dramatically highlighted the need for delineating clinical privileges beyond the traditional medical brotherhood.

Landmark legal decisions have held hospitals to a higher level of accountability for what is done on their premises. The 1965 *Darling vs. Charleston Community Memorial Hospital* (Darling vs. Charleston, 1966) decision involved negligence by a physician covering the emergency room. In this case, the hospital was found liable, along with the physician, because the hospital had not established and followed appropriate quality control procedures. Since this case was decided, the position of corporate and medical staff accountability for the quality of care provided has been adopted and expanded by the courts in several states. At the same time that these and related legal developments occurred, Medical Staff and Board of Governers accountability for the quality of care delivered, (including the functions of credentialing, privileging and quality assurance) has become a critical part of the standards of the Joint Commission on Accreditation of Healthcare Organizations (Joint Commission, 1985).

Shifting resources have added a second type of pressure. There has been a major increase in the number of available physicians. During the 1970s alone, their ranks increased by 40 percent, and it is predicted that we will see a surplus of 30 percent by the year 2000 (United States Department of Health and Human Services, 1980). At the present time, many nonphysician healthcare providers are experiencing dramatic shortages in their numbers. Such personnel shortages create pressures on related professions to expand their scope of practice in an effort to compensate for emerging service gaps. These shortage periods also provide opportunities for disciplines to expand their "turf." (This can clearly be seen with the current nursing shortage. As nurses have less and less time to do patient education, family counseling, interagency liaison work, research, etc., other professions have begun to integrate these activities into their own professional domains.)

In either case, prolonged personnel shortages invariably produce increased rivalries between disciplines. Demonstrated qualifications and competence will be one of the major factors in deciding who will provide which services in the future. These issues of qualifications and competence present challenges particularly to those involved in the education and training of individuals who would become Therapeutic Recreation Specialists in clinical settings. Unfortunately, our field continues to lag well behind most others in its ability to prepare students for the changes taking place in health care today. Too few students are coming into the clinical work setting with the basic skills and/or understanding needed to perform on the level expected of those who would be a part of a modern sophisticated health care team. This growing preparation gap will force more professionally oriented clinical programs to develop credentialing, privileging and staff education systems which reflect realistic expectations of the current health care environment.

A third pressure area may be the most significant of all– economics. Financial pressure is forcing all agencies to examine closely their utilization of resources, with regards to productivity and cost effectiveness. This examination included their largest single resource or budget item, personnel. How effectively and efficiently health care providers can deliver services will determine future resource allocations. Hospitals will have strong incentives to provide only those services which assure effective, efficient treatment. The old "sellers" market has rapidly disappeared in favor of a "buyers-oriented" market. The buyers include the client, the payors (insurance companies, etc.) *and* the providers, (i.e., hospital administration, etc.) along with their governing boards. For a profession to survive, to say nothing of thriving, demonstration of professional competence and efficacy of services provided are essential. The demonstration of staff competencies through credentialing and clinical privileges is one important approach to demonstrating the viability of and need for particular service.

## Understanding Terminology

At this point a common understanding of relevant terminology is necessary.

*Credentialing* is the effort to establish a health care professional's basic qualifications for admission to staff. *Privilege delineation* refers to the process by which individual members of a hospital staff (physician and nonphysicians) are granted the authorization to perform certain specified activities within the hospital. *Medical/Professional Staff* is the group which has overall responsibility for the quality of the professional services provided by individuals within the hospital. *Clinical privileges* refers to the permission provided to medical or other patient-care services in the granting institution, within well-defined limits, based on an individual's professional license and his/her competence, ability and judgement (Joint Commission, 1987).

While the hospital's governing board is considered to be ultimately responsible for the granting of staff membership and privileges, historically, medical staff have made recommendations which were rubber-stamped by the board. As legal and economic events have forced hospitals to rethink their structures, greater flexibility has been given to the organization of medical/professional staffs. A stronger emphasis has been placed on the processes of Credentialing and Privileging staff. A clearer and more direct accountability has also been placed upon Boards of Directors.

## Process of Clinical Privileging

The organizational governing in any hospital is determined by the agency's board. In a Medical Staff structure, the Medical Staff refers to physicians and possibly other selected professionals who, by legal requirement or by the decision of the governing board and the medical staff itself, are to be included. All other professionals practice under the direction of the medical staff. In a Professional Staff structure, those professionals who meet specific criteria established by the agency and its governing board may be a part of the Professional Staff. All others practice under the direction assigned to them by the professional staff. (Professional Staff structures tend not to be as heavily physician oriented as are Medical Staff structures.) The many issues related to quality of care and accountability are the concerns of the Medical/Professional staff and the Board of Directors.

To understand clinical privileging, it is important to realize that Clinical Privileges are just that–privileges. They do not mandate a responsibility on the part of the hospital to allow practice. Privileges are to be granted by the hospital through its designated agents/representatives on the basis of established criteria. They are to be applied uniformly and consistently (Joint Commission, 1987). Privileges are generally delineated in three distinct categories:

1.  *Provisional Privileges*–Privileges granted on a time-limited basis and under close supervision.
2.  *General Privileges*–Privileges considered to be usual and customary.
3.  *Special Privileges*–Privileges granted for activities and procedures which fall outside of the classification of "usual and customary," and which may imply a higher degree of risk to the patient and/or therapist, and may require a higher level of skill on the part of the therapist.

The process of delineating clinical privileges is essentially a three-step procedure. The first step involves verification of credentials for admission to staff. The second step is granting of the right to perform certain activities with the hospital. The third step is the periodic review of performance in relation to the privileges granted.

A critical part of the admission to staff is the application process. In the case of *Johnson vs. Misericordia Hospital (1980)*, the Supreme Court of Wisconsin held that a hospital through its agents should, at a minimum, require completion of an application and verification of the accuracy of the applicant's statements, especially in regards to education, training and experience. This case also ruled as follows: "Additionally, it should (a) solicit information from the applicant's peers, including those not referenced in his application, who are knowledgeable about his education, training, experience, health, competence, and ethical character; (b) determine if the applicant currently is licensed to practice in the state and if licensure or registration has been or is being currently challenged; and (c) inquire whether the applicant has been involved in any malpractice action and whether he has experienced a loss of medical organization membership or privileges or membership at any other hospital. The investigating committee also must evaluate the information gained through its inquires and make a reasonable judgement as to the approval or denial of each application for privileges" (Johnson vs. Misericordia Community Hospital, 1980, p. 32).

The granting of admission to staff does not constitute privileging although a professional usually must be a member of the staff to gain privileges. The initial application is for the purpose of assuring the hospital that the practitioner is legally able to practice and that he is not immoral or incompetent. In the next step, the application for privileges, the hospital is seeking to ensure that the applicant is competent to perform specific services.

The actual privilege delineation process is relatively consistent from one hospital to the next. The process begins with the applicant requesting privileges. The request (and verified credentials) is examined by the appropriate department head and/or the department's clinical privileges or clinical practice committee. Based on the determination of qualifications, a recommendation is made to the governing board through the medical staff credentials committee or the profes-sional staff credentials committee. The governing board then considers recommendations and grants or denies the privileges. Determination of whether or not an individual is qualified for privileges is not easy to accomplish. This process is potentially ladened with subjective decision making.

There are two common methods used in clinical settings: the *"disease-based approach"* (or procedure-based approach) and the *"categorical approach"* (American College of Surgeons, 1986). Within the *disease-based approach,* the applicant checks off those procedures which he/she wishes to perform and is evaluated against recognized standards for these procedures. There are several potential problems associated with this method:

1. There exists the potential problem of establishing an inappropriate set of standards.
2. There is a possibility of granting privileges to an unqualified applicant when using the above approach.
3. There is also the possibility of denying privileges to a qualified applicant.

The *categorical approach* requires the applicant to estimate his level of knowledge in a particular area (i.e., leisure counseling). Based on the applicant's assessment of his/her skills, privileges may be granted or denied. This very general method can easily provide an inaccurate impression of the clinician's competencies. Whatever method is chosen, it is still essential that an accurate picture of the applicant and his/her past practice be obtained. In all probability, past performance may be the very best predictor of future performance. This probability underscores the need for accurate references and work history information.

Once privileges are granted, the clinician is assigned to a "provisional" status which allows his superiors and peers to monitor and evaluate performance based on demonstration of competence. This provisional status may last anywhere from three months to two years.

### Applied Approach in Therapeutic Recreation

In the fall of 1986, the Department of Recreation Therapy at the North Carolina Memorial Hospital undertook the task of developing a clinical privileging procedure for all therapeutic recreation staff. The initial step of information gathering consisted of an extensive literature search and contacts with other Recreation Therapy programs which are involved in privileging systems within their agencies. The result of the search revealed that a limited number of TR staff are involved in privileging systems. The next step involved contacting the NCMH administration and legal staff concerning our desire to develop a clinical privileging system. The hospital administration provided us with valuable procedural information and much appreciated encouragement.

As is true in any case, the organizational structure of our agency has directly affected the privileging system which we eventually developed. The North Carolina Memorial Hospital is organized under a strict medical staff structure. The only other professional services in the hospital which were using a privilege and credentialling system at this time were Respiratory Therapy and Nursing. In our initial discussions with medical staff representatives, hospital administration and hospital legal counsel, concerns were raised that we might be asking for sanction for independent practice. We assured those concerned that we were not seeking independent practice privileges but rather a system aimed at monitoring and assuring quality Recreation Therapy services which would be consistent with the policies and procedures already in place at the North Carolina Memorial Hospital. In a concession to the concerns expressed and in an attempt to avoid future confusion, we decided to officially title the system the "Clinical Practice System for the Department of Recreation Therapy." Once these concerns had been addressed, we were given support and encouragement to proceed. Appendix 12A contains the clinical practice process which has been in place since the Spring of 1987 at the North Carolina Memorial Hospital.

**Conclusion**

The growing financial pressures on the health care system will increase the conflicts between service providers for their "piece of the patient" as well as the health care dollar. The arguments will be familiar ones with one group claiming that it is the most uniquely qualified to provide a particular service. The other group(s) will respond with the argument that there is little if any data to support the former group's claim. There will also be complaints that one group is more concerned about its own survival than with the quality of care being provided. These pressures identified will force a sorting out of professions along lines of effectiveness, efficiency and credentials. As a result, Recreation Therapists can count on a much closer examination of their own qualifications and the effectiveness of the services which they provide. The most intense examinations will come from administrators, third party payors and consumers. In order to prove its effectiveness and efficiency therapeutic recreation will have to establish sound credentialing and privileging procedures at the service-delivery level. We have to be able to say unequivocally which necessary services we can provide and what we specifically require in the way of education, training and experience in order to provide them. If we can not deliver this information, then we cannot and should not survive as a health care profession in the clinical setting.

## References

American College of Surgeons (1986). Medical Staff Accountability for Credentialing and Quality Assurance. *Patient Safety Manual,* Second Edition, p. 94.

Darling vs. Charleston Community Memorial Hospital (1966). 211 N.E. 2nd e 253 (Ill. 1965), cert denied, 383 U.S. 946.

Johnson vs. Misericordia Community Hospital (1980). 294 N.W. 2nd 501, Wisconsin Court of Appeals, (May 12, 1980).

Joint Commission on Accreditation of Hospitals (1987). *Accreditation Manual for Hospitals.* Chicago, IL: JCAHO.

Joint Commission on Accreditation of Hospitals (1985). Issues in Medical Staff Credentialing. *Quality Review Bulletin,* September, pp. 277-78.

United States Department of Health and Human Services (1980). *Graduate Medical Education National Advisory Committee: Summary Report, Volume 1.* Hyattsville, MD: DHHS Pub. No. HRA 81-651.

## Appendix 12A
## Clinical Practice Process Department of Recreational Therapy

### The North Carolina Memorial Hospital

### Open Positions Are Posted

For each TRS position at NCMH there is a job description which details job duties, responsibilities, knowledge skills and abilities as well as minimum education and experience required for the position. The complexity of the position and the responsibility given to it are reflected in the position classification and in the minimum academic and experience requirements for the position. An important part of the application process is the completion of a supplemental employment application. This is a detailed form which focuses specifically on identifying the applicant's professional credentials. The information requested is consistent with that suggested by the Joint Commission on Accreditation of Healthcare Organizations and the office of Personnel, State of North Carolina. Each applicant interviewed for a TRS position must complete this form.

### Applications Are Reviewed

Once the candidate pool is identified, all of the applications are circulated to the staff who will be involved in the interview process. The most viable candidates are then selected for interview offers.

### Reference and Data Verification

Before a position can be offered the department is obligated to verify that all of the application information is accurate and that references are acceptable. If there are inconsistencies or inaccuracies in the application, the applicant is either excluded or further checks are made.

### Screening/Interview Selection

Once the most suitable applicants are identified, interviews are conducted with the appropriate department and hospital staff.

### Selection Is Made

Based on verification of credentials and positive feedback from the interviews, the most suitable candidate is identified. The final decision to offer a position is made by the department director. Once this decision has been made, the position is offered.

## Position Is Offered

The Department Director and the employment counselor contact the finalist candidate and negotiate the offer. If the position is declined, the process returns to a review of the candidate pool and starts over from there. Assuming that a position offer is accepted and the candidate chooses to join the staff, the new staff member is then granted PROVISIONAL GENERAL PRIVILEGES as of his/her employment date. (General Privileges are considered to be usual and customary privileges granted to entry-level TRS staff.) The granting of these privileges is dependent upon the person's ability to demonstrate his/her competence in 17 critical areas of knowledge/ability which have been identified by department staff. Under Provisional General Privileges, the staff member is closely supervised during his/her probationary period. Full General Privileges are granted by the TR Supervisor and must be obtained by the end of the six month probationary period or the employee may be terminated. (As part of the process, resources available for obtaining the competencies required for privileges at all levels are clearly identified for the staff member.) The staff member has the right to appeal any adverse decision by his/her TR Supervisor to the Departmental Clinical Practice Committee. This committee is made up of four members, each representing one of the four KTR levels within the Department; TRSI, TRSII, TR Supervisor, TR Administrator. The individuals sitting on the committee rotate every six weeks. It is the duty of this committee to review appeals and to make final decisions on such matters.

This committee may also be asked to review any staff member's progress from the provisional level to full privileges or settle any disputes over the interpretation of the policies/procedures related to the clinical practice program.

## Special Privileges

Special Privileges are those that are specific in nature and require a higher or more specific level of knowledge/training than do general privileges. These are granted to only those who have demonstrated the specific competencies required. Some examples of areas requiring special privileges would be: Assertiveness Training, Therapeutic Outings, Leisure Education, Pre- and Post Operative Teaching and Relaxation Training.

Competencies required for each area of special privileges have been clearly identified. The TR Supervisor makes the initial determination on whether or not a staff member has met the stated competency requirements for the special privileges in question. As with the general privileges, the staff member requesting special privileges may appeal any adverse decision to the Clinical Practice Committee.

## Annual Review

All privileges which have been granted to staff are reviewed on an annual basis. This is done as a part of each employee's Work Planning and Performance Review. At that time, each employee's performance over the past year is reviewed and evaluated by his/her peers, supervisor and department director. In any instance where the employee privileges are being questioned, the Clinical Practice Committee makes a final recommendation to the department Director. In cases where the employee's ability to perform duties which fall under the umbrella of the privileging system are questioned, the employee may be directed to reestablish his/her credentials and demonstrate his/her competency in the specific areas identified. If directed to do so, the employee may be placed on a Provisional Privilege status until the identified performance/competency goals are met. In extreme cases, the employee may have his/her privileges in question suspended. If the employee is unable or unwilling to follow the plan identified, he/she is subject to disciplinary action through the personnel policies of the hospital.

Clinical oversight of the Department of Recreation Therapy's Clinical Practice System is provided through the four Medical Directors to whom the department provides service. These are all members of the Medical Staff and have representation on the Medical Staff Executive Committee of the hospital. Administrative oversight is provided through the appropriate Division administrator. Ultimately, the Hospital Board of Directors is accountable for the provision of all services and the management of the hospital.

# CHAPTER THIRTEEN

# Systematizing A Quality Assurance Program for State-wide Therapeutic Recreation Services

MATT GOLD, C.T.R.S.

DOROTHY McNAMARA, C.T.R.S.

## Introduction

The overall goal of a therapeutic recreation quality assurance program is to assure that appropriate and effective services are provided to patients. A secondary aspect of a quality assurance program is to provide for every possible opportunity to improve the clinical performance of the staff. The quality assurance process should identify areas of service that are most beneficial to patients and assure the consistency and appropriateness of the services provided, as well as identify areas of the program and/or aspects of a particular practitioner's performance that need improvement.

Application of the above is at best difficult to establish at the facility level. A system-wide adoption of quality assurance methodology is viewed as a monumental task. Illustrative of this point is the fact that, prior to the last decade or so, the New York State Office of Mental Health (NYS-OMH) had established policies and procedures for its facilities by concentrating primarily on administrative issues. Therapeutic recreation departments throughout the state received limited direction from NYS-OMH toward establishing clinical policies and procedures. However, assistance and direction, as well as a uniformity, began to emerge as a result of active communication amongst therapeutic recreation administrators. Through a series of working meetings involving administrators over several years, a comprehensive QA program is now in place within the NYS-OMH system.

Through its Division of Quality Assurance, NYS-OMH is now attempting to provide QA guidance and structure to hospital professional service programs. During the Spring of 1987, the Division of Quality Assurance requested the Joint Commission on Accreditation of Healthcare Organizations (JCAHO) to provide consultation to several psychiatric centers throughout the state. These centers were the first facilities targeted for review under AMH standards. In January, 1988, guidelines for the development and implementation of program indicator monitoring were established. Shortly thereafter, prototypes for the monitoring and evaluation of psychology and social work became available. Later that year, a work group consisting of therapeutic recreators was formed to draft a similar prototype for therapeutic recreation. The members of the work group consisted of both senior therapists and Chief Recreation Therapists within the Department of Mental Health. At present, this prototype is in draft form waiting final approval. The draft includes the following major aspects of care: Activity Assessment, Activity Assessment Updates, Therapeutic Recreation Interventions, Risk Management and Leisure Education. (These aspects are generally the ones now being used by many of NYS-OMH facilities.)

In addition to the above, another NYS-OMH policy that attempts to provide guidance, structure and consistency throughout the state and one in which several Senior and Chief Recreation Therapists from across the state had input was the Policy Directive on Inpatient Programs. This directive established ".... standards related to the development, implementation and monitoring of inpatient treatment programs for adult patients in state-operated psychiatric facilities" (Surles, 1988, p. 2). The primary purpose of this policy was to insure that patients participate in programs that are consistent with the goals and objectives of their individual comprehensive treatment plans. And further, that patient level of participation is consistent with their present assessed needs and level of functioning.

One advantage that this guideline provides is that it lends much needed assistance to those Recreation Therapists who have no other sources of guidance in TR specific programs (i.e., professional conferences, etc.). Another positive aspect is that the guidelines establish a more consistent approach throughout the state. It stands to reason that, to a large degree, approaches to quality assurance in Buffalo should be similar to approaches in the Bronx. With the establishment of the above guidelines, practitioners in Buffalo can now share experiences with peers in the Bronx, without having to translate their terminology. Another advantage to this statewide consistency is that, when outside regulatory bodies such as JCAHO conduct surveys and have suggestions or modifications, these changes can travel statewide through the proper mechanism. One potential drawback is that a Chief or Senior Recreation Therapist might accept verbatim the statewide model without taking the time to adapt it to his/her facility's specific needs.

### Application of a Systemwide Quality Assurance Model

Developing a Quality Assurance Program for a Therapeutic Recreation Department is a continuously evolving process using a variety of resources. Some of these resources are critical (i.e., JCAHO standards, facility policies and procedures, etc.). Other resources are very helpful but are not always considered essential (i.e., professional standards, state of the art professional information, etc.). Figure One illustrates the variety of resources used by the authors in developing their current Quality Assurance Programs. The Department's Quality

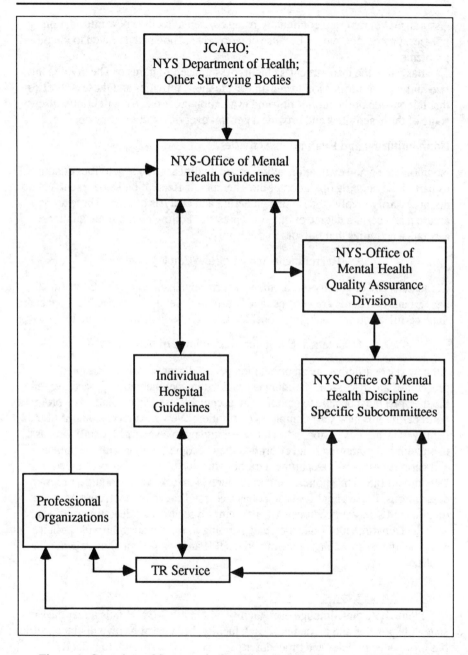

Figure 1–Overview of Systematic Quality Assurance Program NYS-OMH

Assurance Programs are continually being revised to include new information, policies, procedures, etc. or because of corrective action taken related to identified problems.

Basically, the Department's Quality Assurance Programs can be divided into two major categories: Monitoring and Evaluation Activities and those Activities that fall outside of the monitoring and evaluation process. We will briefly discuss some of these activities and provide a general overview of how they operate. *

### Nonmonitoring and Evaluation Activities

Nonmonitoring and evaluation activities are quality assurance activities conducted as part of the ongoing operation of the Therapeutic Recreation Department and do not necessarily involve the routine gathering and analysis of data. These activities assure that a certain degree of quality is present. Following are some quality assurance activities that fall into this category.

#### Recruitment, Screening and Employment

Credentials and eligibility requirements are reviewed and verified. Educational background standards are verified, and "on-the-job" experience and National and State certification are taken into consideration. Only qualified staff are hired.

#### Orientation, Education and Training of New Staff

All new staff participate in an orientation period during which policies and procedures are discussed. Training is provided in documentation procedures, and the therapist must be able to complete an acceptable assessment and write progress notes before this new staff completes orientation. New staff receive a tour of the facility. During this period, new staff are assigned to a veteran TR staff who assist them with programming in an effort that they become familiar with the patients and various programs. Department training includes: organization chart, overall Department functions, policies and procedures, job tasks and standards, program descriptions, Department goals and objectives, staff development, core program training and safety procedures. The new employee attends orientation sessions with the Department of Education and Training to review hospital-wide policies and procedures, as well as to be trained in CPR and Management of Patient Violence.

---

* Please note that although each facility within NYS-OMH falls under the same statewide policies and procedures, each facility, because of its own distinct profile, has refined the policies and procedures to be even more specific to meet its particular needs. Therefore, each TR Service will vary slightly in terms of its Quality Assurance Program.

## Staff Development Activities

Continuous learning opportunities are provided through discipline-specific meetings and workshops, monthly educational meetings, core program training, College Degree Program courses, Education and Training courses, and clinical supervision.

## Clinical Supervision

All staff have an assigned clinical supervisor with whom they meet on a regular basis with minutes of each meeting recorded. Discussions/exchanges include delivery of services, patient needs, program needs, professional development, results of rounds, chart reviews, audits and surveys, training an any other professional concerns.

## Activity Schedules

In order to assure quality and appropriateness of programs, the TR Supervisor must review and approve, in writing, the program schedules of each staff member.

## Department Goals and Objectives

The Department develops yearly goals and objectives which are continually reviewed, adapted, changed or deleted when they are met or when they are not relevant any longer.

## Policies and Procedures Manual

The manual is available to all staff and includes the service's philosophy, goals and objectives, as well as policies and procedures for staff performance and patient participation.

## Program Protocols

Written description of all programs is required which includes a program description, clinical justification/purpose, goal(s), problem(s) addressed, entrance criteria, risk reduction/safety precautions, and exit criteria/patient outcomes. (For a sample protocol, see Appendix 13A.)

## Statistics/Attendance Records

Records of attendance are kept to assist in assuring that each patient attends the programs he/she is assigned to in his/her treatment plan.

## Core Programs

Each facility is divided into functional units (units where patients have similar psychiatric problems, needs and level of functioning). Each discipline then defines certain "core" programs which would benefit the majority of patients and which they would be expected to be involved in at some time during their hospitalization. If a patient is not assigned to any core program, there must be a clinical rationale documented in the chart. (Core Programs for TR at a given facility would include Leisure Education, Physical Fitness and Socialization Skills Development.)

### Safety Check Lists

Each program area is monitored on a regular basis, and safety check lists are used to identify problems which need to be corrected or improved upon.

### Monthly Reports

Monthly reports include information on programs, staffing, scheduling, chart review results, rounds results, staff development activities, results of audits, surveys, etc., clinical supervision, statistics and other pertinent information. Information is analyzed, and plans for any needed corrective action is given. Results of previous corrective action are also discussed.

### Staff Professional Performance Profile Folders

To assure continuing quality staff performance, professional performance profile files are kept on each staff and reviewed regularly. When reviews suggest corrective action, it is implemented. The folders include staff evaluations, summary compliance rates for chart reviews and rounds, staff development activities, and any counseling related to clinical performance.

### Patient Satisfaction Surveys

In order to meet the needs/interests of those patients being served, as well as to improve upon the quality of the existing TR program, patient satisfaction surveys are conducted. (For a sample Survey, see Appendix 13B).

### Equipment and Supplies

Equipment and supplies should be adequate and selected on the basis of appropri-ateness, safety, durability and programmatic and treatment needs.

## Monitoring and Evaluation Activities

Monitoring and evaluation activities are those strategies which involve a continu-ous system of collecting and analyzing data. These activities focus on important aspects of patient care and staff performance in order to identify and correct/ improve problem areas. The data is measurable and objective.

The selection of most forms of monitoring and evaluation activities is dictated by a number of variables. The most obvious factor is the interest and requirements of outside accrediting agencies such as JCAHO and HCFA. As these agencies place more and more emphasis on the collection and analysis of data related to the important aspects of care, the Department has become more concerned about its ability to document its services.

Another influence on monitoring and evaluation activities is the internal policies and procedures required by NYS-OMH. As stated previously, these policies are limited at present, but are growing steadily as more emphasis is placed on clinical areas. Guidelines for discipline-oriented aspects of care are in the final stages of development and will soon be a standard component for monitoring and evaluation activities statewide.

Individual hospital policies, state-of-the-art professional methods, and, of course, the Department members themselves, also influence QA activities. The last two items mentioned are not deemed obligatory in the QA process, but without them, the process would be directly hampered.

The authors strongly believe that each member of the Department should have input into the Department's Quality Assurance System. This input should include determining what is to be evaluated, as well as staff members being part of the evaluation process themselves (peer review). Following are some monitoring and evaluation activities currently in place within the therapeutic recreation services of NYS-OMH.

## Chart Review

Chart review includes the following areas: assessment, the treatment plan, progress notes and the treatment plan. The assessment should be completed before the treatment plan is developed. Recommendations should take into consideration the patient's strengths, interests, problems, disabilities/limitations and needs. The recommendations should then be incorporated into the treatment plan, or, if not, a rationale for not including it should be documented. Progress notes should correspond to the treatment plan and give the reviewer a good picture of the patient's progress or lack of progress toward the treatment plan goal.

Chart reviews include audit questions involving technical aspects, as well as those checking for quality and appropriateness. These forms have been revised several times, thus eliminating items that are no longer a significant problem or including items where more refinement was needed. Monthly compliance rates on each item are computed for each staff as well as for each unit. From this information, quarterly and yearly summary reports are drafted for each staff and each unit. Data is analyzed and corrective action is instituted where needed. Individual results become part of each staff's professional profile folder.

Reviews are conducted by the Department Head, the Unit TR Supervisor and a TR Peer Reviewer from another unit. Copies are sent to the TR staff, the TR Supervisor, the Department Head and the unit. Reviewed results from all these areas are used by the clinical supervisor as a learning/teaching tool during clinical supervision, as well as for determining compliance rates for the Department's Aspects of Care.

Reviews contain a section for needed corrective action (with a due date). Unit TR Supervisors must document to the Department that corrective action was completed. The Department spot checks these charts to ensure that the corrective action was completed. (For sample chart review forms and summary of chart review results forms, see Appendix 13C).

## Rounds and Clinical Rounds

Unannounced rounds are made by the TR Service, as well as unit supervisory staff and hospital administrative staff, to assure that program activity schedules are posted and scheduled programs are conducted. Clinical rounds are made by Department and Unit TR supervisory staff as well as Peer Unit TR supervisory staff to observe the quality of the programs being conducted.

Additionally, the level of patient participation and staff performance is evaluated. Written results are sent to the Department, the Unit, the Unit TR Supervisor and the TR conducting the program. If corrective action is required, it must be implemented and a memo sent to all concerned as to how and when this was done. The Department spot checks these programs again to see that corrective action was indeed completed.

Clinical rounds address a variety of areas including: safety, program appropriateness, leadership and interaction techniques, programs to meet patients physical, cognitive, social and emotional needs. Results of rounds are used as a learning/teaching tool and are considered part of clinical supervision as well as staff evaluation. Each item reviewed is computed and a compliance rate is formulated for each staff as well as for each program. Individual staff results become part of each staff's professional profile folder. From all of this information quarterly and yearly summary reports are formulated. (For samples of Clinical Rounds forms, see Appendix 13D).

## Aspects of Care

The TR Service, with input from each member of the Service, identifies the diagnostic, treatment and therapeutic activities it considers the most important for its Service. Indicators and criteria for each aspect of care are developed. Methods for evaluating whether each criterion is being met and a method for corrective action is included. For the most part, the results from several monitoring and evaluation activities are used to determine overall essential compliance. (For sample Aspects of Care Monitoring Forms, see Appendix 13E.)

## Summary

As presented, many of the functions included as part of our Quality Assurance Program have been existing functions of the TR Department long before we understood them to be a formal part of a Quality Assessment. The more sophisticated the Department's Quality Assurance programs become, the more we comprehend the interrelationships among these activities. Included in the appendices are samples of Quality Assurance tools. These tools are continually being revised and improved upon as new information is received and/or as better methods are found.

The future forecasts a more decentralized direction for the New York State–Office of Mental Health with respect to policies and procedures. Input from Therapeutic Recreation will increase as discipline heads take a more active role in the development of policies and procedures through statewide discipline work groups. State professional organizations will also be more actively involved as evidenced by their recent involvement in the development and sponsorship of workshops and conferences. The future for quality services within the NYS-OMH looks positive. Increased professional involvement in quality assurance will not only promote improved Therapeutic Recreation services but also provide more qualified staff to conduct these services.

## References

Riley, B. (1987). *Evaluation of Therapeutic Recreation Through Quality Assurance:* State College, PA: Venture Publishing, Inc.

Surles, R. C. (1988). Personal Correspondence of the Authors, *NYS-OMH Official Policy Manual Transmittal Letter #88-02.*

**Appendix 13A**
**Program Protocol**

| MANHATTAN PSYCHIATRIC CENTER | SUBJECT: Core Programs/Physical Fitness for Short Term Patients |
|---|---|
| DEPARTMENT/UNIT: REHABILITATION SERVICES | SECTION: THERAPEUTIC & LEISURE RECREATION PROGRAM/ PSYCHOSOCIAL PROGRAMS |
| POLICY AND PROCEDURE POLICY | DATE ISSUED: 1/4/89  PAGE 1 OF 5 |

TRANSMITTAL LETTER NUMBER:   89-14

PROGRAM DESCRIPTION:
      The physical fitness program consists of an exercise program
or game/sport activity that encompasses these four components:
1) relaxation, 2) exercises of the endurance type to condition the heart,
lungs and circulation, 3) muscle-strengthening exercises and
4) stretching exercises to improve joint mobility.  Programs progress
from simple tasks to difficult, sequential ones so as to also improve
attention span, concentration and problem-solving and decision making
abilities.  Programs also progress from individual to cooperative and/or
competitive activities which promote social skills and self expression.
Selection of programs are based on individual patient needs and are
adapted to meet individual disabilities and/or limitations.  Patient
interests and strengths are also strongly considered in the selection of
the activites.  Programs may include but not limited to the following
activities:
        Exercises
        Active Sports
        Active Games
        Nature Walks
        Bowling
        Swimming
        Weight-Training
        Adapted Sports/Games

MPC-4 (1-81)

| MANHATTAN PSYCHIATRIC CENTER | SUBJECT: Core Programs/Physical Fitness for Short Term Patients |
|---|---|
| DEPARTMENT/UNIT: REHABILITATION SERVICES | SECTION: THERAPEUTIC & LEISURE RECREATION PROGRAMS/ PSYCHOSOCIAL PROGRAMS |
| POLICY AND PROCEDURES POLICY | DATE ISSUED:  1/4/89  PAGE 2 OF 5 |

TRANSMITTAL LETTER NUMBER:   89-14

Dance
Movement to Music
Hatha Yoga
Jogging

CLINICAL JUSTIFICATION/PURPOSE:
      A good, regular physical fitness program can control obesity, improve body image and provide an acceptable outlet for feelings of aggression, hyperactivity stress and frustration.  Many of our patients are sendentary or are consistantly acting out and hostile.  A regular physical fitness program would not only improve the physical functioning of their body but would also help them relieve stress and tension, improve self-image, attention span and concentration as well as improve their socialization skills.

GOALS:
      Patient will improve his overall muscle tone and physical functioning and develop a more positive way of dealing with stress and feelings of hostility and aggression.

PROGRAMS ADDRESSED:
      Angry, acting-out behaviors
      Restlessness, tension
      Limited attention span

MPC-4 (1-81)

| MANHATTAN PSYCHIATRIC CENTER | SUBJECT: Core Programs/Physical Fitness for Short Term Patients |
|---|---|
| DEPARTMENT/UNIT: REHABILITATION SERVICES | SECTION: THERAPEUTIC & LEISURE RECREATION PROGRAMS/ PSYCHOSOCIAL PROGRAMS |
| POLICY AND PROCEDURE POLICY | DATE ISSUED: 1/4/89  PAGE 3 OF 5 |

TRANSMITTAL LETTER NUMBER:    89-14

Limited social skills
Impaired sense of reality
Poor concentration
Preoccupation
Obesity
Low self-esteem
Anxiety
Poor self-image
Poor impulse control
Depression

ENTRANCE CRITERIA:
–Medical clearance from the Doctor to participate (with or without modifications or adaptations).
–Patient does not exhibit any behaviors that severely interfere with the group process.

PROCESS:
The program involves patients participating on an individual as well as on a team basis. At the beginning of each session, the therapist communicates th purpose of the sessions and the expectations expected through the patient's participatiition. Rules and safety precautions are discussed and any necessary

MPC-4 (1-81)

| MANHATTAN PSYCHIATRIC CENTER | SUBJECT: Core Programs/Physical Fitness for Short Term Patients |
|---|---|
| DEPARTMENT/UNIT: REHABILITATION SERVICES | SECTION: THERAPEUTIC & LEISURE RECREATION PROGRAMS/ PSYCHOSOCIAL PROGRAMS |
| POLICY AND PROCEDURE POLICY | DATE ISSUED: 1/4/89  PAGE 4 OF 5 |

TRANSMITTAL LETTER NUMBER:  89-14

adaptations are made. Each patient is encouraged to participate at his/her own level. The therapist is supportive and focuses on each patient's problem/s. Continual encouragement is given. Tasks proceed from easy to more difficult and are adapted according to the patient's capabilities and needs.

RISK REDUCTION/SAFETY PROCEDURES:
Group is conducted in a safe, therapeutic environment.
Sufficient space and lighting is available.
Temperature is conductive to group functioning.
Supplies and equipment are safe, age appropriate, properly supervised and adapted where necessary.
Rules and Safety Procedures are explained at the beginning of each sessions.

EXIT CRITERIA/PATIENT OUTCOMES:
–Patient will achieve and/or maintain "ideal" weight.
–Patient will, upon request, demonstrate the ability to follow directions involving sequential steps by accurately responding to the task directions given.
–Patient will demonstrate improved coordination, flexibility and strength by successfully completing at least five advanced physical tasks/exercises.
–Patient will independently practice relaxation techniques when he feels stressed or tense.

MPC-4 (1-81)

| MANHATTAN PSYCHIATRIC CENTER | SUBJECT: Core Programs/Physical Fitness for Short Term Patients |
|---|---|
| DEPARTMENT/UNIT: REHABILITATION SERVICES | SECTION: THERAPEUTIC & LEISURE RECREATION PROGRAMS/ PSYCHOSOCIAL PROGRAMS |
| POLICY AND PROCEDURE POLICY | DATE ISSUED: 1/4/89  PAGE 5 OF 5 |

TRANSMITTAL LETTER NUMBER:    89-14

   –Patient will exercise or participate in some active sport/game rather than act out or be involved in hostile/violent behavior.
   –Patient will independently participate daily in some form of physical fitness program.

MPC-4 (1-81)

# Appendix 13B
## Patient Satisfaction Survey

NEW YORK STATE PSYCHIATRIC INSTITUTE
DEPARTMENT OF RECREATIONAL THERAPY
PATIENT SATISFACTION SURVEY

NAME: _____ DATE _____

                     CC
SERVICE: _____ # _____ ADMISSION _____ DC _____
                                    DATE                 DATE

The Recreation Therapy Department welcomes your feedback regarding your satisfaction with the Recreation Therapy activities you attended during your hospitalization. Please take a moment to complete this questionnaire. It will be used to help us re-evaluate the program that we offer. Thank you for your cooperation.

I.   The following is a list of general goals that the various Recreational Therapy groups intend to meet. Next to each goal statement, please indicate the number that best describes your level of satisfaction with the role that your individualized Recreation Therapy program played in your treatment.

CODE:      0 – not applicable
           1 – extremely dissatisfied
           2 – dissatisfied
           3 – satisfied
           4 – extremely satisfied

____ 1.  To improve/ maintain physical fitness, and physical functioning (coordination, endurance, strength, stamina).
____ 2.  To improve/maintain social skills (communication, frustration tolerance, impulse control) and to decrease isolation and dependence.
____ 3.  To improve and maintain feelings of self-esteem, self-worth, and self-confidence.
____ 4.  To improve/maintain cognitive skills.
____ 5.  To facilitate appropriate expression of emotions and creativity.
____ 6.  To decrease atypical behavior and mannerisms.
____ 7.  To improve/maintain task skills (concentration, attention span, cooperation, organization, ability to follow directions, decision making, ability to assume responsibility, problem solving ability).
____ 8.  To teach and encourage healthy attitudes towards competition, rules, regulations, and authority figures.
____ 9.  To develop awareness of leisure and its significance.

___ 10. To explore and develop personal leisure attitudes, values, and philosophies.

___ 11. To teach/expand kmowledge of leisure resources and opportunities.

___ 12. To facilitate intergration into community recreation programs.

___ 13. To stimulate self-directed leisure behavior.

___ 14. To provide exposure to new leisure-skills areas.

___ 15. To teach new leisure skills.

___ 16. To develop leadership or community service skills.

___ 17. To improve/maintain goal setting ability.

___ 18. To facilitate participation in previously acquired leisure skills.

___ 19. To facilitate self expression.

___ 20. To provide opportunites for development of physical, cognitive and social skills.

___ 21. To provide opportunities for experiencing enjoyment and fun.


II.    The following is a list of the Recreational Therapy groups that you attended during the course of your hospitalization.  Please circle the number that best describes your level of satisfaction with the role that the group played in your treatment.

|     |                          | DISSATISFIED |   |   | SATISFIED |
|-----|--------------------------|:---:|:---:|:---:|:---:|
| 1.  | _____ | 1 | 2 | 3 | 4 |
| 2.  | _____ | 1 | 2 | 3 | 4 |
| 3.  | _____ | 1 | 2 | 3 | 4 |
| 4.  | _____ | 1 | 2 | 3 | 4 |
| 5.  | _____ | 1 | 2 | 3 | 4 |
| 6.  | _____ | 1 | 2 | 3 | 4 |
| 7.  | _____ | 1 | 2 | 3 | 4 |
| 8.  | _____ | 1 | 2 | 3 | 4 |
| 9.  | _____ | 1 | 2 | 3 | 4 |
| 10. | _____ | 1 | 2 | 3 | 4 |


COMMENTS AND SUGGESTIONS:

_____

_____

_____

_____

_____

_____

_____

RT (7/88)

# Appendix 13C
# Chart Review Forms

## SUMMARY OF CHART REVIEW RESULTS FORMS

MANHATTAN PSYCHIATRIC CENTER    QUALITY ASSURANCE MONITORING
RECREATION SERVICES    CHART REVIEW
RECREATION THERAPY    DATE OF REVIEW: _____
    REVIEWER: _____

Patient's Name: _____ Hospital#: _____ Unit/Ward ___ Date of Birth _____
Date of Admission: _____ Physical Disability (if any): _____ RT Staff _____

or

## SECTION 1-ACTIVITY ASSESSMENT:

| | NOT MET | MET | COMMENT |
|---|---|---|---|
| 1.01: Current Activity Assessment is present | | | |
| 1.02: Assessment and/or addendum is completed by the 10th day | | | |
| 1.03: Current skills, talents, aptitudes and cultural/ recreational interests cited | | | |
| 1.04: Relevant life experiences including past and/or current utilization of leisure time cited | | | |
| 1.05: Problems, strengths, motivations, disabilities/ limitations cited | | | |
| 1.06: Treatment recommendation(s) incorporate positive characteristic(s) of patient | | | |
| 1.07: Treatment recommendation(s) include a goal statement followed by measureable objectives | | | |
| 1.08: Recommended treatment modality takes any limitations/disabilities into consideration and any necessary adaptations or modifications are specified | | | |
| 1.09: Recommended treatment modality clearly addresses the patient's needs/problems | | | |
| 1.10: There is evidence that the patient participated or was involved in his/her proposed plan | | | |

## SECTION 2-TREATMENT PLAN:

| | | | |
|---|---|---|---|
| 2.01: Recreation is a method for at least one measureable and realistic objective that clearly addresses the patient's needs/problems | | | |
| 2.02: Assessment recommendations are incorporated into Plan or there is evidence they were considered and a rationale is given as to why they were not included | | | |

| | NOT MET | MET | COMMENT |
|---|---|---|---|
| 2.03: If a patient has a physical disability, programs are adapted to his/her needs where necessary | | | |
| 2.04: Patient is assigned to Leisure Education | | | |

## SECTION 3-PERIODIC TREATMENT PLAN REVIEW:

| | NOT MET | MET | COMMENT |
|---|---|---|---|
| 3.01 Rational for continuation, deletion, revision and/ or additions of Recreation is explicitly made | | | |

## SECTION 4-PROGRESS NOTES:

| | NOT MET | MET | COMMENT |
|---|---|---|---|
| 4.01: Notes have date and time and are appropriately titled and written in DAP form | | | |
| 4.02: Notes are written weekly/monthly as appropriate | | | |
| 4.03: Notes contain goal number and objective letter and are cross-referenced to the Treatment Plan | | | |
| 4.04: Notes reflect progress or lack of progress toward treatment goal(s) and objectives | | | |
| 4.05: Notes reflect patient involvement in nonreferred activities | | | |
| 4.06: Patient is assigned to and participates in Leisure Education | | | |
| 4.07: Patient participates in all TR programs recommended in the Treatment Plan | | | |
| 4.08: Patient participates in some TR programs recommended in the Treatment Plan | | | |

Comments and Corrective Action:

Corrective Action to be made by: _____

(Staff)                          (Date)

cc:  F. Chondris          Unit Cheif          RT
     D. McNamara Team Leader

3/30

MANHATTAN PSYCHIATRIC CENTER
REHABILITATION SERVICES
THERAPEUTIC RECREATION
QUALITY ASSURANCE MONITORING– CHART REVIEWS
SUMMARY FORM

UNIT:          WARD:          RT:

NUMBER OF CHARTS REVIEWED:          MONTH:          YEAR:

## SECTION 1-ACTIVITY ASSESSMENT:

| | MET | NOT MET | N/A | UNIT % RATES |
|---|---|---|---|---|
| 1.01: Current Activity Assessment is present | | | | |
| 1.02: Assessment and/or addendum is completed by the 10th day | | | | |
| 1.03: Current skills, talents, aptitudes and cultural/ recreational interests cited | | | | |
| 1.04: Relevant life experiences including past and/or current utilization of leisure time cited | | | | |
| 1.05: Problems, strengths, motivations, disabilities/ limitations cited | | | | |
| 1.06: Treatment recommendation(s) incorporate positive characteristic(s) of patient | | | | |
| 1.07: Treatment recommendation(s) include a goal statement followed by measureable objectives | | | | |
| 1.08: Recommended treatment modality takes any limitations/disabilities into consideration and any necessary adaptations or modifications are specified | | | | |
| 1.09: Recommended treatment modality clearly addresses the patient's needs/problems | | | | |
| 1.10: There is evidence that the patient participated or was involved in his/her proposed plan | | | | |

## SECTION 2-TREATMENT PLAN:

| | MET | NOT MET | N/A | UNIT % RATES |
|---|---|---|---|---|
| 2.01: Recreation is a method for at least one measureable and realistic objective that clearly addresses the patient's needs/problems | | | | |
| 2.02: Assessment recommendations are incorporated into Plan or there is evidence they were considered and a rationale is given as to why they were not included | | | | |

|  | MET | NOT MET | N/A | UNIT % RATES |
|---|---|---|---|---|
| 2.03: If a patient has a physical disability, programs are adapted to his/her needs where necessary |  |  |  |  |
| 2.04: Patient is assigned to Leisure Education |  |  |  |  |

## SECTION 3-PERIODIC TREATMENT PLAN REVIEW:

| 3.01: Rationale for continuation, deletion, revision and/or additions of Recreation is explicitly made |  |  |  |  |
|---|---|---|---|---|

## SECTION 4-PROGRESS NOTES:

| 4.01: Notes have date and time and are appropriately titled and written in DAP form |  |  |  |  |
|---|---|---|---|---|
| 4.02: Notes are written weekly/monthly as appropriate |  |  |  |  |
| 4.03: Notes contain goal number and objective letter and are cross-referenced to the Treatment Plan |  |  |  |  |
| 4.04: Notes reflect progress or lack of progress toward treatment goal(s) and objectives |  |  |  |  |
| 4.05: Notes reflect patient involvement in nonreferred activities |  |  |  |  |
| 4.06: Patient is assigned to and participates in Leisure Education |  |  |  |  |
| 4.07: Patient participates in all TR programs recommended in the Treatment Plan |  |  |  |  |
| 4.08: Patient participates in some TR programs recommended in the Treatment Plan |  |  |  |  |

SENIOR RECREATION THERAPIST: _____

RECREATION THERAPY DEPARTMENT
SUMMARY OF CHART REVIEWS

MONTH/YEAR _____

TOTAL NUMBER OF CHARTS REVIEWED _____

| _____ 4 South | _____ | (CC #) |
| _____ 5 South | _____ | (CC #) |
| _____ 6 North | _____ | (CC #) |
| _____ 7 South | _____ | (CC #) |

## COMPLIANCE/DEFICIENCY SUMMARY

| | COMP | DEF | NA |
|---|---|---|---|
| A. ASSESSMENTS: | | | |
| 1. Completed on time | | | |
| 2. Signed and dated | | | |
| 3. Includes: | | | |
| a. past recreational interests | | | |
| b. social relationships | | | |
| c. motivation re: leisure involvement | | | |
| d. current recreational skills, talents, interests | | | |
| e. recreational possessions | | | |
| f. ability to structure time | | | |
| 4. Summaries strengths/assests, liabilities/barries, recommendations | | | |
| 5. Activities Schedule present | | | |
| | | | |
| B. TREATMENT PLAN: | | | |
| 1. Interim Treatment Plan entry | | | |
| 2. Comprehensive Treatment Plan signed | | | |
| 3. Comprehensive Treatment Plan Service Needs addressed | | | |
| 4. Objectives are: | | | |
| a. stated in behavioral, measureable terms | | | |
| b. related to strengths, liabilities identified in assessment | | | |
| 5. Methods include activities, dates and leaders | | | |

| C. PERIODIC TREATMENT PLAN REVIEW: | COMP | DEF | NA |
|---|---|---|---|
| 1. Entry signed | | | |
| 2. Entry completed on time | | | |
| 3. All current objectives are referred to by number | | | |
| 4. Review includes description of behavior and progress re: current objectives, consistant with progress notes. | | | |
| D. PROGRESS NOTES: | | | |
| 1. First note within 14 days of assessment | | | |
| 2. Subsequent notes every two weeks | | | |
| 3. Entries labeled, signed and dated | | | |
| 4. Entries refer to all current objectives by appropriate number | | | |
| 5. Entries describe behavior/progress re: all current objective | | | |
| 6. Entries refer to RT groups attended | | | |
| TOTALS | | | |

Totals # of Items Rated _____
  (# of charts Reviewed x 26)

Percent of compliance _____


_____
REPORT PREPARED BY

10/88

# Appendix 13D
# Clinical Rounds Forms

MANHATTAN PSYCHIATRIC CENTER
REHABILITATION SERVICES
THERAPEUTIC RECREATION
QUAILITY ASSURANCE ACTIVITIES
CLINICAL ROUNDS

UNIT: _____    MONTH: _____    YEAR: _____

WARD: _____    STAFF: _____    REVIEWER: _____

|   | 1. | 2. | 3. | 4. | 5. |   |
|---|---|---|---|---|---|---|
| A. Date of Rounds: |   |   |   |   |   | A |
| B. Time of Rounds: |   |   |   |   |   | B |
| C. Number of Patients in Group: |   |   |   |   |   | C |
| D. Name of Group in Progress: |   |   |   |   |   | D |

(Circle either (Y)es or (N)o)

Comp. Pct

|   | 1. | 2. | 3. | 4. | 5. |   |   |
|---|---|---|---|---|---|---|---|
| 1. Is the Approved Schedule posted? | Y N | Y N | Y N | Y N | Y N |   | 1 |
| 2. Is the Activity in progress as per approved schedule? | Y N | Y N | Y N | Y N | Y N |   | 2 |
| 3. Is a Special Event in progress? | Y N | Y N | Y N | Y N | Y N |   | 3 |
| 4. Is Special Event posted? | Y N | Y N | Y N | Y N | Y N |   | 4 |
| 5. Is an approved cancelation notice posted? | Y N | Y N | Y N | Y N | Y N |   | 5 |
| 6. Level of patient involvement is: <br> A: Almost every patient is involved on some level. | Y N | Y N | Y N | Y N | Y N |   | 6A |
| B: The majority of patients are involved on some level. | Y N | Y N | Y N | Y N | Y N |   | 6B |
| C: Very few patients are invloved on any level. | Y N | Y N | Y N | Y N | Y N |   | 6C |
| 7. The program is conducted in an area of sufficient space. | Y N | Y N | Y N | Y N | Y N |   | 7 |
| 8. The air temperature is conductive to the activity. | Y N | Y N | Y N | Y N | Y N |   | 8 |
| 9. The surroundings are distraction-free so as not to seriously hamper participation. | Y N | Y N | Y N | Y N | Y N |   | 9 |
| 10. There is sufficient light availible to afford participants maximum visibility. | Y N | Y N | Y N | Y N | Y N |   | 10 |
| 11. Supplies and equipment are age appropriate. | Y N | Y N | Y N | Y N | Y N |   | 11 |
| 12. Supplies and equipment are population appropriate. | Y N | Y N | Y N | Y N | Y N |   | 12 |
| 13. The program is organized. | Y N | Y N | Y N | Y N | Y N |   | 13 |

| | | | | | | |
|---|---|---|---|---|---|---|
| 14. Adaptations are made where necessary. | Y N | Y N | Y N | Y N | Y N | 14 |
| 15. There is a safe enviornment. | Y N | Y N | Y N | Y N | Y N | 15 |
| 16. Supplies and equipment are safe. | Y N | Y N | Y N | Y N | Y N | 16 |
| 17. The appropriate leadership technique is used. | Y N | Y N | Y N | Y N | Y N | 17 |
| 18. Program content is presented clearly and in an orderly sequence. | Y N | Y N | Y N | Y N | Y N | 18 |
| 19. There are enough participants for the activity. | Y N | Y N | Y N | Y N | Y N | 19 |
| 20. Interaction techniques are appropriate. | Y N | Y N | Y N | Y N | Y N | 20 |
| 21. Patients have emotional controls necessary for participation. | Y N | Y N | Y N | Y N | Y N | 21 |
| 22. Patients have cognitive skills necessary for participation. | Y N | Y N | Y N | Y N | Y N | 22 |
| 23. Patients have social/interaction skills necessary for participation. | Y N | Y N | Y N | Y N | Y N | 23 |

24. Comments:

## Appendix 13E
## Aspects of Monitoring Forms

MPC 29(12/87)

### MANHATTAN PSYCHIATRIC CENTER
### MONITORING AND EVALUATION REPORT

UNIT/DEPT. Rehab Services/Recreation    FOR MONTH(S)_____

---

ASPECTS OF CARE: <u>Activity Assessment</u>    QUESTION#: <u>1.02</u>
INDICATOR: <u>Every patient has a current assessment and it is completed before the</u>
<u>treatment plan is developed.</u>
CRITERION: <u>85%</u>    NO. OF RELEVANT CASES REVIEWED ____
WAS CRITERION TRIGGERED? Y ( ) N ( )
IF TRIGGERED, PLEASE PROVIDE ANALYSIS & CORRECTIVE ACTION(S) IF
NECESSARY: _____

---

ASPECTS OF CARE: <u>Activity Assssment</u>    QUESTION#: <u>1.10</u>
INDICATOR: <u>The patient participated or was involved in the assessment process for the</u>
<u>current treatment plan</u>
CRITERION: <u>85%</u>    NO. OF RELEVANT CASES REVIEWED ____
WAS CRITERION TRIGGERED? Y ( ) N ( )
IF TRIGGERED, PLEASE PROVIDE ANALYSIS & CORRECTIVE ACTION(S) IF
NECESSARY: _____

---

ASPECTS OF CARE: <u>Activity Assessment</u>    QUESTION#: <u>1.08</u>
INDICATOR: <u>Patient limitations/disabilities are identified and the treatment modality</u>
<u>recommended takes it/them into consideration and any necessary adaptations or</u>
<u>modifications are specified.</u>
CRITERION: <u>85%</u>    NO. OF RELEVANT CASES REVIEWED ____
WAS CRITERION TRIGGERED? Y ( ) N ( )
IF TRIGGERED, PLEASE PROVIDE ANALYSIS & CORRECTIVE ACTION(S) IF
NECESSARY: _____

---

SIGNATURE: _____ DATE REPORTED COMPLETED: _____

## Monitoring and Evaluation
## Recreational Therapy Department

IMPORTANT ASPECT OF CARE: All phases of charting (assessments, treatment plans and progress notes)

INDICATORS:
1. Asessments will be timely, will identify strengths, liabilities and treatment recommendations, and comprehensively describe leisure lifestyle.
2. Treatment plans will be timely and will set appropriate treatment goals/objectives.
3. Progress notes will be timely, and will accurately describe progress towards idendified goals/objectives.

SCOPE OF CARE: Inpatients' charts

RESPONSIBILITY:
DATA COLLECTION: Recreational Therapy staff
DATA AGGREGATION/ANALYSIS: Head Recreational Therapist

THRESHOLD FOR EVALUATION: 85% compliance rating

CRITERIA: Chart Review Form

SAMPLE SIZE: 20 percent of admissions (to be determined by the number of admissions per unit during previous six month period).

DATA SOURCE: Patients' charts

METHODOLOGY: Director of Recreational Therapy will identify the charts to be reviewed and assign the reviews to the Recreation Therapists, using the Chart Review Form. During each six month period (January-June, July-December), 20 percent of each unit's admissions will be reviewed. Data will be aggregated quarterly. Trends will be noted and discussed between the Recreation Therapist and the Head Recreation Therapist if an individual therapists' compliance rating falls below the departmental threshold of 85 percent, over the course of two consecutive quarters, then two additional charts will be reviewed by the Head Recreation Therapist, for determination of the need for corrective action.

CHAPTER FOURTEEN

# A Staff Inclusion Model for QA Development

GEORGE D. PATRICK, Ph.D., C.T.R.S.

## Introduction

Numerous authors have defined the QA process from a therapeutic recreation (TR) perspective (Navar and Dunn, 1981; Reynolds and O'Morrow, 1985; Riley, 1987). While gaining conceptual clarity from these sources, professional literature available to TR practitioners does not include models of implementation other than conference presentations on "this is what we do" and perhaps "these are the forms we use." Sometimes the professional literature can be seen as contradictory or overwhelming.

The TR practitioner may note that various authors and conference presenters express many different perspectives when deliniating the scope of TR practice and, therefore, the QA prescriptions offered may not seem to fit their unique circumstances. The resulting confusion is in part due to these sources vacillating between bureaucratic rigidity and total nondirection. To add to this confusion, professional organizations have made vague statements of standards of practice and definitions of the profession. Many TR practitioners have continued to struggle with professional identity crises, often uncomfortably parallel to the painful developmental tasks of adolescence. Especially in the creation of QA plans, scope of service statements, and delineation of clinical privileges, TR practitioners have wrestled with the underlying issues of professional identity. The model offered in this paper presents a systematic approach toward a consensus building direction for QA management.

Many TR departments lack adequate statements of (1) scope of service, (2) standards of practice, or (3) a QA plan tailored to their specific service (see Appendix 14A). Too often, these are seen as a mere paper exercise with the result that one person is given the job of writing the statements . . . not infrequently borrowed from another cooperative facility willing to loan a copy of their policies. These statements end up in a manual of procedures or in a file drawer and have little or no impact on patient care (Marker, 1987).

What is suggested is not that we ignore outside resources (books, chapters, articles, presentations, or manuals from professional networks), but in addition, that we recognize fully the ethical responsibility of departmental staff to develop service-specific standards. Huston (1987) has noted that TR QA programs "must be continually revised and evaluated at least annually." The inclusion of all clinical staff . . . is also encouraged. A staff inclusion model based on the development of QA activities for the Patient Activities Department of The Clinical Center, National Institutes of Health is presented. This model involves TR staff in the process so that all interested persons have an equal voice in the development of the QA agenda. Because our staff inclusion model relies on a modification of a research strategy called the Delphi technique, a short review of this methodology is presented.

## The Delphi Technique

Originally developed by Helmer (1967) as a method of predicting future events for the purpose of decision making and policy setting (McLaughlin, 1976), the Delphi technique has been developed and successfully implemented to facilitate group consensus (Dalkey, Rourke, Lewis, and Snyder, 1972).

According to Miller and Knapp (1979), the Delphi technique is a simple and efficient method of assuring participatory decision making, policy setting and planning. The Delphi method incorporates the use of a questionnaire to determine individual views and attitudes regarding a specific topic or area of concern. It is most effective when the outcome of the question is not predictable, thus allowing for personal judgment and value clarification (Donabedian, 1982).

The actual implementation process of the Delphi technique varies from application to application but, according to Isaac and Michael (1985, p. 115), usually contains the following steps:

1. Group Selection:     Identify and select experts in the area(s) of inquiry.

2. Questionnaire One:     Solicit opinions from group members in an attempt to formulate a structured and valid questionnaire.

3. Questionnaire Two:     Develop a second questionnaire using an appropriate format for rating or ranking. Have each member complete the instrument.

4. Questionnaire Three: Present feedback by informing each panel member of the panel about the opinions of the entire group (statistical summary). Each member is then asked to reconsider his/her initial opinions in light of the consolidated group response.

5. Questionnaire Four:    Reconstruct the instrument using the results of questionnaire three. Each member rates or ranks each item for a third and final time, mindful of the emerging pattern of group consensus.

6. Results:    Tabulate the results of the Delphi process (questionnaire four) and present as the final statement of group consensus.

As Quade (1975) stated: "The anonymous debate among experts as conducted by Delphi procedures, in the many instances where a valid comparison can be made, has proved superior to the same experts engaging in a face to face discussion in arriving at a group decision in a given question" (p. 194). However, caution must be exercised in determining whether the Delphi technique is the appropriate method for a given investigation. Donabedian (1982) indicated that ". . . it also seems reasonable to assume that with the Delphi technique, one still cannot create valid information where none exists, and that group opinion can serve to consolidate error just as readily as it can reveal truth" (p. 157). In general, it may be concluded that the Delphi technique, when used within appropriate parameters and guidelines, serves as a very effective procedure for soliciting individual opinion and for facilitating group consensus (Riley, 1989).

**The Staff Inclusion Model**

In our model, interested staff were recruited for the TR department QA committee. This model accepted Quade's conclusion (1975) that all staff are not equal when placed in a group discussion format (where departmental politics, reputations, and positions are taken into account), so the Delphi technique was employed to overcome potential inequity of influence in the determination of group values. The process began with the distribution of a list of broad elements of TR service provision (See Table 14.1, p. 202). Elements are defined as major aspects of professional service that serve as the focus of monitoring and evaluation activities (Riley and Wright, 1990). The rationale for beginning at this point is to identify important or essential aspects of care, a first step toward defining quality professional services at the local facility (or program) level. While these broad elements used by Riley and Wright were not intended to fit every facility, they were sufficiently broad to provide a basis for choosing those elements that were more important or essential to our specific service.

In our adaptation of the Delphi technique, sample elements were distributed (equivalent to Questionnaire Two from Isaac and Michael, 1985, p. 115) to the group without discussion, asking for individual input in terms of a seven-point Likert-type rating scale using even points from very important to unimportant. Data were collated and ranked by averaging the numerically weighted responses.

This method gave each respondent equal influence initially unhindered by the stated opinion of others. A second round (repeat of the same rating sheet) was then conducted, but this time the group rankings (average scores) were available to each rater. This allowed the rater to consider the influence of the entire group via the average rating, to solidify their individual responses, and to think through the values behind their rating. After the second round, scores were averaged and

| Table 14.1–Major Elements of Therapeutic Recreation from Riley and Wright, 1990 |
|---|
| Elements |

| | |
|---|---|
| Assessment Credentialing | Standards of Practice |
| Treatment Program Plan | Leisure Education Program |
| Treatment Program Implementation | Ethical Practice |
| Documentation | Utilization Review |
| Patient/Client Safety | Follow-up Plan |
| Treatment Program Evaluation | Patient Family Education |
| Intervention Approaches | Normalization Principles |
| Discharge Plan | Diversionary Activities |
| Staff Development | |

placed in rank order (from most important to least important). At this point the group then received the second round of rankings (similar to results of Isaac and Michael). The TR QA committee was then convened and prepared for a group discussion of the rankings in terms of the department's priorities. Differences of opinion, variable interpretations, and misunderstandings all became topics for discussion, but based on considerably strengthened individual values/opinions. From this discussion the TR QA committee accepted 13 priority elements (See Table 14.2).

The same model was used to determine priority indicators for the top 13 elements. *Indicators* are the subdimensions of the elements that delineate more specifically, the level of quality performance (structure, process, and outcome) within each important element of care (Riley & Wright, 1990). Thirteen lists of indicators varying in number from eight to 21, were given to each QA committee member. They ranked the indicators for each selected element and went through a repeat of the previous two rounds (except for using indicators for the selected elements) before bringing the results to the group discussion (See Table 14.3). After becoming familiar with the modified Delphi format and the consensus-

Table 14.2–Elements of TR Service QA Committee Ranking

| Rank Order | | Mean |
|---|---|---|
| 1. | Treatment Plan | 6.3 |
| 2. | Documentation | 6.1 |
| 2. | Assessment | 6.1 |
| 4. | Treatment Program Evaluation | 5.8 |
| 5. | Treatment Program Implementation | 5.7 |
| 6. | Patient/Client Safety | 5.6 |
| 7. | Standards of Practice/Written Plan | 5.5 |
| 8. | Staff Development | 5.1 |
| 9. | Credentialing | 5.0 |
| 9. | Professional Ethical Practice | 5.0 |
| 11. | Intervention Approaches | 4.7 |
| 12. | Recreational Activity Programs | 4.5 |
| 12. | Playroom Programs | 4.5 |

Nonpriority Elements

| | | |
|---|---|---|
| 14. | Discharge Plan | 4.0 |
| 15. | Patient/Family Education | 3.5 |
| 16. | Normalization Principles | 3.3 |
| 17. | Utilization (Resource) Review | 3.0 |
| 18. | Follow-Up Plan (Post Discharge) | 2.9 |

building discussions from the first round, the indicator discussion should have been routine. However, more conflict was experienced by our committee during this step. The quality of the conflict was substantive . . . based more on principles and concepts than on personality and opinion. Perhaps this conflict came as a result of the greater specificity of indicators as compared with elements which are more general. Finally, the QA committee was ready to discuss the implementation of monitoring and evaluation . . . now that they had preliminarily set priorities for what (elements and indicators) needed to be assessed. Not enough emphasis can be given to the importance of using the Delphi technique to give form to committee derived priorities. The strength and energy of well-prepared individuals and the value of a self-generated document to discuss gave focus to our QA process. The staff inclusion model empowered committee members with their own clarified values and prepared each with a process by which all were considered equal participants.

Table 14.3–Is It Important to Monitor ...?
Indicators:  QA Committee Ranking

| Element Rank | | Mean Indicator Rank |
|---|---|---|
| **1.** | **Treatment Plan** | |
| 1.1. | Treatment plan is based upon outcome findings of the assessment process. | 6.0 |
| 1.1 | Treatment plan contains behavioral written criteria that are measurable. | 6.0 |
| 1.3. | Therapeutic recreation treatment plan is an integral part of the overall client treatment plan. | 5.8 |
| 1.3. | Documentation of goal achievement is directly related to need statement and assessment (i.e., diagnostically related). | 5.8 |
| 1.5. | Client, when appropriate, is involved in the treatment plan. | 5.5 |
| **2.** | **Documentation** | |
| 2.1. | Documented progress notes reflect individual client's response to treatment. | 5.6 |
| 2.2. | Charts and subsequent documentation are reviewed on a timely basis. | 5.5 |
| 2.3. | All documentation is specific to assessed need and client-specific treatment goals. | 5.4 |

Table 14.3 (continued)–Is It Important to Monitor ...?
Indicators:  QA Committee Ranking

| Element Rank | | Mean Indicator Rank |
|---|---|---|
| 2.3. | Documentation is accurate and contains no errors or falsifications. | 5.4 |
| 2.3. | Standardized terminology is used in accordance with policy and procedures. | 5.4 |
| **3.** | **Assessment** | |
| 3.1. | Assessment results identify strengths and weaknesses of the client. | 6.0 |
| 3.2. | Assessment is documented within client's record | 5.9 |
| 3.3. | Assessment is conducted by qualified staff | 5.6 |
| 3.4. | Referral for assessment is initiated by physician or multi-disciplinary team. | 5.5 |
| 3.5. | Assessment is completed in a timely manner. | 5.4 |

NOTE: Only the top rated indicators are listed.

The next step for our QA committee was to look at ways to collect data (monitor) the indicators identified. Our question became this: "What is the most efficient way to study our priority elements?" For our QA committee, concern was focused on monitoring documentation through a proposed chart audit form. We assigned several members to estimate this chart audit form's suitability for monitoring as many of the relevant indicators as possible.

The selection of relatively easy-to-monitor indicators was the next obvious step. We did recognize that clinical privileging (related to credentialing and staff work could be done on rewriting scope of service documents for each unit or development elements) was a desirable future step, but postponed that issue until identifiable program. Similarly, the remainder of (unselected) elements and indicators were postponed for future consideration. A pictorial schemata of the staff inclusion model as applied to QA is presented in Figure 14.1.

### Summary

*Step 1* identified individual values related to each element of TR service. This endeavor was based on personally held theories of TR. QA committee members were assured that there were no "right" answers or ratings. TR staff may not be used to being asked their opinion on the relative importance of various aspects of TR. Use care to reassure them of this matter. *Step 2* allowed restatement of individually held values, but relative to the aggregated (averaged) rankings of their peer group. The influence of the peer group was impersonal and anonymous. The private endeavor of restating rankings in the face of collective data from one's own work group is a valuable experience that prepares the individual for the following step. *Step 3* was the group discussion in light of the results gathered from the second Delphi round. Each TRS came prepared by its personal evaluation of elements to discuss outcomes in the political arena of face-to-face group process. The theory behind this process was that concepts and principles develop strength over personalities or unexamined opinions. *Steps 4 to 6* were essentially the same except that they focused on indicators. *Steps 7 to 10* were the practical aspects of determining how to monitor (collect data) on the elements/indicators. At this point, criteria may begin to develop based on previous experience, but in the absence of data, it is recommended that a data collection period precede the setting of objective standards (performance criteria) by which the department QA committee evaluates the quality of the department's service. A concrete example of this was that chart audits were carried on for a year before setting numerical criteria for an acceptable chart.

The staff inclusion model has a strong measure of respect for individual values while steadfastly moving toward group consensus. The inclusion of TR staff in the QA process is more likely to be successful if it is accomplished in the spirit of professional respect rather than a judgmental attitude. The latter is inherently problematic in the process of evaluation whether it is summative or formative

**Step 1**
Individually rank elements.

**Step 2**
Re-rank elements with knowledge of average score from QA committee.

**Step 3**
QA Committee discussion of second round rankings to determine agenda priorities and nonpriorities.

**Step 4**
Individually rank indicators for priority elements.

**Step 5**
Re-rank indicators with knowledge of average score from QA committee.

**Step 6**
QA committee discussion of second round rankings to determine priority indicators.

**Step 7**
Decisions as to how best monitor prioritized elements and indicators.

**Step 8**
Data collection and analyzing results.

**Step 9**
Setting departmental standards (performance criteria).

**Step 10**
Determine evaluation schedule.

Figure 14.1–Schedule of Procedures for QA Development

(Bloom, Hastings, and Madaus, 1971) and must be carefully finessed by the astute manager of the QA process. The QA committee has the constant task of deciding what to monitor and evaluate. The staff inclusion model offers a rational decision-making process. Obviously only a small portion of all possible items brought to a QA committee's attention can be selected for monitoring and evaluation at any one time. Priorities must be set for near term action and many items will have to wait for future consideration.

There are no final stages for the QA process; it is a self-repeating loop. Some indicators can be put to rest, at least temporarily, but mostly it is a cyclical process. The model of staff inclusion offered here has a strong chance for success because respect for individual values is inherent in the process. Any QA program without staff support seems unlikely to develop the cooperation and compliance based on shared professional pride that is chronicled by organizational visionaries such as Peters and Waterman (1987).

## References

Bloom, B., Hastings, J., and Madaus, G. (1971). *Handbook of Formative an Summative Evaluation of Student Learning.* New York, NY: McGraw-Hill.

Bull, M. (1985). Quality Assurance: Its Origins, Transformations, and Prospects. In Meisenheimer, C. (Ed.), *Quality Assurance.* Rockville, MD: Aspen Systems Corp.

Dalkey, Rourke, Lewis, and Snyder (1972). *The Quality of Life: Delphi Decision Making.* Lexington, MA: Lexington Books.

Donabedian, A. (1986). Criteria and Standards for Quality Assessment and Monitoring. *Quality Review Bulletin,* March, p. 104.

Donabedian, A. (1985). *Explorations in Quality Assessment and Monitoring, Volume III: The Methods and Findings of Quality Assessment and Monitoring.* Ann Arbor, MI: Health Administration Press.

Donabedian, A. (1982). *Explorations in Quality Assessment and Monitoring, Volume II: The Criteria Standards of Quality.* Ann Arbor, MI: Health Administration Press.

Donabedian, A. (1978). The Quality of Medical Care. *Science,* 200, p. 856-864.

Helmer, O. (1967). *Analysis of the Future: The Delphi Technique.* Santa Monica, CA: Rand Corp.

Huston, A. (1987). Clinical Application of Quality Assurance in the Therapeutic Recreation Setting. In Riley, B. (Ed.) *Evaluation of Therapeutic Recreation through Quality Assurance.* American Therapeutic Recreation Association, State College, PA: Venture Publishing.

Isaac, S. and Michael, W. (1985). *Handbook In Research and Evaluation,* Second Edition, San Diego, CA:  Edits Publishing.

Marker, C. (1987).  The Marker Model: A Hierarchy for Nursing Standards, *Journal of Nursing Quality Assurance,* 1:2, 7-20.

McLaughlin, C. (1976).  Delphi Process. *Health Care Management Review.* 16:11, 51-52.

Miller, M. and Knapp, R. (1979). *Evaluating Quality of Care.* Rockville, MD: Aspen Publications.

Navar, N. and Dunn, J. (Eds.)(1981). *Quality Assurance: Concerns for Therapeutic Recreation.* Urbana-Champaign, IL:  University of Illinois.

Peters, T. and Waterman, F. (1982). *In Search of Excellence.* New York, NY: Harper & Row.

Quade, E. (1975). *Analysis for Public Decision.* New York, NY:  American Elsevier  Publishing Co.

Reynolds, R. and O'Morrow, G. (1985). *Problems, Issues, & Concepts in Therapeutic Recreation.* Englewood Cliffs, NJ:  Prentice-Hall.

Riley, B. (1987). *Evaluation of Therapeutic Recreation through Quality Assurance.* State College, PA:  Venture Publishing, Inc.

Riley, B. (1989).  "An Exploratory Study of QA Methodology in Therapeutic Recreation Using the Delphi Technique." Unpublished Doctoral Dissertation, Pennsylvania State University, University Park, PA.

Riley, B. and Wright, S. (1990).  Establishing Quality Assurance Monitors for the Evaluation of Therapeutic Recreation Service. *Therapeutic Recreation Journal,* 24:2, 25-39.

## Appendix 14A
## The National Institute of Health Clinical Center Patient Activities
## Department Quality Assurance Plan

I.  OVERVIEW

A.  PURPOSE
The Patient Activities Department (PAD) is committed to providing quality care to patients and families who are participating in biomedical research. The PAD believes that every therapeutic recreation specialist (TRS) should participate in the improvement of patient care. The desire to provide appropriate services and quality work emanates from our collective sense of professional ethics. This quality assurance (QA) plan serves as one measure of the level of achievement toward fulfillment of this commitment.

B.  GOALS
1.  Maintain a program to objectively and systematically monitor and evaluate patient care in order to ensure delivery of optimal therapeutic recreation services to Clinical Center (CC) patients, consistent with the profession's established Standards of Practice and PAD's Policies and Procedures.
2.  Identify patient care deficiencies and potential problems and develop appropriate strategies to resolve them, monitoring the effectiveness of corrective actions.
3.  Recognize and validate outstanding care.
4.  Disseminate QA information to all the TRS's in the PAD so that the interchange of relevant information is assured.
5.  Promote continued development and modification of standards for all sections of the PAD.

C.  DEFINITIONS: The *QA process* is a systematic approach to the evaluation of therapeutic recreation service.
The *evaluation* process involves a comparison of performance with standards (discrepancy analysis). Standards of practice are self-imposed as part of the responsibility of professional, accountable behavior. When discrepancy information exists, it is then used to:
(a) terminate or change program standards or
(b) direct efforts at changing clinical performance.
Thus conceived, evaluation is seen as a program improvement feedback cycle.

II.  ORGANIZATIONAL COMPONENTS

A.  AUTHORITY/ACCOUNTABILITY
1.  The chief of the PAD has overall responsibility for the conduct of the department's activities.
2.  The PAD Special Assistant is assigned responsibility for development of departmental QA standards, monitoring, and that findings are reviewed and corrective actions are instituted in order to ensure the quality and appropriateness of care. The PAD Special Assistant serves as Chair of the PAD QA Committee and, as department representative to the Clinical Center QA Committee, keeps the PAD informed of CC QA efforts and expectations.
3.  Section Supervisors are accountable for the quality of patient care rendered by TRS's in their respective patient care units (pcu). With assistance from the PAD Special Assistant, supervisors define the scope of specialty practice and services. They ensure clinical involvement of their service on units assigned.
4.  The PAD QA Committee consists of the Chief, Special Assistant (as Chair), Section Supervisors (3), and one TRS appointed from each section (4) on a rotating (two-year) basis. The committee identifies and addresses problems and recommends solutions; develops standards of care and practice, key elements, indicators, and criteria; and provides input on matters affecting quality and appropriateness of TR service provision.

III.  CLINICAL ASPECTS OF CARE

A.  STANDARDS OF CARE AND PRACTICE
The PAD QA committee has chosen to adopt the following published standards as guides:
1.  *Standards of Practice for Therapeutic Recreation Service* (1980) published by the National Therapeutic Recreation Society (NTRS).
2.  *Guidelines for Administration of Therapeutic Recreation Service in Clinical and Residential Facilities* (1980) NTRS.
3.  *Evaluation of Therapeutic Recreation Through Quality Assurance,* (1987) Bob Riley, American Therapeutic Recreation Association (ATRA).
4.  *Accreditation Manual for Hospitals* (most recent edition) JCAHO.

The following list summarizes the standards of care and practice for the PAD within the priorities established under "Unit Evaluation" and updated by section supervisors as needed.

1. The patient is provided leisure activities in order to develop, maintain, and express an appropriate leisure/social lifestyle in the face of physical, mental, emotional or social limitations, imposed by hospitaliztion in a biomedical research facility.

2. The patient is assessed for leisure, social, and recreational abilities, deficiencies, interests, barriers, needs and potential in order to develop a plan of services which may include (a) treatment to improve function by removing barriers; (b) leisure education designed to help the patient acquire knowledge, skills, and attitudes needed for independent leisure/social involvement, adjustment in the community, decision- making ability, and appropriate use of free time; and (c) recreational opportunity for maintaining physiological, psychological, and cultural equilibrium while hospitalized.

3. The patient maintains the highest level of leisure wellness possible along the health-illness continuum by being informed of therapeutic, educational and recreational resources in the hospital and/or community environment.

4. The TRS will implement these standards of care by:
    a. The Initial Assessment, which screens the patient for participation in recreational activities, elicits basic patient information related to leisure activity preferences and interests, and the patient's desire for TR services.
    b. Full Assessment and Treatment Plan

1. Assessing a patient's ability to be involved in leisure activities from physical, social, and emotional perspectives;
2. Developing an individualized treatment plan based on the assessment;
3. Implementing the treatment plan;
4. Evaluating the results of TR service.
5. The TRS promotes open communication among the patient, the family, and health care professionals assigned in order to maintain a sense of independence, self-worth, and autonomy in the patient.
6. The TRS will maintain continuity of care through multiple admissions and discharges frequently occurring in biomedical research protocols.

B.  ELEMENTS OF CARE
    These standards of care and practice reflect the various major clinical
    functions identified by the PAD. They are called components of care and
    are activities that may involve one or more of the following:

    - High Volume
    - High Risk
    - Problematic

    Elements of care will be identified as priority components by the PAD
    QA Committee.

C.  CLINICAL INDICATORS OF CARE
    A clinical indicator is one dimension of an element of care that, if
    monitored over time, would detect trends in the quality or appropriateness
    of care. The indicator is what is being measured. A minimum of three
    clinical indicators are recommended to monitor an element of care.

D.  MONITORING
    Monitoring of Incident/Occurrence Reports includes tracking or trending
    patient occurrences. A method of electronic reporting, the Medical
    Information System (MIS) has been developed for the CC. The adverse
    occurrence reporting system was designed to document incidents in the
    following four categories relevant to TR services:

    - Medical/behavioral problem
    - Accident/injury or equipment problem
    - Environment hazards
    - Others (e.g., dietary, program, transportation)

    The MIS report is completed by the PAD staff. Copies go to the PAD
    Chief, Supervisor, and QA Coordinator. The latter facilitates immediate
    follow-up when needed. Various problem-solving approaches can be
    used. The monthly PAD QA Committee meeting provides a forum for
    considering and developing the occurrence as an indicator and including
    it in the ongoing monitoring. In addition, prompt and direct administra-
    tive action can be taken before presentation to the QA Committee.

E.  DOCUMENTATION AND REPORTING OF THE PAD QA PROGRAM

The minutes of the monthly PAD QA Committee are distributed in a timely manner. The PAD QA Coordinator reports monthly (on or before the fourth Friday) to the CC QA Coordinator on discovered matters of concern to the CC or to the Institutes. The PAD QA Coordinator submits a quarterly report to the Chief and to the CC QA Coordinator summarizing the findings of QA monitoring and the efforts of the PAD QA Committee over the previous three months.

CHAPTER FIFTEEN

# Surviving The Audit

LINDA HUTCHINSON-TROYER, C.T.R.S.

**Introduction**

Darwin probably did not conceive that his "survival of the fittest" would extend to the arena of Quality Assurance in health care. But given recent developments, the health care arena has become a type of jungle. The key to surviving in the competitive health care market lies in the successful development of an integrated quality assurance plan. Essential to the development of this plan is a complete understanding of the following areas:

**Knowledge**–how your service integrates with all other services within the system.

**Positive Attitude**–reflecting a commitment from the clinician to the governing board that fosters effective communication and encourages involvement in the quality of patient care; and

**Practice**– providing the highest quality of patient care that is well-documented through the use of outcome indicators.

In addition to the above points the specific departmental QA plan should be integrated within the ongoing systematic plan of the agency. If done properly, this integration provides for a framework for the QA activities you conduct and for their ongoing monitoring. This departmental plan should include provisions for the following procedures:

- monitoring of clinical indicators are planned and ongoing;
- comprehensive approach is provided so that all services are reviewed;
- there is a review of indicators and criteria that are agreed on by the department facility;
- routine collection of the data that must be evaluated on a set schedule is provided;
- problems are identified and result in opportunities for resolution;

- once problems are resolved monitoring should continue to assure improved patient services/care; and
- information derived through each department should be integrated into the facility's overall plan. (JCAHO, 1987, p. 9)

## Key To Survival

The survey process is a necessary "evil" to survive in the competitive health care industry. In successfully completing a JCAHO or CARF survey, your facility will gain an additional marketing tool to show to insurance carriers and (more importantly) to health care consumers. The intent of the survey process is to help assure that both appropriate and high quality care are delivered to the consumers you serve. This is accomplished through an ongoing monitoring and evaluation process. Generally speaking, the survey process consists of an interview and the review of written materials (policy/procedure manuals and QA plans). All information presented is considered as part of the verification process. The amount of time to accomplish required survey procedures varies from facility to facility. Often the process is initiated by a brief meeting between the survey team and the administrative personnel of the facility. The survey process culminates with a summation conference. Persons attending the summation meeting are selected at the discretion of the hospital. Representatives usually include staff members from nursing, the medical staff, the governing body and administration, and clinical department heads.

The specific areas of service that the survey auditors hone in on vary considerably with each auditor. It is to your advantage to network with other Certified Therapeutic Recreation Specialists in your region to determine the "hot" issues with respect to the auditing process. JCAHO auditors are often assigned to a geographic area and do a circuit of audits during a given period of time. The following areas were the main areas of concern in our region during the past year:

- credentialing and continuing education of staff;
- policy/procedures for acute events on a community reentry outing;
- contracts/agreements with afflicting schools;
- infection control/disposal issues of contaminated materials within a given treatment area;
- quality improvement/program evaluation by diagnosis as distinct from department.

It is assumed that, prior to the audit, the department has an operational policy and procedure manual that has been read and signed off on by each staff member (clinical and support). Additionally, the department should have an updated quality assurance plan with responsibility for monitoring the identified indicators assigned to a specific individual. Often, the primary responsibility for QA lies with the department director, but it may be delegated to others. If so, such action should be documented in the respective job descriptions.

The first step in preparing for the audit is to review the department manuals and compare them to the standards manual of the accrediting organization you are being surveyed by. Note all areas where your department is required to have a documented policy or procedure to reflect compliance with a standard. An example of this point within a physical rehabilitation facility being surveyed by JCAHO is compliance with *Standards RH.2.5 Recreational Therapy*. Any item in the *JCAHO, Accreditation Manual for Hospitals (1988)* with an asterisk (*) is a key factor in the accreditation decision process. It is therefore imperative to review all of the standards that apply to the organization's request for accreditation. For example, *Standard RH.1.1.5 of the JCAHO Accreditation Manual for Hospitals*, states:

> Each individual who provides physical rehabilitation services has been determined to be competent to provide such services by reason of education, training, experience, and demonstrated adherence to current standards of care.

This is not a duplicate of the Recreational Therapy Standards. Therefore, your department manual should contain job descriptions that delineate professional standards and indicate the proper certification required, expiration date and a monitoring system for follow-up.

Standards from other integrated services that overlap with the roles and services performed by therapeutic recreation include but are not limited to:

- **Infection control**. If you have a pet therapy program—what are the health standards required for the animal involved to reduce any potential risk of infection or disease? Animal health certificates should be on file and regular review of expiration dates documented. Do all your staff know where the universal precaution supplies are kept? And how to use them?
- **Medical record services**. What is the written criteria for persons in the department who document in the patient chart? Are co-signatures required for therapeutic recreation students and those awaiting certification? What is the department standard related to routine documentation in the patient medical record?
- **Plant technology and safety**. Are staff required to attend annual fire and safety in-services? How are these in-services monitored and documented? Does your department keep an updated copy of a safety sheet listing all hazardous substances within easy access?

Each of the areas noted above requires a policy and/or a procedure to denote how the topic is addressed within the department. All such policies should be dated and reviewed annually. Any revision to the manual should be so noted under the date of the original document. If a policy or procedure is deemed critical to quality care, it should be considered as a quality assurance indicator and systematically monitored. When trends are noted during the monitoring process or problems are identified regarding this policy, a method for reporting and resolving the problem needs to be identified.

At Montebello Rehabilitation Hospital each department has a quality review program. Each department is required to present a departmental QA plan to the QA Committee for approval. The plan should identify the important aspects of care provided by department (i.e., assessment). Additionally, indicators are established that will allow for the monitoring of this aspect of care. Monitors can be reviewed monthly, quarterly or as a special study. With each indicator a threshold for compliance must be identified, (i.e., 95 percent of all assessments must meet or exceed *Standard RH.2.5* content). Upon review of the monitor(s), if the threshold(s) is not within acceptable range, an intensive evaluation is conducted to show why the threshold is not being met (See Appendix 15A).

The department assigns a person to be responsible for monitoring the department QA indicators. It is that person's responsibility to attend the hospital-wide meetings and to report department findings. The department findings are summarized in a quarterly written report. After these reports are reviewed at the monthly meetings, a summary of the findings, including outstanding problems, are sent on to the Medical Executive Committee of the hospital. After review and input from the department, the findings are summarized and sent to the hospital's Board of Directors. At this point, the upward communication concludes, and comments, concerns and/or solutions are transmitted down through the same system. When this communication process is implemented, each person must document their involvement because this information will be requested by the hospital's quality assurance coordinator at the time of the audit.

Auditors prefer to see six months of monitoring data. A copy of the most recent annual QA report can serve as an overview of the department's findings/problems. Again, have the paper trail to document each finding. Highlight any findings that reflect trends in patient care/needs; patterns of performance of the clinical staff, and/or problems that affected your overall department. To satisfy the JCAHO, your plan should describe a monitoring process that evaluates care based on objective indicators. The monitoring process should promote continuous improvement in the quality of patient care (Fromberg, 1988).

It is impossible to walk someone through every step of the audit process. Each surveyor makes individual determinations regarding the department's compliance with the standards under which it is being evaluated. The department director receives feedback at both the one-on-one level with the surveyor at the summation conference and in a written report the organization receives post audit. In summary, in preparing for the audit, professional efforts should be directed toward: *Documentation* of what it is the department does: delineating a *Plan* of how it accomplishes those tasks; *Preparation* for the audit by becoming familiar with the standards under which you will be reviewed; and above all, open lines of *Communication*. The latter will provide the avenue to coordinate, resolve conflict, and integrate the overall services of the facility. Provided in Appendix 15B is a "Checklist for Survival." Although this list is not all inclusive nor is it fool-proof, it should, nevertheless, serve as a guide to help a department prepare for the audit.

## References

Fromberg, R. (1988). *The Joint Commission Guide to Quality Assurance.* Chicago, IL: Joint Commission Publications.

Joint Commission on Accreditation of Healthcare Organizations (1988). *Accreditation Manual for Hospitals.* Chicago, IL: Joint Commission Publication.

Joint Commission on Accreditation of Healthcare Organizations, (1987). *Monitoring and Evaluation in Support Services.* Chicago, IL: Joint Commission Publication.

## Appendix 15A

### Montebello Rehabilitation Hospital
University of Maryland Medical System
2201 Argonne Drive • Baltimore, Maryland 21218 • (301) 554-5200

QUALITY IMPROVEMENT
PROBLEM IDENTIFICATION/CORRECTION PROCESS

Description of Problem:_____

_____

Action Taken at Time Problem Occured:_____

_____

_____

_____    _____
Signature of Person Preparing Report             Date

Is Problem Resolved? _____ Yes _____ No   Forwarded to:_____

_____    _____
Signature of Supervisor                    Date

Subsequent Action Intradepartmentally or Interdepartmentally:_____

_____

Is Problem Resolved? _____ Yes _____ No

Anticipated Resolution Date _____

_____    _____
Signature of Person Initiating Action            Date

Send a copy of completed form to:  Person Identifying Problem
Quality Review Department

BBM 2/88
  1/89
  9/89

Accredited by Commission on Accreditation of Rehabilitation Facilities for
Comprehensive Inpatient Rehabilitation • Spinal Cord Injury Programs • Brain Injury Programs

Accredited by Joint Commission on Accreditation of Healthcare Organizations
Member of National Association of Rehabilitation Facilities
Member of Maryland Hospital Association

# Appendix 15B
## Your Checklist for Survival

[ ]  Records of Departmental Meetings

[ ]  Staff Credentials/Licenses

[ ]  Job Descriptions and Performance

[ ]  Written QA Plan and Review

[ ]  Written Agreements with Affiliating Schools

[ ]  Records of Staff Training/Development

[ ]  Policy and Procedure Manual

[ ]  Fire and Safety/Infection Control Plan:
    - Incident report format
    - Preventative maintenance schedule
    - Hazardous materials/waste
    - Smoking regulations

[ ]  Plan of Care for Patients

# CONTRIBUTORS

Cynthia P. Carruthers, Ph.D, C.T.R.S.
University of Nevada, Las Vegas
Las Vegas, Nevada

Peg Connolly, Ph.D., C.T.R.S.
Executive Director
National Council for Therapeutic Recreation Certification
Spring Valley, New York

Julia K. Dunn, Ph.D., C.T.R.S.
Department of Leisure Studies
University of North Texas
Denton, Texas

Carolyn Ebgert, RN
Director, Quality Assurance
South Carolina Department of Mental Health
Columbia, South Carolina

Matt Gold, C.T.R.S.
Director, Therapeutic Recreation
New York State Psychiatric Institute
New York, New York

Richard Hatfield, C.T.R.S.
Associate Director
Recreation Therapy Department
North Carolina Memorial Hospital
Chapel Hill, North Carolina

Linda Hutchinson-Troyer, C.T.R.S.
Director, Therapeutic Recreation
Montebello Rehabilitation Hospital
Baltimore, Maryland

Dan Johnson, C.T.R.S.
Department of Recreation and Parks
University of Wisconsin–LaCrosse
LaCrosse, Wisconsin

Mary Ann Keogh-Hoss, Ed.D., C.T.R.S.
Director, Rehabilitation Services
Easter State Hospital
Medical Lake, Washington

W.B. (Terry) Kinney, Ph.D., C.T.R.S.
Department of Recreation and Leisure Studies
Temple University
Philadelphia, Pennsylvania

Lanny Knight, C.T.R.S.
Director of Activity Therapy
Kings View Center
Reedley, California

Dorothy McNamara, C.T.R.S.
Rehabilitation Services
Manhattan Psychiatric Center
New York, New York

Nancy Navar, Re.D.
Department Recreation and Parks
University of Wisconsin–LaCrosse
LaCrosse, Wisconsin

George Patrick, Ph.D., C.T.R.S.
Patient Activity Department
National Institutes of Health
Bethesda, Maryland

Michael Rhodes, C.T.R.S.
Therapeutic Recreation Services
Sinai Hospital
Detriot, Michigan

Bob Riley, Ph.D., C.T.R.S.
Department of Recreation and Leisure Studies
Green Mountain College
Poultney, Vermont

Carmen Russoniello, C.T.R.S.
Institute Review Board
Sacred Heart Medical Center
Spokane, Washington

Richard Scalenghe, R.M.T.
Department of Standards
Joint Commission on Accreditation of Healthcare Organizations
Oakbrook Terrace, Illinois

John Shank, Ed.D., C.T.R.S.
Department of Recreation and Leisure Studies
Temple University
Philadelphia, Pennsylvania

Janiece J. Sneegas, Ph.D., C.T.R.S.
Department of Leisure Studies
University of Illinois
Champaign, Illinois

# BOOKS FROM VENTURE PUBLISHING

Acquiring Parks and Recreation Facilities through Mandatory Dedication:
A Comprehensive Guide,
   by Ronald A. Kaiser and James D. Mertes

Adventure Education,
   edited by John C. Miles and Simon Priest

Amenity Resource Valuation: Integrating Economics with Other Disciplines,
   edited by George L. Peterson, B.L. Driver and Robin Gregory

Behavior Modification in Therapeutic Recreation: An Introductory Learning
Manual,
   by John Dattilo and William D. Murphy

Benefits of Leisure,
   edited by B. L. Driver, Perry J. Brown and George L. Peterson

Beyond the Bake Sale—A Fund Raising Handbook for Public Agencies,
   by Bill Moskin

The Community Tourism Industry Imperative—The Necessity, The Opportunities,
Its Potential,
   by Uel Blank

Dimensions of Choice: A Qualitative Approach to Recreation, Parks, and Leisure
Research,
   by Karla A. Henderson, Ph.D.

Doing More With Less in the Delivery of Recreation and Park Services: A Book
of Case Studies,
   by John Crompton

Evaluation of Therapeutic Recreation Through Quality Assurance,
   edited by Bob Riley

The Evolution of Leisure: Historical and Philosophical Perspectives,
   by Thomas Goodale and Geoffrey Godbey

The Future of Leisure Services: Thriving on Change,
   by Geoffrey Godbey

Gifts to Share—A Gifts Catalogue How-To Manual for Public Agencies,
by Lori Harder and Bill Moskin

Great Special Events and Activities,
by Annie Morton, Angie Prosser and Sue Spangler

Leadership and Administration of Outdoor Pursuits,
by Phyllis Ford and James Blanchard

The Leisure Diagnostic Battery: Users Manual and Sample Forms,
by Peter Witt and Gary Ellis

Leisure Diagnostic Battery Computer Software,
by Gary Ellis and Peter Witt

Leisure Education: A Manual of Activities and Resources,
by Norma J. Stumbo and Steven R. Thompson

Leisure Education: Program Materials for Persons with Developmental
Disabilities,
by Kenneth F. Joswiak

Leisure in Your Life: An Exploration, Third Edition
by Geoffrey Godbey

A Leisure of One's Own: A Feminist Perspective on Women's Leisure,
by Karla Henderson, M. Deborah Bialeschki, Susan M. Shaw
and Valeria J. Freysinger

Marketing for Parks, Recreation, and Leisure,
by Ellen L. O'Sullivan

Outdoor Recreation Management: Theory and Application,
Revised and Enlarged, by Alan Jubenville,
Ben Twight and Robert H. Becker

Planning Parks for People, by John Hultsman,
Richard L. Cottrell and Wendy Zales Hultsman

Playing, Living, Learning: A Worldwide Perspective on Children's Opportunities
to Play,
by Cor Westland and Jane Knight

Private and Commercial Recreation,
   edited by Arlin Epperson

The Process of Recreation Programming: Theory and Technique, Third Edition
   by Patricia Farrell and Herberta M. Lundegren

Recreation and Leisure: An Introductory Handbook,
   edited by Alan Graefe and Stan Parker

Recreation Economic Decisions: Comparing Benefits and Costs,
   by Richard G. Walsh

Recreation Programming And Activities For Older Adults
   by Jerold E. Elliott and Judith A. Sorg-Elliott

Risk Management in Therapeutic Recreation: A Component of Quality Assurance,
   by Judy Voelkl

Schole VI: A Journal of Leisure Studies and Recreation Education,

A Social History of Leisure Since 1600,
   by Gary Cross

Sports and Recreation for the Disabled—A Resource Manual,
   by Michael J. Paciorek and Jeffery A. Jones

A Study Guide for National Certification in Therapeutic Recreation,
   by Gerald O'Morrow and Ron Reynolds

Therapeutic Recreation Protocol for Treatment of Substance Addictions,
   by Rozanne W. Faulkner

Understanding Leisure and Recreation: Mapping the Past, Charting the Future,
   edited by Edgar L. Jackson and Thomas L. Burton

Wilderness in America: Personal Perspectives,
   edited by Daniel L. Dustin

Venture Publishing, Inc
1999 Cato Avenue, State College, PA 16801
814-234-4561